Sculpture in Silver

Art of the Future

by

Bill Harmsen, Author/Publisher

Illustrating Twenty-Four Silver Sculptures
Cast by the Lost Wax Method
and
Featuring the
Harmsen Hopi Silver Overlay Kachina Collection

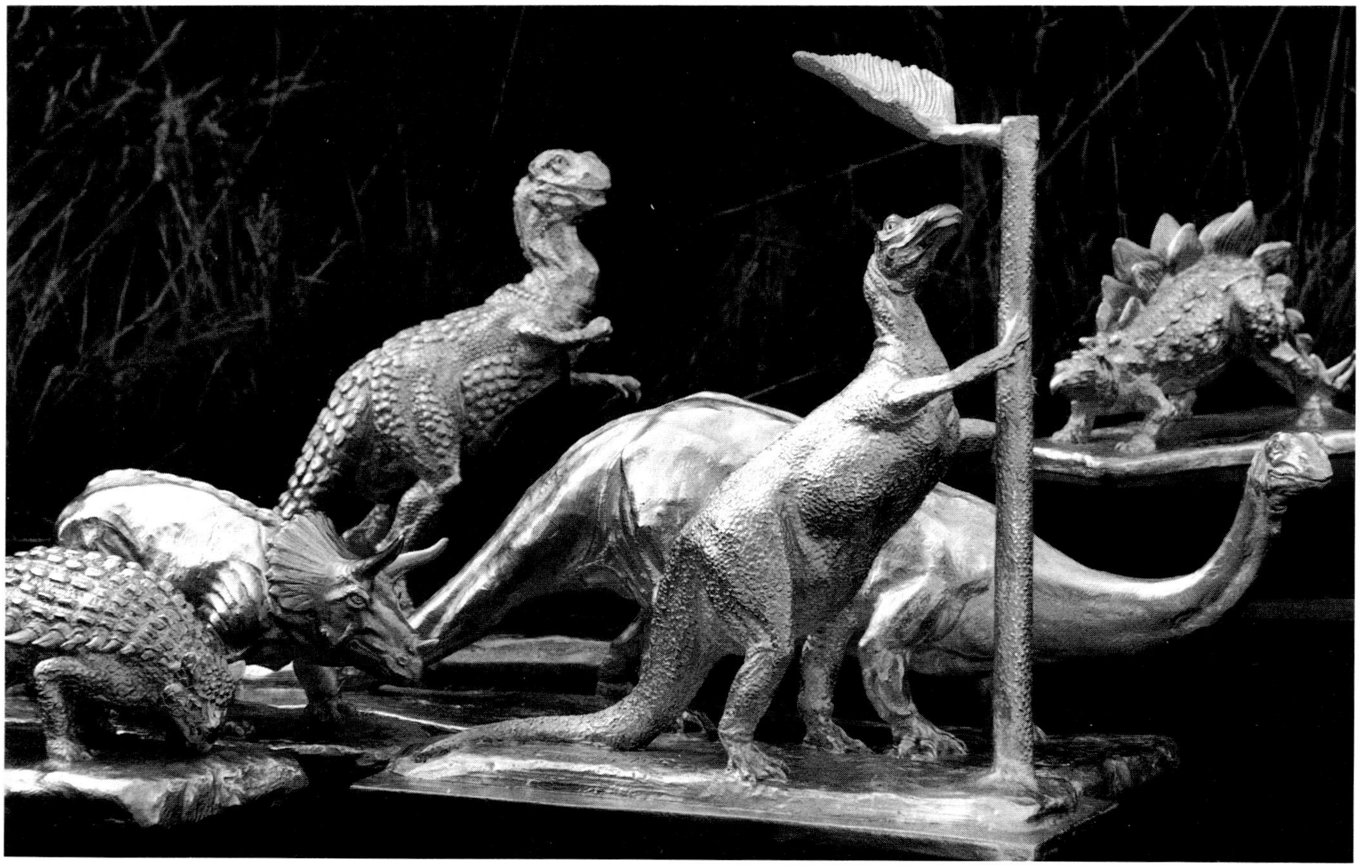

Editor
Melody Sears

Art Director
Josh Young

Book Production
Casa Cold Type, Inc., Tucson, Arizona

Photography
F.C. Hilker, Denver, Colorado
J. De Lorenzo, Colorado State Historical Museum, Denver, Colorado
Balfour Walker, Tucson, Arizona

Film Assembly
Precise Pre-Press, Inc., Tucson, Arizona

Printed in the United States of America by
Walsworth Publishing Company, Inc.

First published in 1988 by The Harmsen Publishing Company

3131 E. Alameda Avenue, Denver CO 80209, 303/777-4030
Revised Edition Second Printing 1992
Library of Congress No. 92-090212
ISBN No. 0-9601322-8-7

All silver sculptures shown and listed in this book are from the
Bill and Dorothy Harmsen Collection

Front Cover: "Requiem" by Buck McCain
Back Cover: "Salako Mana" sterling silver overlay Hopi kachina

To Dorothy . . .

A classy gal,
A Western lady,
A woman of charm,
An inspiration to all who know her,
A devoted mother to our three great sons,
A loving grandmother to eight fine grandkids,
An astute partner in all our business projects,
An expert author and historian for all our art collecting,
A loyal and understanding booster for all my endeavors,
The epitome of a loving, encouraging, and beautiful wife for 52 years.

What more could a man ask for?
With admiration and love,

Bill

ACKNOWLEDGMENTS

After publishing the first edition of *Sculpture in Silver* in 1988, my enthusiasm for collecting artworks in silver intensified. During the next year, I added six new cast silver sculptures to the collection, thus creating the need to update this book as a revised edition. After much thought and planning, I decided to add the collection of 118 Hopi Kachinas crafted in silver overlay to this book, since a book had already been planned for that collection. It is my hope that by combining the two collections in this new version of *Sculpture in Silver,* the reader will enjoy the artistic possibilities of both fine silver (99.9% pure) and sterling silver (92.5% pure) as mediums for sculpture.

For inveterate collectors such as Dorothy and myself, collecting becomes almost a profession. It requires thorough study, more than a little ingenuity, and a great deal of enthusiasm before any collector realizes the result he or she is trying to accomplish. The sage advice, "It's not only what you know but who you know," has been proven over and over again with our art and artifact collections, which are the results of great friendships and help from many inspiring people. In attempting here to remember and credit all the people who have added so much to this book, I hope I miss no one, and apologize in advance if I do.

I want first and foremost to acknowledge the talent and vision of the artists whose works are shown here. Likewise, special thanks goes to Jim Turpen, who first planted the notion of a silver sculpture collection in my mind. There would be no book without these people.

I would very much like to thank Barton Wright for his valuable suggestions and help with organizing the silver kachina collection; Mike Maiden of Maiden Foundry for his expertise in casting all of the cast silver sculptures and his publicist, Jeff Chose, for information on silver casting; Earl and Shawn Starr of Starr Gems for supplying me with silver and for putting me in touch with Native American silversmiths; Trinkle Jones for information on the Petrified Forest; Everett Fry for supplying, sawing, and polishing the petrified wood bases upon which all of the silver kachinas and some of the cast silver sculptures are mounted; Emory Sekaquaptewa for his expertise and information about the Hopi religion and kachina dolls; Jim Hartman of the Colorado State Historical Museum for all his help with our collections; and the Museum's photographer, J. De Lorenzo, for photographing the silver Hopi Kachinas.

I also extend my sincere thanks to the many talented people I relied upon for the production of this book, including Mark Bahti, Laurence Ferguson, Raelee Frazier, Bud Hilker, Debra Huffman, Richard Kandik, Clara Lee Tanner, Balfour Walker, Josh Young, and two great gals, Anne Olson and Melody Sears, who assisted me in all stages of this project.

FOREWORD

William Harmsen developed an interest in Indian art as he accompanied his wife Dorothy to antique shows. This resulted in his acquisition of an appreciable collection of old and contemporary Western and Indian arts and crafts, and the eventual publication of books such as *Patterns and Sources of Navajo Weaving,* and now this volume, *Sculpture in Silver.*

What is silver? What is the lost wax method of silver casting and how is it accomplished? These and other basic queries pertinent to this metal are significantly discussed in this book. There is information regarding contemporary masters of cast silver sculpture, including, among others, James C. Turpen, Jr. and Buck McCain, as well as information about the great historical sculptor of American Indians, Adrien Voisin. In addition to the Indian subjects represented here, Voisin accurately depicted the great and now extinct animals of ancient times—the dinosaurs.

Also in this book, an emphasis is placed on Hopi life in a brief but significant discussion of the religion of this tribe. Emory Sekaquaptewa, a most knowledgeable Hopi, emphasizes the importance of this tribe's religion in his discussion, "The Heart of Hopi Life." Kachinas, most commonly represented in carved and decorated wooden likenesses of Hopi religious spirits, are here richly represented in 118 silver overlay examples from the Harmsen collection. Descriptions of the kachinas include discussions of kachina performances during Powamu, Salako, and other ceremonies performed by this tribe.

The Harmsens have made significant collections of Western and Indian art which they have carefully identified and recorded. These collections are valuable to students of today and tomorrow, and are available for loan to museums and other public institutions throughout the country where they are viewed by vast numbers of people. Certainly this reflects the generosity of Bill and Dorothy Harmsen.

This book, like earlier Harmsen publications, is abundantly, richly, and meaningfully illustrated, providing an interesting, relevant, and valuable record of the sculptures in silver from the Harmsen Collection.

Clara Lee Tanner
Professor Emeritus of Anthropology
University of Arizona, Tucson

TABLE OF CONTENTS

INTRODUCTION

When I first began to collect fine art, sculpture held little appeal for me. I considered it a second-cousin to painting because most bronze sculptures are produced in editions or multiples, not as "one-of-a-kind" pieces. It took my friend, the fine painter Olaf Wieghorst, now deceased, to enlighten me as to the artistry and craftsmanship entailed in casting fine art sculptures.

After his two-hour lecture on the intricacies of this art form, I realized that sculpturing is a complicated, technical, and time-consuming business. The resulting artwork, when cast into metal, becomes almost immortal by nature. My fervor for collecting sculpture had been ignited.

Years later, Jim Turpen, a friend and fine artist, showed me the Zuni Shalako and Koyemshi figures he had sculpted and cast into silver. This new form of sculpture produced by the lost-wax method greatly intrigued me, and my mind soared while contemplating how beautiful a collection of fine art sculptures would be if cast in fine silver.

I decided to visit my friend Adrien Voisin a short time later. On an earlier visit, he had shown me a group of six clay dinosaurs that he had created in 1958. They were fashioned in a collaboration with the Smithsonian Institute, and the six sculptures served as models for life-size sculptures to be exhibited at the Dinosaur National Monument in Utah. They had never been produced in metal, so Voisin agreed that I should have molds of them made to enable them to be cast into bronze.

The six clay pieces were very brittle and broke irreparably when released from the new molds, but, fortunately, the molds emerged in perfect condition. The series was cast into bronze, to Voisin's delight, and he then agreed that I should go on to have them reproduced in fine silver, as the nucleus of this silver sculpture collection.

Liking the results of these first attempts, I plunged into my new project by commissioning sculptures in silver by several contemporary Western and wildlife artists. I went on to explore

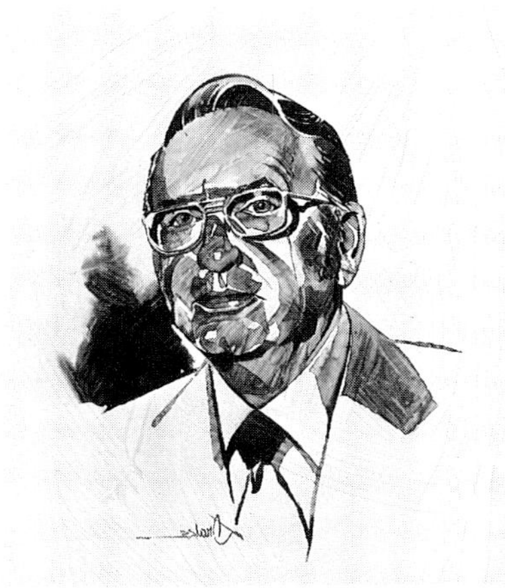

the artistic possibilities of the metal by commissioning Native American craftspeople to create 118 Hopi kachinas in sterling silver. These were all produced using the beautiful Hopi silver overlay technique. Today, our collection contains more than 150 works sculptured in silver.

Since that day in Wieghorst's studio, I have become ever more fascinated by American sculpture. From its emergence out of the woodcarvers' and stonecutters' art of Colonial America, today's American sculpture in bronze and silver represents the pinnacle of technical achievement built upon a solid foundation of artistic talent and vision.

This book, *Sculpture in Silver,* is an attempt to document just one facet of our Western Americana collection of paintings, sculptures, Indian jewelry, rugs, baskets, and other artifacts. It is one of a series of books printed by the Harmsen Publishing Company in an effort to share the beauty of these artworks with many people.

In 1983, Dorothy and I established the Harmsen Foundation to administer our collections of Indian and Western art. Our sons, William Jr., Robert, and Michael Harmsen, serve as members of the Board of Trustees to ensure that the collections will continue to be available to museums and other organizations who want to learn more about America's rich cultural past and the creative accomplishments of its people, both past and present. More than a third of our collection is always on loan to universities, civic agencies, and public or private institutions where it becomes, in a very real sense, a public asset.

We hope readers will enjoy and appreciate these sculptures in silver as much as we do.

Bill Harmsen

THE ORIGINS OF AMERICAN SCULPTURE

Aside from prehistoric, three-dimensional works made by our native inhabitants, the humble beginnings of historic, European-influenced sculpture in America occurred in the seventeenth century with the production of utilitarian objects, wooden Bible boxes, and gravestones. Remnants of the first century of this sculptural heritage can be found today on slate gravemarkers dotting churchyards from Maine to South Carolina.

The early colonists were from the middle and lower classes—working men and their families with little time or training for artistic endeavors. Merchants, ministers, craftsmen, laborers, and vagabonds abounded, but few artisans and perhaps no trained artists populated the Colonies.

Burial markers were at first simply rough-hewn slate or limestone slabs engraved with names and dates. Later, bas-relief designs were introduced and gravemarkers became more elaborate. By 1740, native-born artisans began to create portrait busts and full-figure statues of deceased Colonists.

Colonial woodcarvers decorated the surfaces of furniture, and by 1730, cabinetmakers and woodcarvers began to copy design books from England. It was in the shops of these gifted, unschooled craftsmen that America's first true sculptural art flourished and the "native school" of sculpture had its beginnings.

America's shipyards produced master woodcarvers who adorned sailing ships with massive figureheads and decorative stern boards. Later, carved tavern signs, standing figures of cigar-store Indians and sailors, circus-wagon figures, weather vanes, duck decoys, toys, and treenware (kitchen utensils made from the wood of a tree) were other commercially inspired, yet artistically conceived, examples of the woodcarver's art prior to the 1840s.

William Rush of Philadelphia was considered America's finest wood sculptor in the late eighteenth and early nineteenth centuries. Primarily a figurehead carver, he was also the first consistent and successful sculptor of larger dramatic images, such as "Charity" for Philadelphia's Masonic Hall. Rush was also one of the first artists here to attempt sculpturing in plaster and in clay or terra cotta.

Shortly after his death, modeling in wax was introduced in America. One of this country's first recognized professional sculptors was Patience Wright, whose wax sculptures brought her fame in New York and then London. Because wax was so abundant in the colonies, her work fostered a tradition of wax artists in America. The better wax sculptures created by these artists were sent to Europe for casting into bronze, but many early wax bas-relief portraits, small figures, and larger wax-museum figures still survive.

French and Italian professional sculptors began to visit the United States after the Revolution. They sought work as decorative carvers and portrait artists in stone for the new United States Capitol, as well as for other monuments to the new government and its founding fathers. Their European influence helped establish the classical ideal as an important component of America's artistic sensibilities.

The American ideal was advanced by John Frazee of Rahway, New Jersey, who created several intensely realistic works in stone after 1823. Frazee's most popular bust was a marble portrait of John Marshall, which the artist reproduced and sold as plaster copies.

The first known bronze sculpture cast in the United States was created by Robert Ball Hughes in the 1850s. Although initially he cast it in his own Boston foundry, the bronze's speedy deterioration compelled him to have it recast in a Parisian foundry.

America's capability to cast art bronzes of quality has grown tremendously since Hughes' day. Over the past century and a half, American fine art sculpture has matured so much that our artists now produce some of the finest sculptures in the world, both technically and aesthetically.

ABOUT SILVER

Throughout the ages, people have valued and venerated the precious metal silver. Its rarity and beauty inspired ancient peoples to fashion it into religious and ceremonial objects, while its willingness to be shaped induced later craftsworkers to fashion more utilitarian objects with it, such as bowls and spoons. Today, silver's unique properties assign it a prominent place in our current technological revolution. This lustrous, brilliant metal is undeniably as precious today as it was 5000 years ago.

Silver is a rare metal: miners consider a ton of ore yielding three ounces of silver as a rich strike. Although found occasionally in pure form as a native element, silver is more often extracted from compounds and obtained as a byproduct of lead, copper, and other ore processing. Mexico is currently the world's largest producer of this metal, followed by Peru, the Soviet Union, Canada, the United States, and Australia. Together, these six countries produce more than seventy percent of the world's silver supply.

Pure silver is almost pure white in color. When polished, it reflects ninety-five percent of the light striking it—the source of its unmatched, luminous beauty. Nevertheless, it is practical as well as beautiful: in outer space, its high reflectivity is put to use collecting solar energy.

The best conductor of heat and electricity known to man, silver is the next most malleable and ductile of the elements (only gold is more malleable), which allows it to be stretched, hammered, and shaped without breaking. Pure silver is so workable, it can be hammered into leaf measuring 1/100,000 of an inch thick, and, when drawn into fine wire, one ounce will stretch thirty miles.

Pure, unalloyed silver is known as fine silver. Although too soft for daily use, pure silver can be alloyed or combined with other metals to improve its mechanical strength and resistance to wear and tarnish. Sterling silver, strong enough to function as tableware, jewelry, and decorative articles, is an alloy of

92.5% silver with 7.5% copper. To guarantee the quality of objects made of silver that had passed official inspection, the practice of hallmarking was developed in England almost 700 years ago. The same hallmarks, "sterling" and "925," are still used today to assure the quality of sterling silver jewelry and tableware.

Precious metals such as silver and gold are measured in troy ounces, a system that differs from our ordinary avoirdupois system used to weigh food and other commercial products. See the table on page 8 for a comparison between these two systems.

Silver can be alloyed with various elements to change its characteristics. Combined with antimony and arsenic, it is less prone to tarnish, which makes the metal useful for electrical contacts. Tin and silver combine to form a dental amalgam which is initially pliable but quickly hardens into a corrosion-resistant material used to fill cavities. Alloys with palladium and platinum are also used in dental work.

The compound silver nitrate is used to "silver" mirrors and to produce light-sensitive silver halides, or silver salts, for photographic films and papers. Silver iodide, another silver salt, has a crystalline structure very similar to ice and provides the "seeds" to seed clouds and make rain.

Nickel silver, or German silver, is an alloy of copper, zinc, and nickel containing no silver whatsoever. It is widely used for inexpensive decorative items, tableware, and imitation silver objects. Mexican silver, on the other hand, is a common name for silver of at least ninety percent purity. It has frequently been used over the years by Mexican and Native American artisans.

Silver's use as currency can be traced back to ancient Babylon. Since antiquity, it has been cast or minted into coins, then those coins, in turn, have been melted down for other purposes. Many of the silver teapots, sauceboats, spoons, and silver objects made by Paul Revere and other silversmiths in Colonial America were produced from melted coins of that era, the purity of which often varied greatly.

Before 1966, coins officially minted by the United States government contained ninety percent silver and ten percent copper, a material called coin silver. Today, our common "silver" coins—dimes, quarters, and half-dollars—are really no more than copper sandwiched between two sheets of nickel. Nevertheless, thirteen million ounces of silver were used in the minting of other United States coins during 1987.

Silverwork is often considered a traditional art form of Native Americans, although there are no evident indigenous artifacts made of silver prior to European contact. The first record of a silversmith among the Navajo was a blacksmith named Atsidi Sani, who learned to work silver from a Mexican man around 1850 in order to earn more money making bridles. At about the same time, the Zuni Indians of western New Mexico, who had already been making brass and copper jewelry, began to fabricate jewelry of silver.

Until the turn of the century, Native American craftspeople produced silver jewelry only for their own native markets. As increasing numbers of Anglos arrived by rail from the East, these artisans began to produce jewelry for the tourist trade. They used coin silver in their work, melting American silver coins until the government forbade the defacing of United States money. They switched to melting down Mexican pesos after that.

The lost-wax casting of silver jewelry in this country is not a new technique. In the Southwest, native silversmiths casting silver jewelry traditionally hand carved two-piece molds of tuff or tufa, a porous rock originating from volcanic ash and found in many locations of the Four Corners area, where the Hopi and Navajo Reservations are situated. These silversmiths also adopted a technique of casting metal into sand molds. This process requires a matching pair of casting flasks to hold the sand, creating, in essence, a two-piece mold. Fine windblown sand with rounded edges, when viewed under a magnifier, can be obtained in many areas of the Southwest and provides a good medium for the sand casting of silver jewelry.

The lost-wax casting process has recently been refined by fine art foundries to accommodate the casting of sculptures into silver. In principle, it is an identical process to the lost-wax casting of bronze used for fine art sculptures. Both are labor-intensive and time-consuming, but both result in the finest detail of any other metal casting techniques. What differs between them is the environment where casting takes place. While contaminants are not an issue in bronze casting, they are of crucial importance in silver casting, where the integrity of the finished silver sculpture must be preserved.

From electronics to computers, telephone systems to pharmaceuticals, and rockets to auto windshields (where an ounce of silver added to the glass makes the defroster work better), silver has proven itself a valuable and valued commodity in our world. Works of art cast into silver are an investment in metal as well as in art. The artworks in this book go far to prove that, like all successful "marriages," a sculpture in silver is more valuable and more beautiful than either component alone.

Comparative Table of Avoirdupois and Troy Weights

Avoirdupois	Troy	Avoirdupois	Troy
1 oz.	.91 oz.	5 lb.	72.90 oz.
2 oz.	1.82 oz.	6 lb.	87.48 oz.
3 oz.	2.73 oz.	7 lb.	102.06 oz.
4 oz.	3.64 oz.	8 lb.	116.64 oz.
5 oz.	4.55 oz.	9 lb.	131.22 oz.
6 oz.	5.46 oz.	10 lb.	145.80 oz.
7 oz.	6.37 oz.	15 lb.	218.70 oz.
8 oz.	7.28 oz.	20 lb.	291.60 oz.
9 oz.	8.19 oz.	25 lb.	364.50 oz.
10 oz.	9.10 oz.	30 lb.	437.40 oz.
11 oz.	10.01 oz.	35 lb.	510.30 oz.
12 oz.	10.92 oz.	40 lb.	583.20 oz.
13 oz.	11.83 oz.	45 lb.	656.10 oz.
14 oz.	12.74 oz.	50 lb.	729.00 oz.
15 oz.	13.65 oz.	60 lb	874.80 oz.
1 lb.	14.58 oz.	70 lb.	1010.60 oz.
2 lb.	29.16 oz.	80 lb.	1166.40 oz.
3 lb.	43.74 oz.	90 lb.	1312.20 oz.
4 lb.	58.32 oz.	100 lb.	1458.00 oz.

WHY SILVER?

Silver has an intrinsic value. As a precious metal, it has been cherished thousands of years around the world for its exotic beauty. By combining the beauty of silver with the artistic talent of a sculptor, the resulting work becomes the finest of artistic expression.

Sculpture made from the lost-wax or vanishing-wax method is perhaps the least understandable art technique for the layperson, although it has been known to humankind for some 6000 years. Early artisans using the method appeared in China, India, Afghanistan, Egypt, the Near East, Italy, and Greece. Because of its durability, cast metal sculpture survives all other art forms and one can find early masterpieces formed in bronze, silver, and gold made by the lost-wax method in museums worldwide. The identical lost-wax process is used by today's artists, and, with developments in science and technology, the quality of cast sculpture has been much improved.

When we visit museums, galleries, and collectors of fine art, it is unusual to see sculpture in silver. The intent of this book is to show the beauty of this precious metal when it is combined with the extraordinary talent of our past and contemporary artists. What is depicted within these pages is not simply art for today, but "art of the future" with artistic and intrinsic value that will live on for generations.

FROM WAX TO SILVER BY THE

LOST-WAX METHOD

In 1981, the Harmsen Publishing Company introduced the book *Sculpture to Bronze* by Bill Harmsen. The book included a detailed article with drawings to explain the lost-wax process of metal casting. For readers not familiar with the lost-wax method, there is no better way to explain this process than to include the article again in this publication, reproduced here on pages 12 to 23.

The twenty-four fine silver sculptures depicted through page 67 have all been cast by the lost-wax method. Lost-wax casting can be used for all metals—bronze, silver, or gold—but pouring with precious metals takes additional experience and specialized foundry equipment.

The properties of silver demand that allowances be made to create a chemically nonreactive ceramic mold. Though the mold-making materials involved in silver and bronze casting are similar, creating the mold for a silver sculpture takes twice the time as for bronze.

While bronze can be heated and poured in the most primitive of circumstances, unusual pouring difficulties arise when casting in silver. In a molten state, silver will absorb oxygen in an amount several times its volume. As the metal cools, it spits out this oxygen, creating flaws and pitting in the casting. To eliminate this phenomenon, modern techniques have been devised to ensure gas-free metal. Another difficulty arises because silver is so efficient at conducting heat. The molten metal can lose fluidity very quickly, dropping temperature by 125 degrees each minute.

Pouring silver also requires a larger crew. For example, two foundry workers with 150 pounds of molten bronze can pour twelve castings in one heat, taking about four minutes for the entire procedure. In contrast, a crew of five must work together in a controlled atmosphere to pour just one silver casting, although the pour takes less than forty-five seconds from start to finish.

After the casting has cooled, the ceramic shell is broken away and the cleaning process begins. Being a hard metal, bronze easily withstands the effects of impact tools and blasting with glass beads. Silver, however, requires careful and meticulous cleaning to avoid damaging its softer surface. A typical bronze can be cleaned in about fifteen minutes, while the same image cast into silver requires up to eight hours.

Once clean, bronze can be assembled and finished rather aggressively by means of welding, hammering, and filing. With silver, every piece of metal that is not part of the finished work must be vacuum-captured, recovered, and reprocessed as 99.9% fine silver—cuttings, filings, and even silver sawdust has value. Silver welding demands expert craftswork, because heat applied to the weld point is rapidly conducted away and transferred throughout the casting.

The laborious procedures called for in silver casting lead to doubling or tripling the time expended to create a sculpture in silver, compared to an identical casting in bronze. Add the actual value of silver into the equation and one begins to appreciate that a casting in fine silver is perhaps the ultimate tribute to the art of sculpture.

FROM WAX TO BRONZE BY THE LOST WAX METHOD

LOST WAX

Sculpture made from the lost-wax or vanishing-wax method is perhaps the least understood of all the art forms produced today. To fully comprehend this ancient art, a person would have to put in much time and effort with an artist at a foundry observing the intricate procedures that must be undertaken.

In the early days, ornate designs were made from the sand-casting method, which is still popular today and was used a great deal by the Navajos in making much of their jewelry. At present, however, ninety percent of all bronzes are made by the lost-wax method. This term is derived from the process itself, as the wax is actually "lost."

This chapter presents a comprehensive, elementary look at what takes place from the time the original model is formed by the artist to the point where the sculpture emerges complete. To make the study easier to assimilate, an artist has made schematic drawings that outline the procedures.

1 Plaster Elk

For illustrative purposes, we will first examine the original model of THE FAWN ELK, which is small and "plain" and will be easier to follow and to understand than a large and more complicated form. Voisin sculptured this piece in clay in 1936.

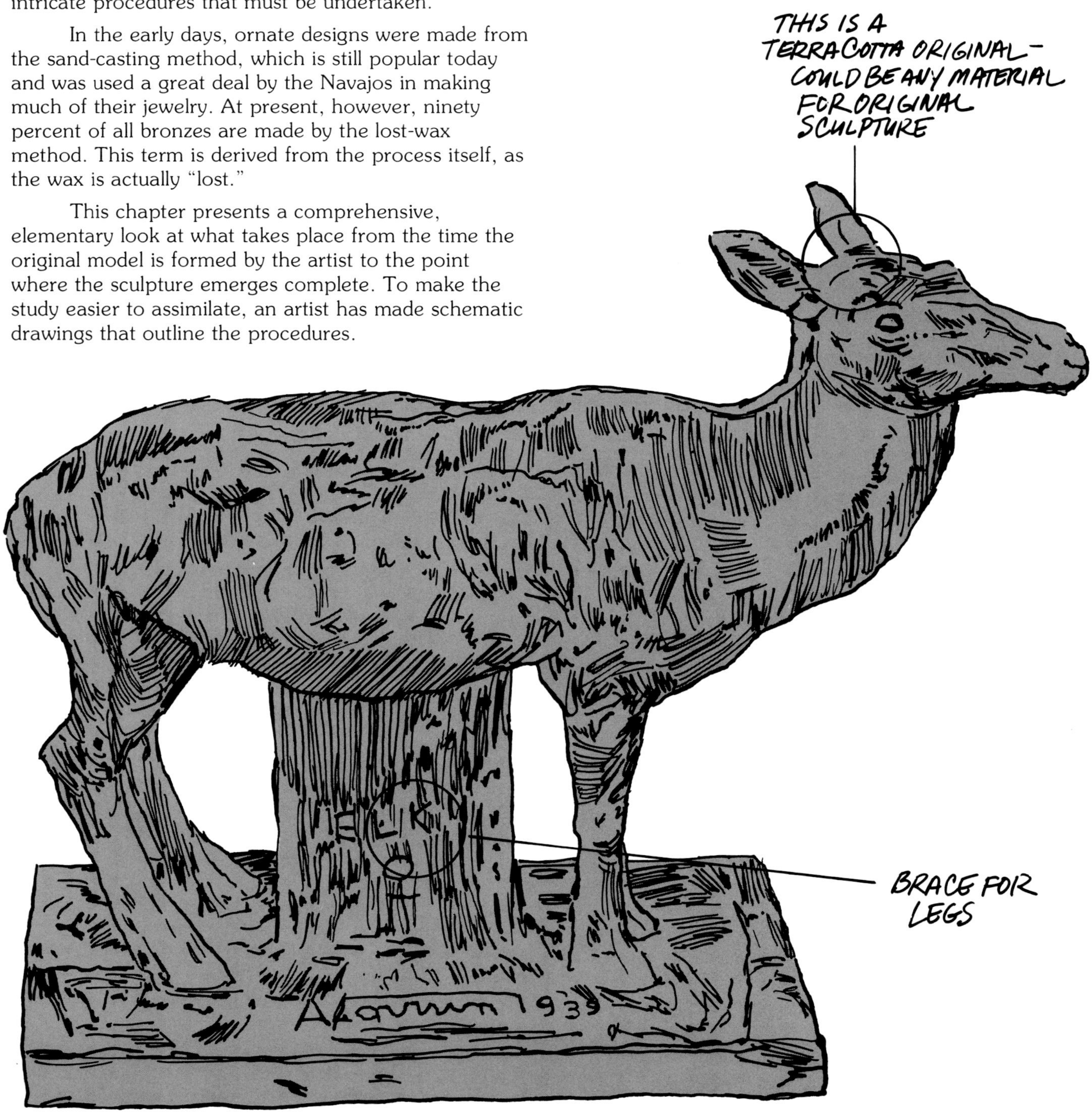

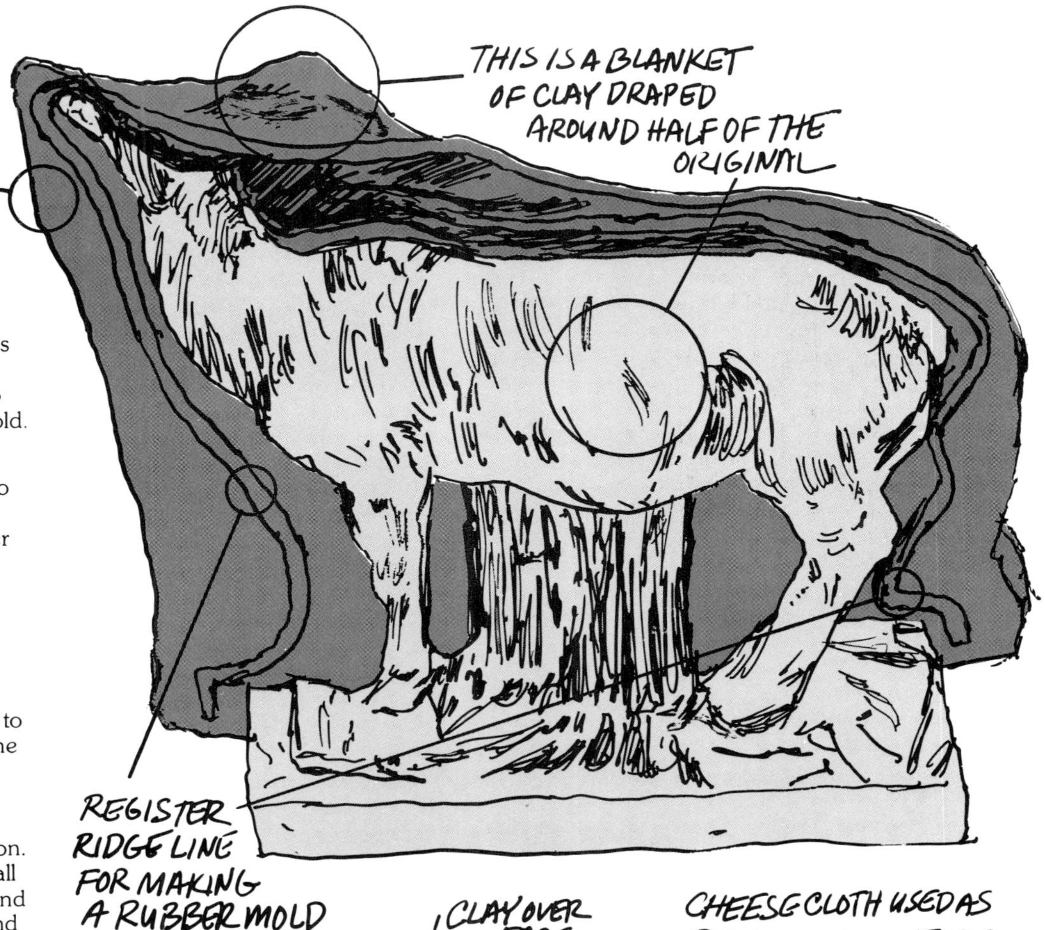

2 Rubber Mold

From this original, one of the first steps of the "Sculpture to Bronze" process is the molding of the original art work. There are many molding techniques; two of them are the **blanket** and the **pour** mold.

BLANKET MOLD: For a blanket mold, the original art is sectioned into two halves by chosing a common center line over the entire piece; and once this center line is established, of modeling clay or plasticine a clay wall is laid up to the first section to be molded, and the "cold molding compound" (CMC) is then painted on this half. The first layer is the "detail coat," meaning that it will pick up all the surface detail. This coat is allowed to "cure," and then several more layers of the CMC are applied for added strength.

When the final application of the CMC has cured, a "mother mold" of plaster of paris is applied to the first section. The piece is then turned over, the clay wall that is next to the sculpture is removed, and the same steps are repeated on the second section. In this mold are formed alignment keys or notches to properly adjust the two halves together.

POUR MOLD: This is a more modern method which is being used by many moldmakers today.

Once again, the art work is sectioned into two halves by the use of a common center line. Sometimes the work will require more than two sections for molding, particularly if it is a more involved sculpture. This time, the moldmaker "paints" a thin line on the sculpture as to where the dividing line will be for easy location later. A thin sheet of saran is wrapped around the sculpture and secured with cellophane tape. This is for easy removal of the two mold halves. Clay that has been pounded or rolled out to a quarter-inch thickness is then molded over the art work. A larger, thicker section of clay is build up over the predetermined dividing lines that were painted on the art work. This will serve as a division for the plaster halves and a thicker cutting section, for dividing the rubber mold.

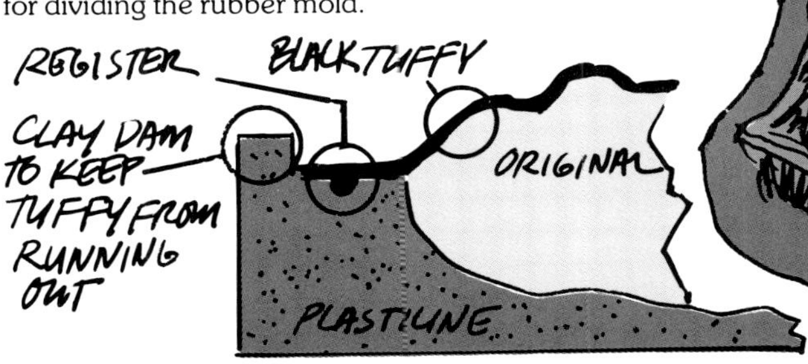

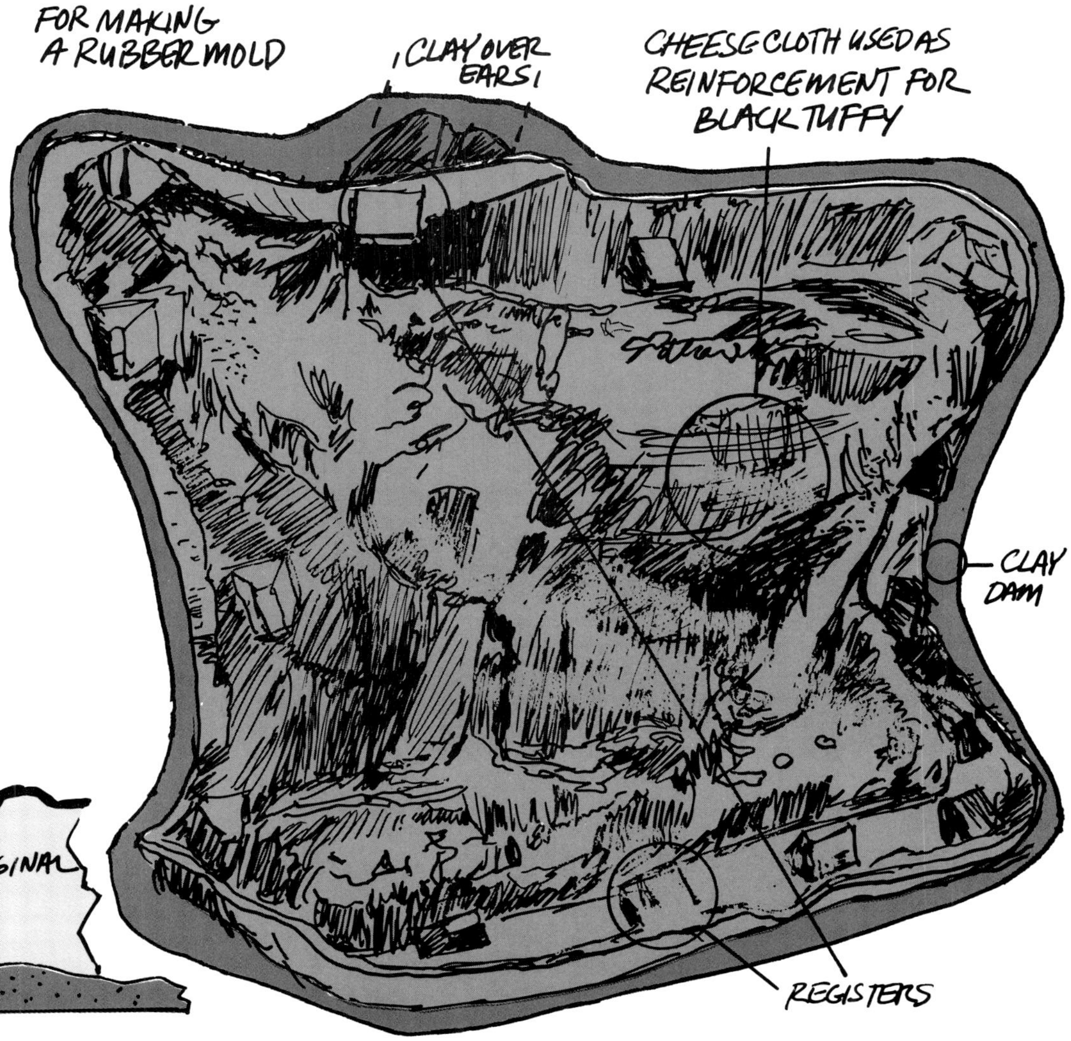

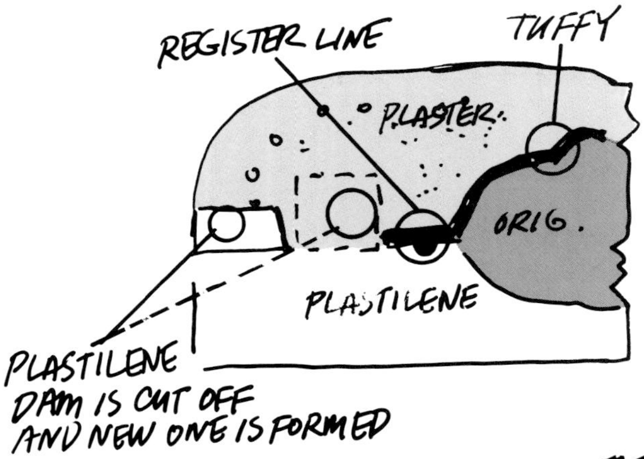
REGISTER LINE
TUFFY
PLASTER
ORIG.
PLASTILENE
PLASTILENE DAM IS CUT OFF AND NEW ONE IS FORMED

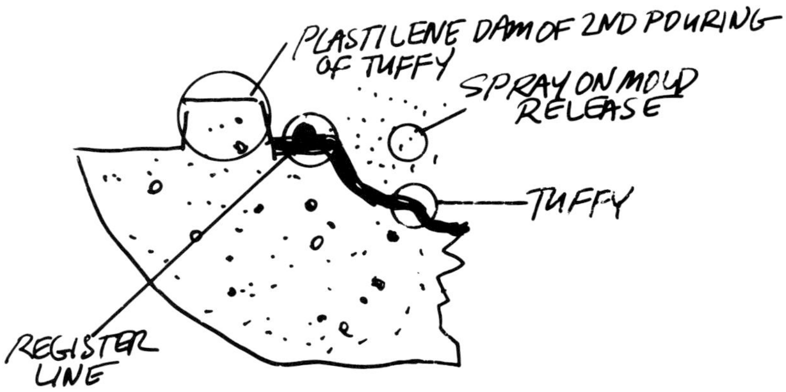
PLASTILENE DAM OF 2ND POURING OF TUFFY
SPRAY ON MOLD RELEASE
TUFFY
REGISTER LINE

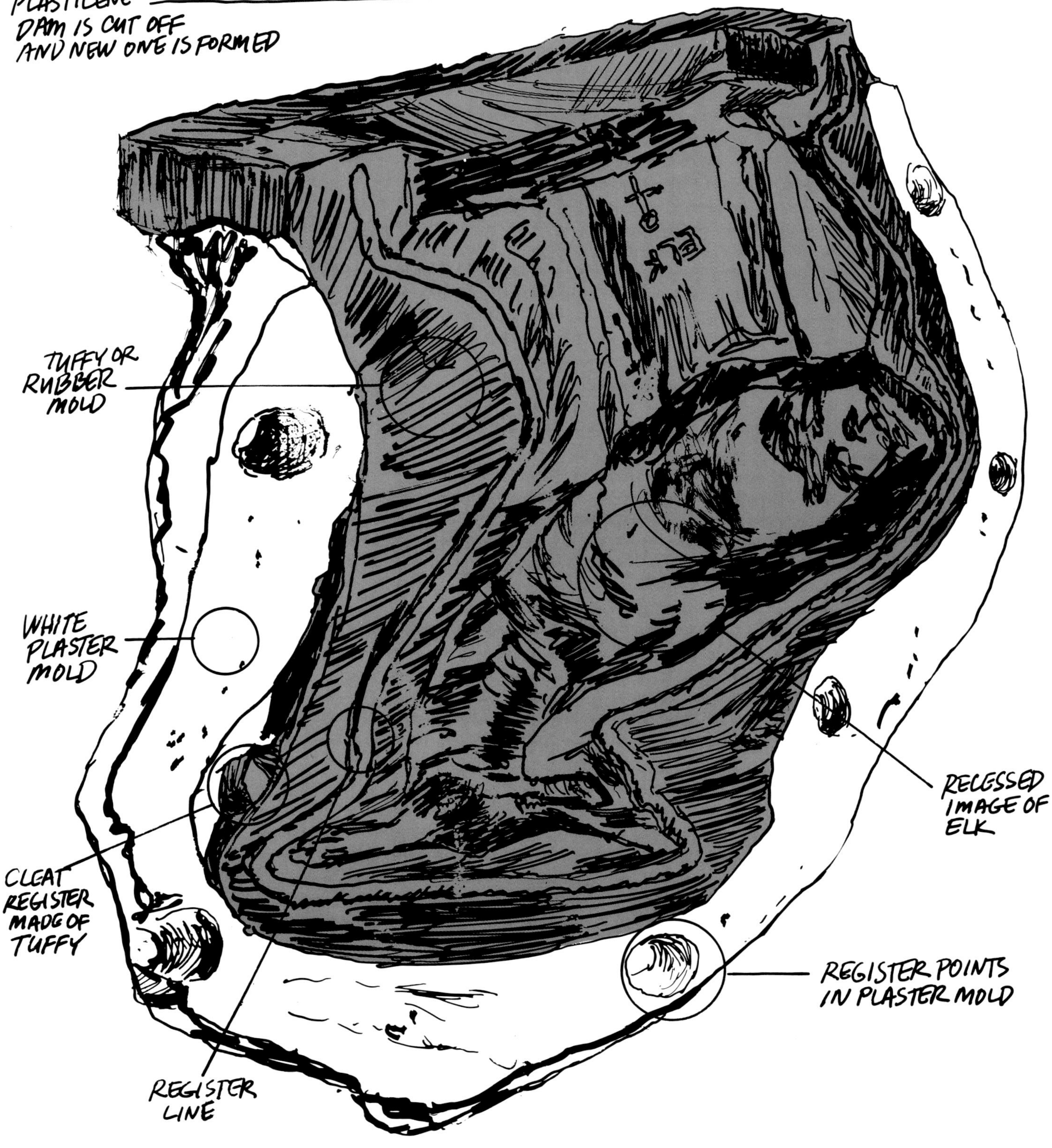
TUFFY OR RUBBER MOLD
WHITE PLASTER MOLD
CLEAT REGISTER MADE OF TUFFY
RECESSED IMAGE OF ELK
REGISTER POINTS IN PLASTER MOLD
REGISTER LINE

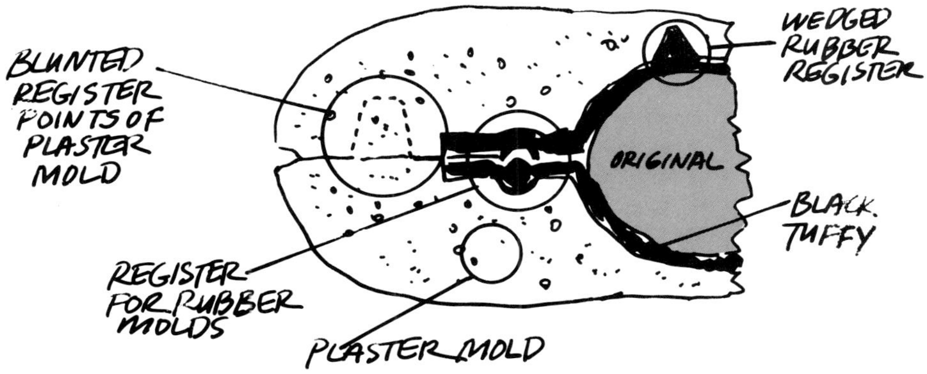

3 Plaster and Rubber Molds

Plaster of paris is then applied to the clayed-up sections of the mold. After the plaster has dried, it is removed from the clay. The clay, in turn, is removed from around the art work. At this point, the saran wrap is removed. The plaster sections are then placed back around the original art work. There will be a quarter-inch negative space around the original where the clay once was. The moldmaker then will pour CMC through a pour spout in the mold. The rubber will flow into the space that was left by the clay.

The rubber is allowed to cure, and the plaster mother mold is removed. The original art work is encased in the rubber now so that the moldmaker can open the rubber mold along the built-up edges. The rubber is cut open with a scalpel or sharp instrument in a zigzag or serrated pattern, which gives accurate alignment to the two halves; and the white line that was painted on the original art work in the beginning makes the cutting operation more certain.

After the rubber mold has been cut, the sections are placed in the plaster mother molds. These molds will be used each time a wax is made.

4 Pouring the Wax

Our next step is the forming of the wax, which will also be an exact duplicate of the original model. The two halves of the molds (rubber inside and plaster outside) are placed and locked together; then in an inverted position, the heated wax in liquid form is poured into the mold cavity. As the material hardens from the mold surface toward the center, the excess is poured out. Timing and temperature again are of the utmost importance, for it is necessary to pick the right moment to pour out the excess wax to form an exact duplicate with a wall thickness of one-eighth inch.

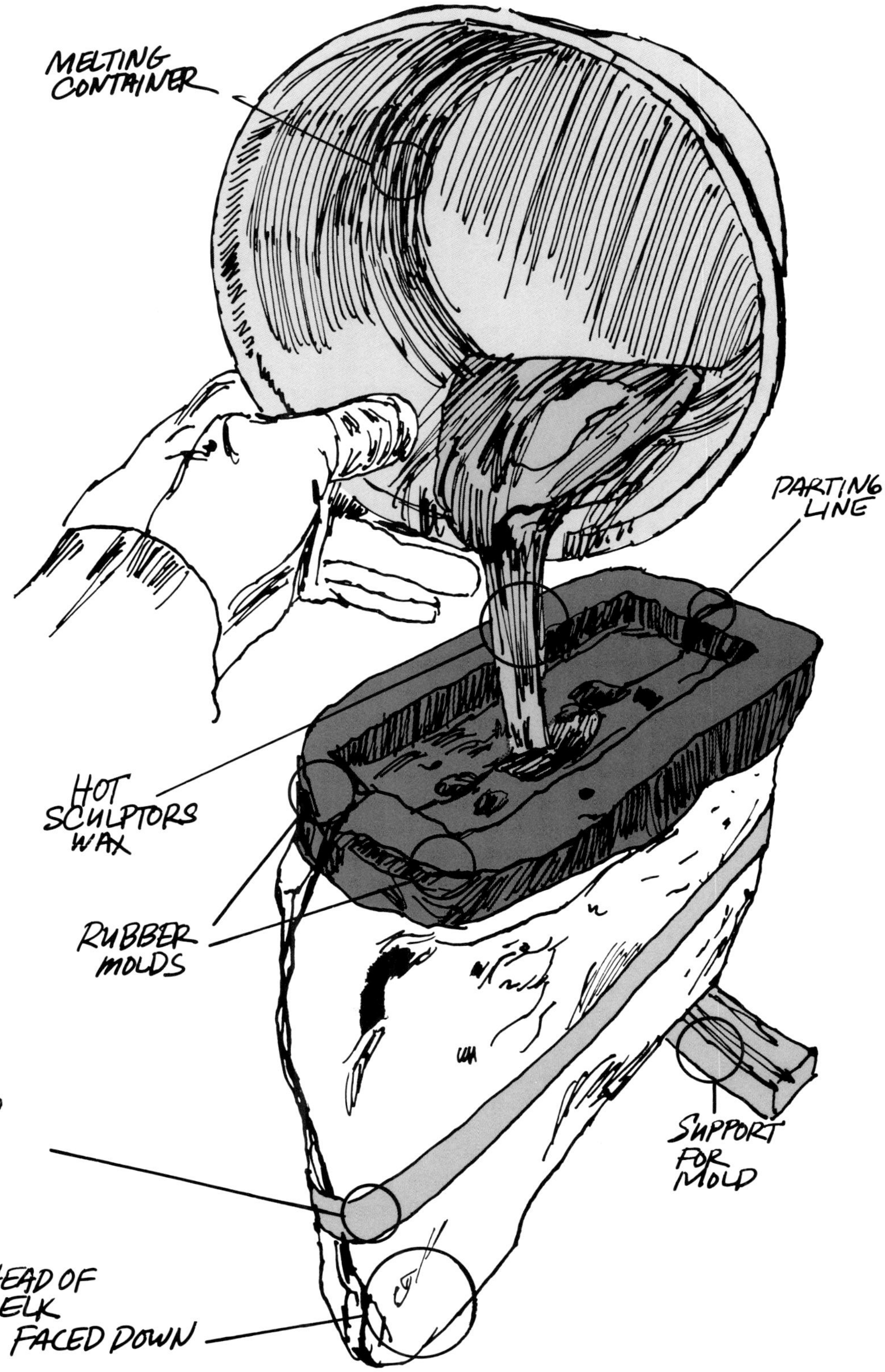

5 Removing the Mold
After the wax is set up and cooled, the plaster mother mold is removed, and the rubber mold is carefully peeled from the hollow wax replica.

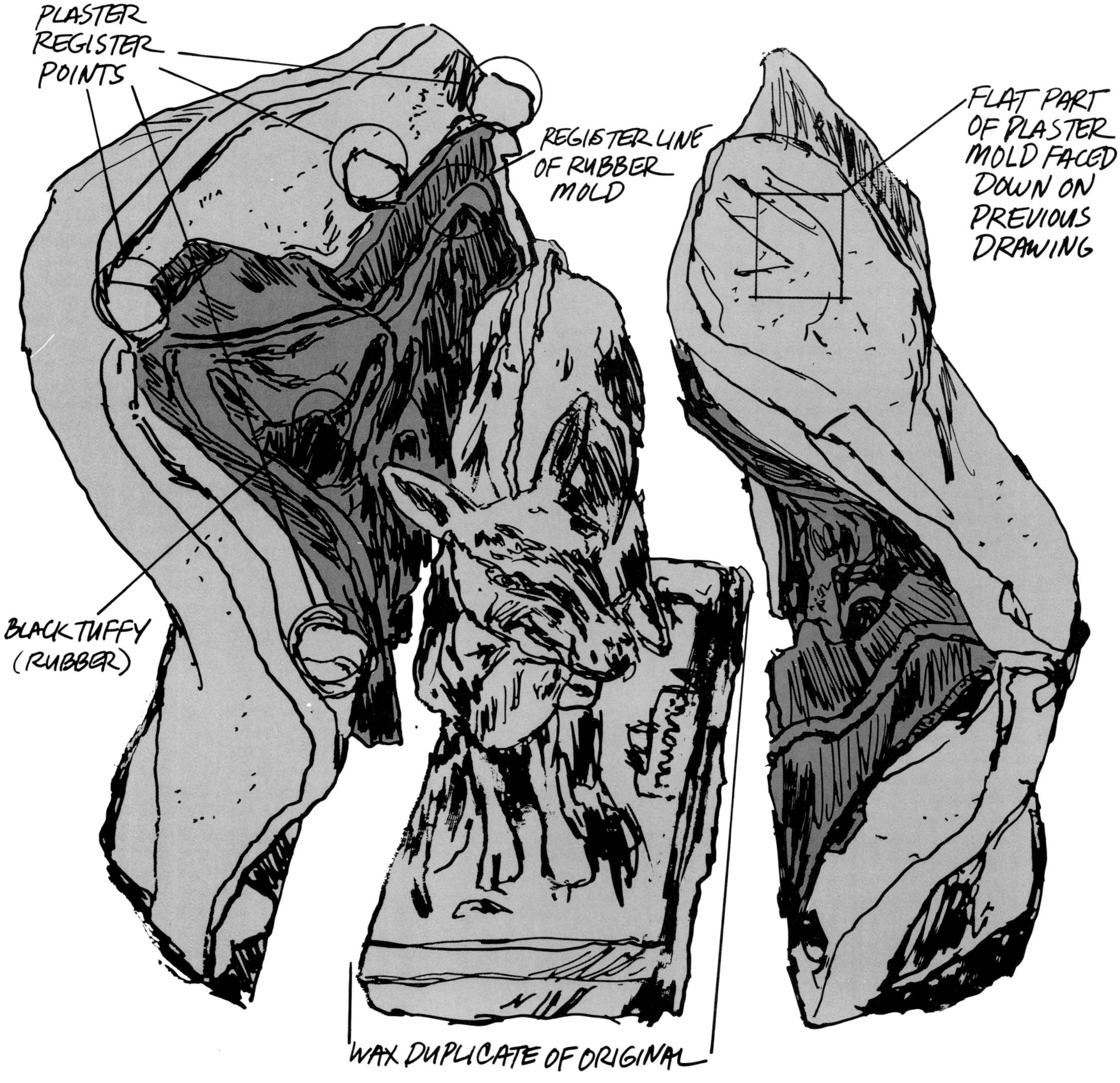

6 **Chasing the Wax**

The wax reproduction is carefully chased and prepared for attaching the gating and sprews necessary for the metal delivery system and venting.

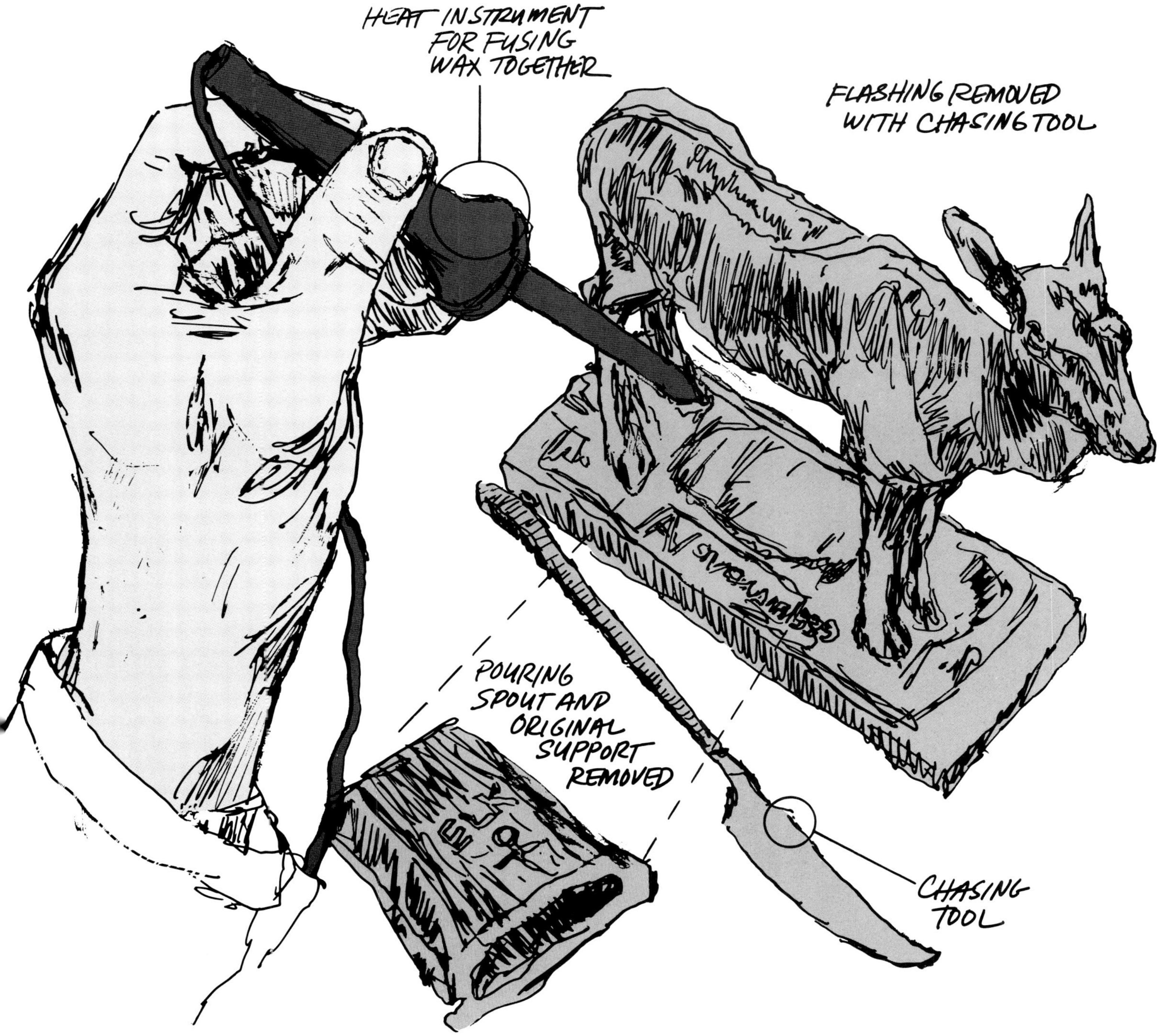

7 Ceramic-Coating Procedure

The wax pattern, properly prepared and attached to the casting sprue, which is also wax, is now ready for the ceramic shell to be started. It is dipped into a silicone slurry from five to eight times, depending on the size and type. Between each dipping, sand is sprinkled on the form. The first two dippings are sprinkled with 120 grain sand which is for detail in the sculpture. The following dippings are of 30 grain sand to give it strength and make it permeable after curing. It is important between each one of these steps to have proper curing and drying; otherwise it could end up with a weak shell, causing a failure in the metal casting process.

The drawing shows a section in the body of the elk cut out. This permits the entry of the slurry into the hollow of the wax, for it is important to ensure the production of a thin-wall casting. (Metal shrinks as it cools, and the thinness of the wall is important).

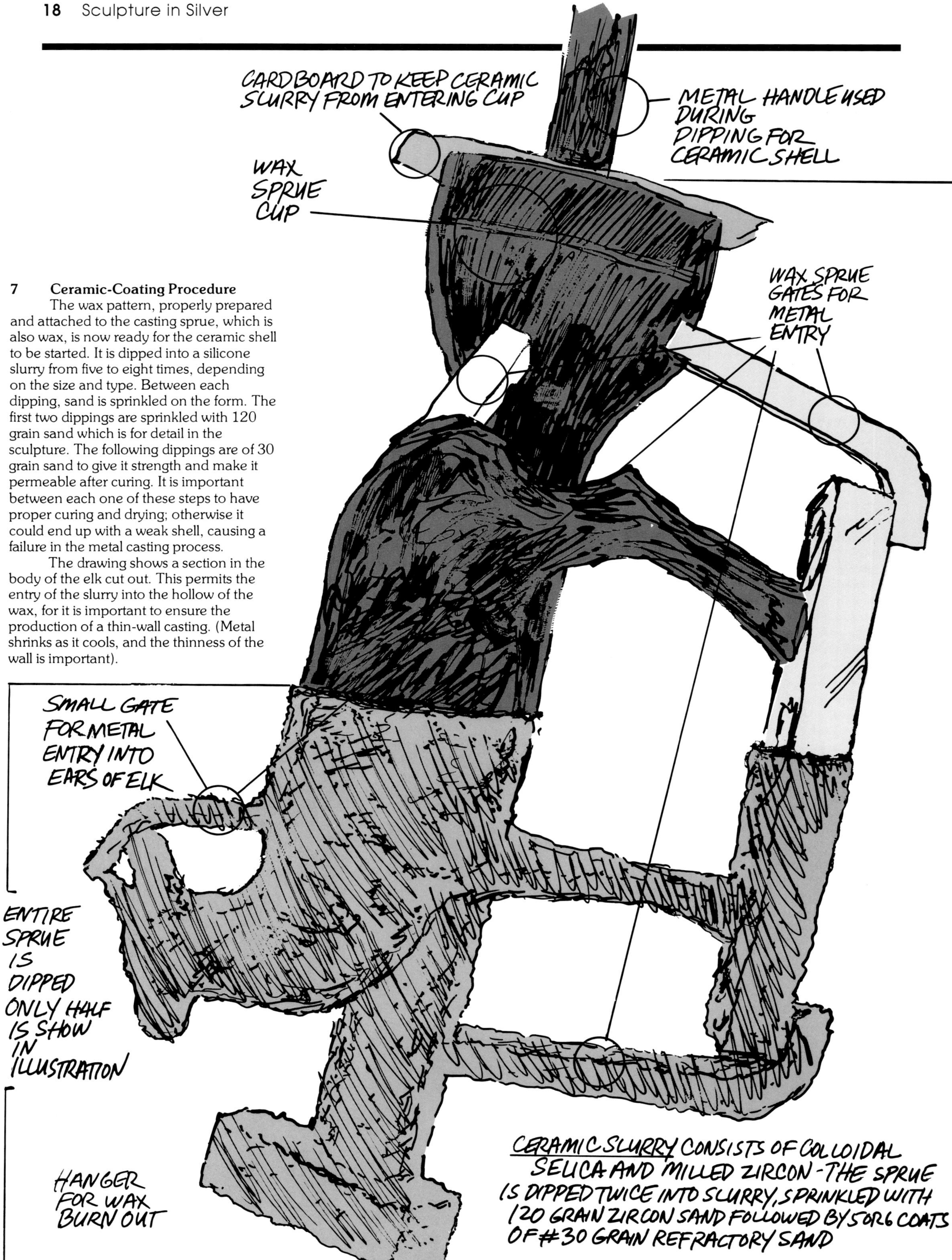

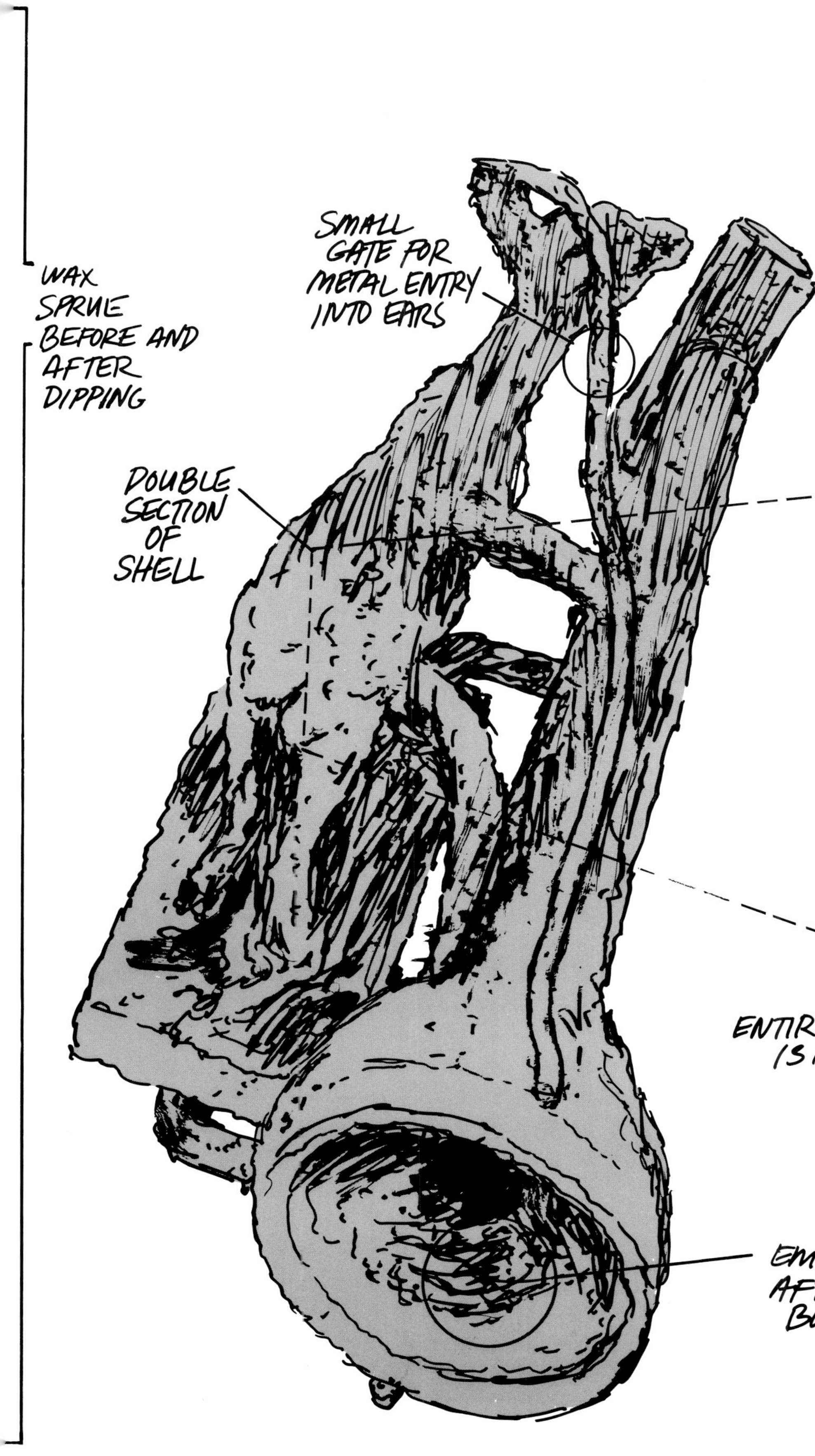

8 Melt-out—Lost Wax

At this point, the ceramic-filled mold is placed into a burn-out oven. This is the stage of the "lost-wax" procedure when the wax is actually melted out, leaving the hollow mold clean, dried, and cured. Some foundries add another step at this point by first heating the shell in an autoclave where a generator introduces steam under pressure at approximately 300°. The steam melts out approximately 98% of the wax, and then the shell is again heated in a dry-heat chamber to complete the melt-out, cure, and harden the investment.

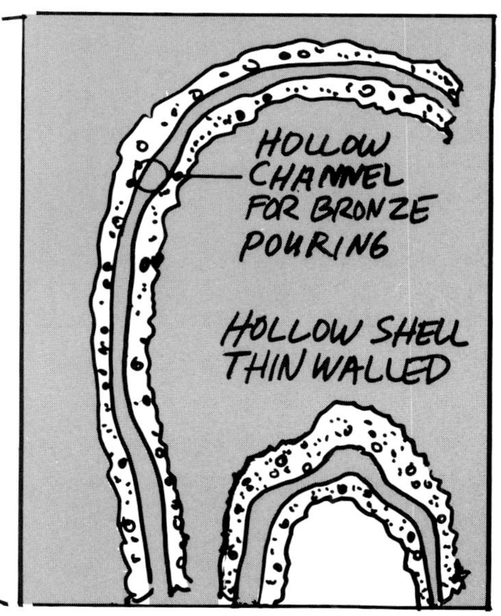

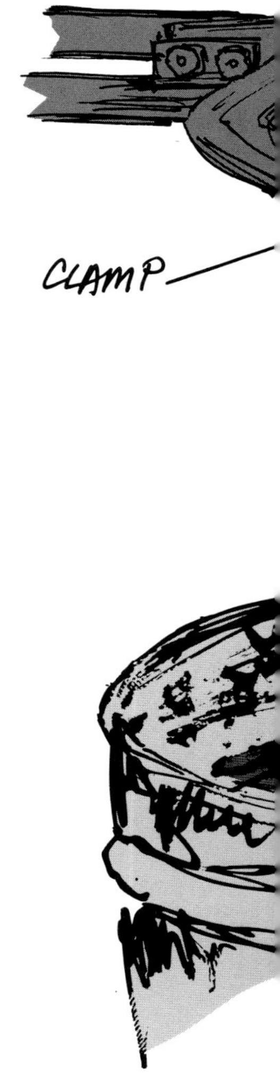

9 Positioning the Ceramic Mold

With the mold readied, it is put into an oven and heated to approximately 1400° and then placed on a pouring table or buried in a container of sand with the pouring cup up. This is a safety feature, for if the mold should break, the hot fluid bronze would be contained. It also adds strength to the mold.

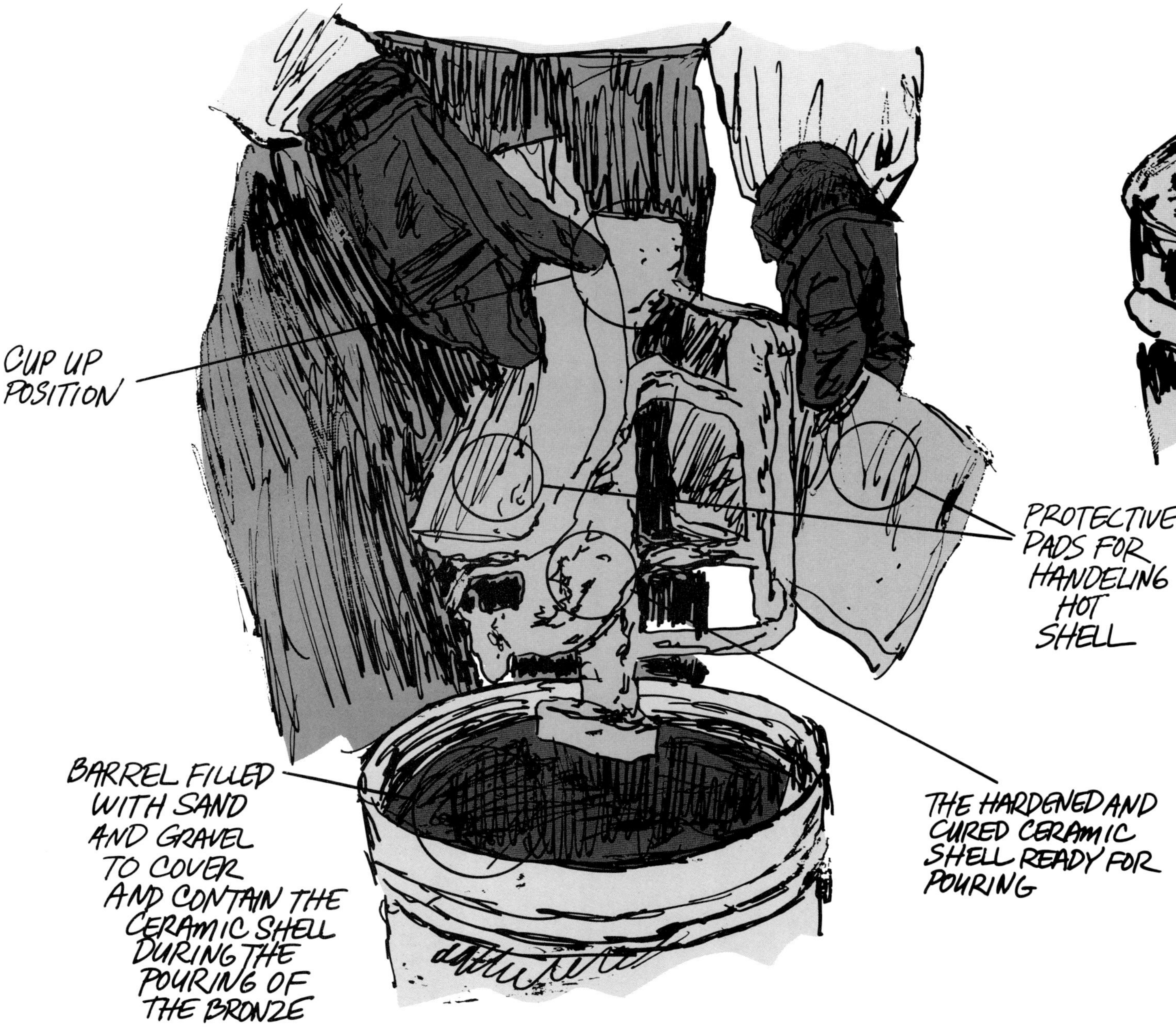

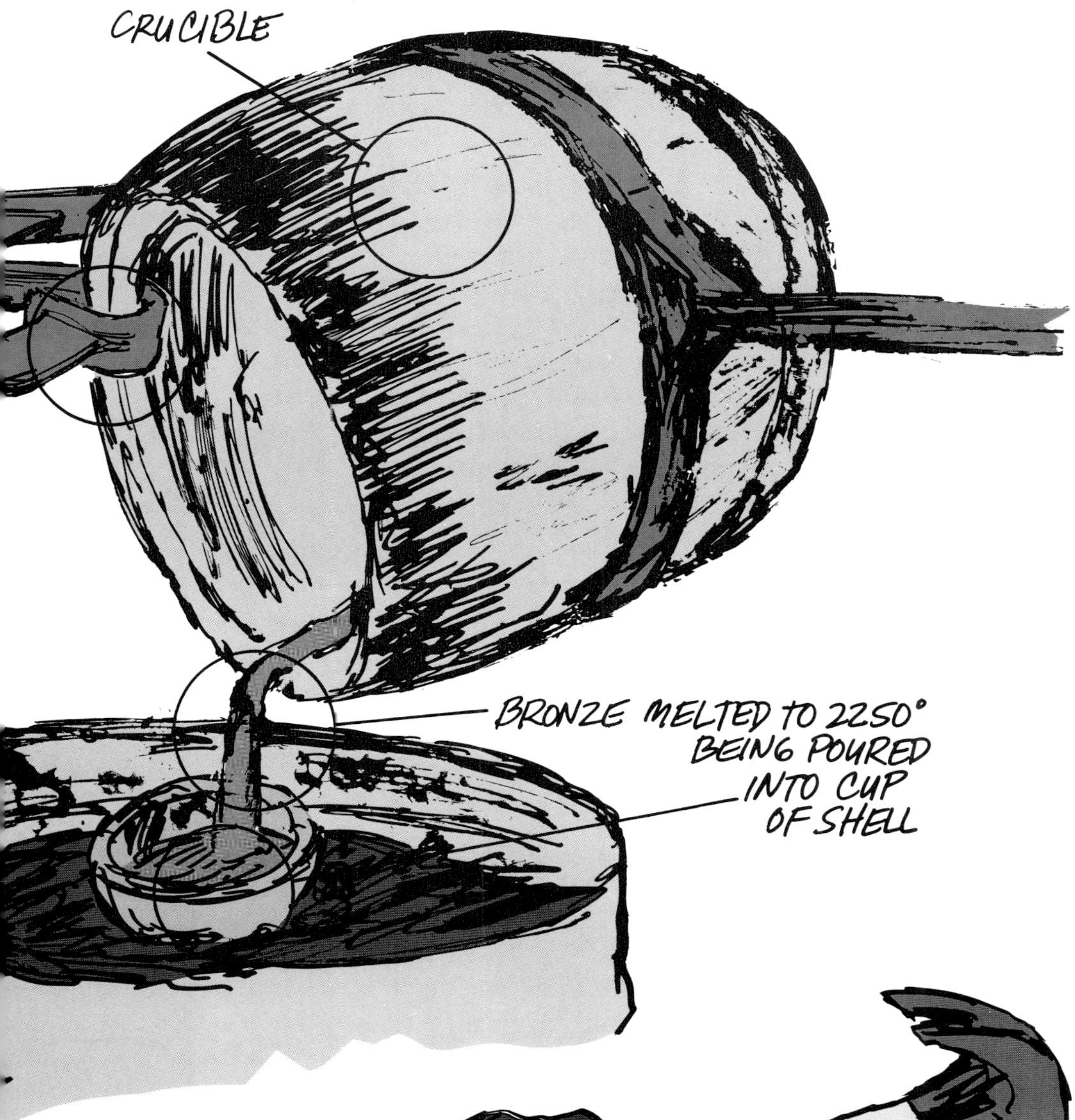

10 Pouring the Molten Metal

The metal, which is heated to approximately 2200° is then poured into the mold.

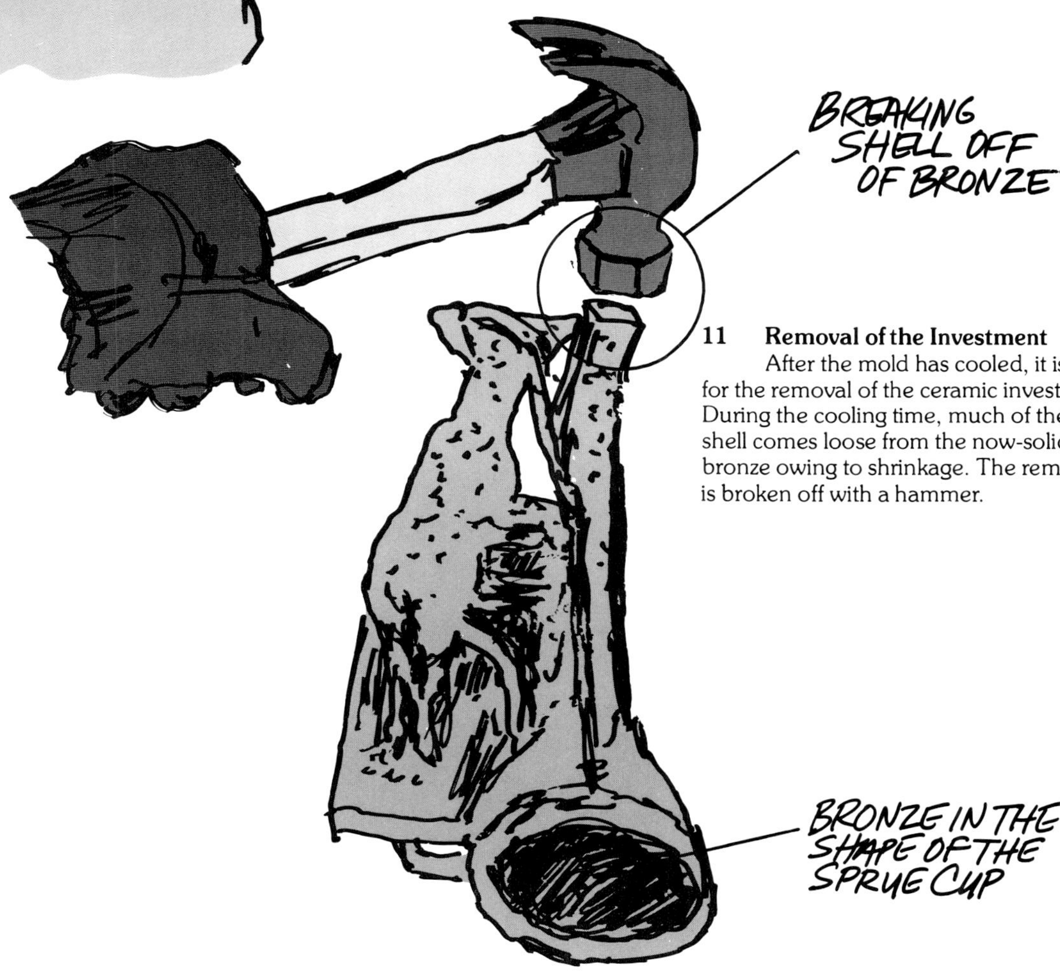

11 Removal of the Investment

After the mold has cooled, it is ready for the removal of the ceramic investment. During the cooling time, much of the shell comes loose from the now-solid bronze owing to shrinkage. The remainder is broken off with a hammer.

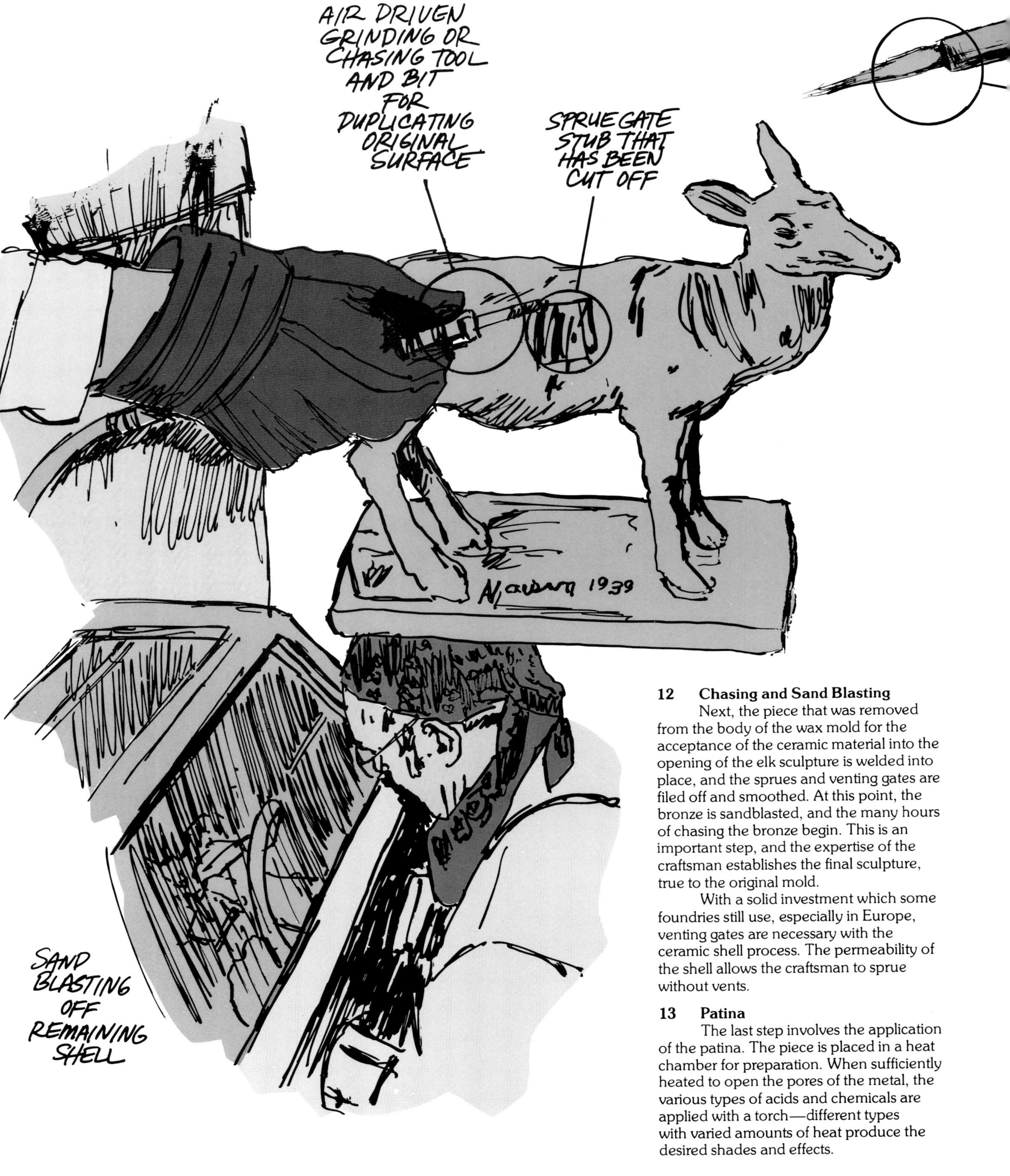

12 Chasing and Sand Blasting

Next, the piece that was removed from the body of the wax mold for the acceptance of the ceramic material into the opening of the elk sculpture is welded into place, and the sprues and venting gates are filed off and smoothed. At this point, the bronze is sandblasted, and the many hours of chasing the bronze begin. This is an important step, and the expertise of the craftsman establishes the final sculpture, true to the original mold.

With a solid investment which some foundries still use, especially in Europe, venting gates are necessary with the ceramic shell process. The permeability of the shell allows the craftsman to sprue without vents.

13 Patina

The last step involves the application of the patina. The piece is placed in a heat chamber for preparation. When sufficiently heated to open the pores of the metal, the various types of acids and chemicals are applied with a torch—different types with varied amounts of heat produce the desired shades and effects.

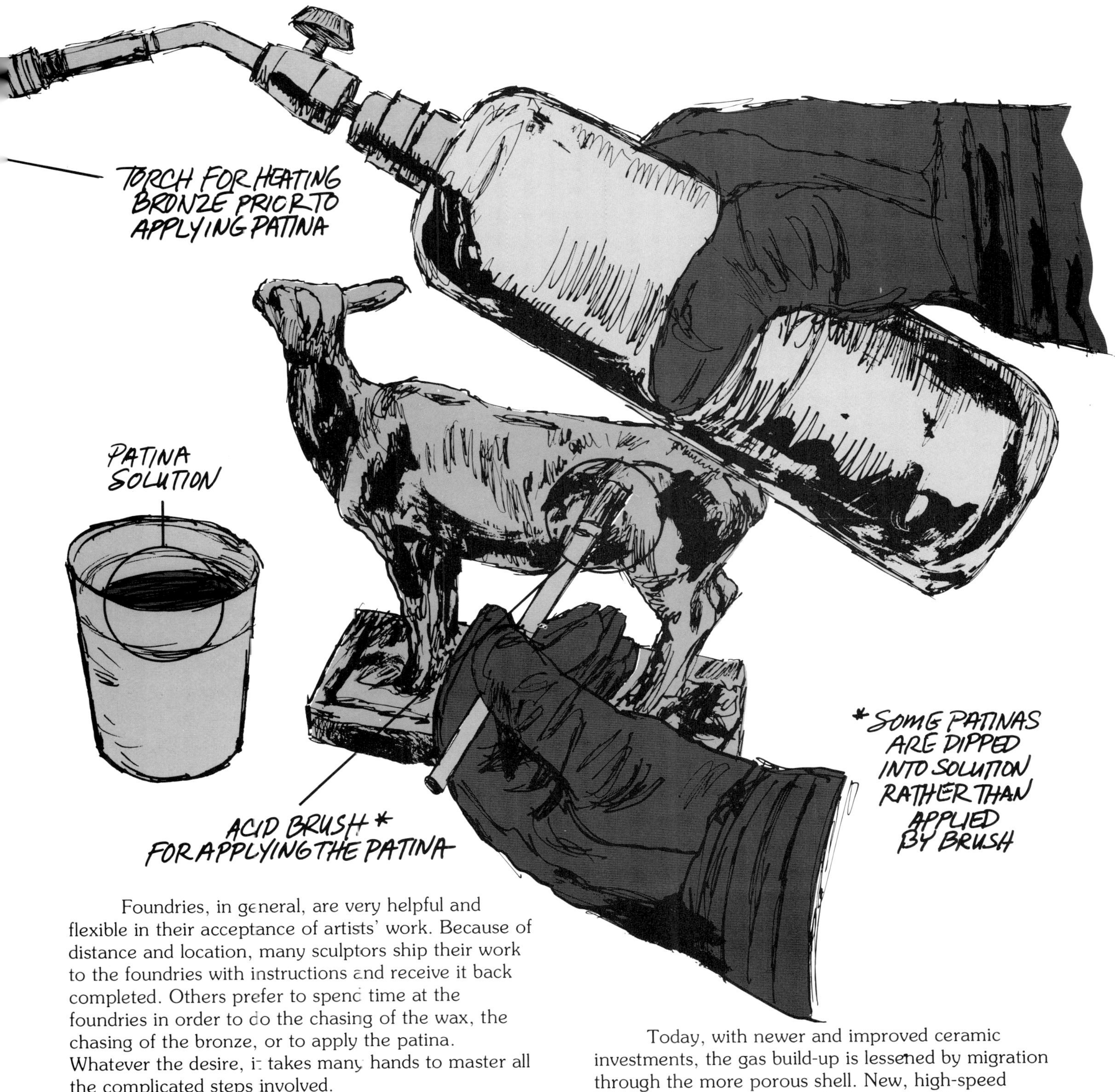

Foundries, in general, are very helpful and flexible in their acceptance of artists' work. Because of distance and location, many sculptors ship their work to the foundries with instructions and receive it back completed. Others prefer to spend time at the foundries in order to do the chasing of the wax, the chasing of the bronze, or to apply the patina. Whatever the desire, it takes many hands to master all the complicated steps involved.

As in many professions, there is no one set way to complete a bronze. This art, handed down from father to son, has many variations. In the past, it took days to build a hot fire in a brick oven to accomplish the burn-out or "lost wax." Today, with electric furnaces and high-speed blowers, the process is greatly speeded up. Also, much emphasis was put on the gating system and venting for the release of gas build-up.

Today, with newer and improved ceramic investments, the gas build-up is lessened by migration through the more porous shell. New, high-speed grinding tools and chemicals also add to the efficiency and beauty of the work.

Sculpture to bronze has many variations. With this new and advanced technology, much of the process has been improved, which adds to the quality and diversity of the finished work. It is hoped that with a better understanding of this art form, a greater appreciation of the talent of the creator and the expertise of the craftsman will result.

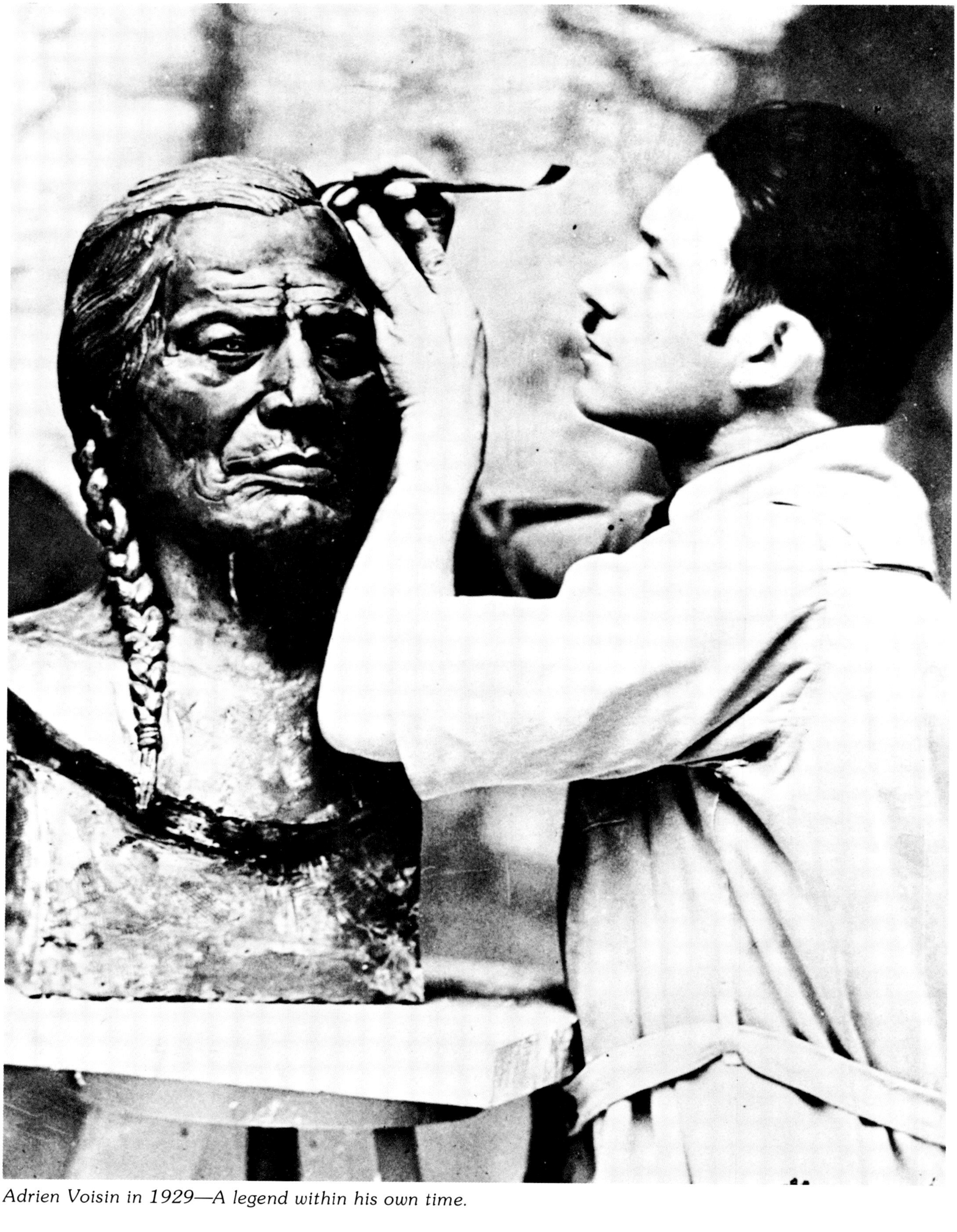

Adrien Voisin in 1929—A legend within his own time.

PAST MASTER —

ADRIEN VOISIN

A noted art critic once called Adrien Voisin one of the four greatest sculptors of the American Indian, with good reason. This American-born artist spent a substantial portion of his life capturing in bronze the nobility and dignity of his contemporary Native Americans, leaving us a valuable visual and artistic record.

Adrien Voisin was born October 4, 1890, on Long Island, although most of his early days were spent in Newport, Rhode Island. In Newport, he enjoyed the acquaintance of many artists, whose studios he often visited, since the city was a gathering spot for cultured Americans.

Voisin's early aspiration was to become a naturalist, but he did not enjoy his school studies. After dropping out of school, he apprenticed himself to a taxidermist. In that capacity, he learned to improvise animal forms of wire, foreshadowing his eventual pursuit of sculpturing. His budding interest in art led Voisin to apprentice himself to a master woodcarver for four more years while painting part-time under the tutelage of Sargent Kendall from the Yale School of Fine Arts. At Kendall's urging, Voisin decided to study in France.

In Paris, he first enrolled in the Academe Colorossi in 1912, then went on to the Ecole National des Arts Decoratifs and the famous Ecole des Beaux Arts. He also studied at the ateliers of Mercer and Injalbert, and medalist Victor Peters. Under their guidance, Voisin realized that sculpture was his calling.

During his schooling in Paris, Voisin had made many idle sketches of Indians. His drawings attracted the attention of his teachers, who encouraged him to try to sculpt the figures. He eagerly followed their advice and began to model the Indians of his own country.

Art studies were interrupted for Voisin by the onset of World War I. After serving his country in the European trenches and suffering exposure to mustard gas, Voisin relocated to California because of poor health. Upon arriving, he was appointed head sculptor at the San Simeon estate of William Randolph Hearst. He then traveled to Spokane, Washington, to mold decorative designs for the Paulsen Building. There, he met and established a lifelong friendship with Vachel Lindsay, the poet and writer of Blackfeet descent. The two friends traveled together, meeting many of the northwestern Indians.

Voisin's wife, Frances, was the daughter of an Indian agent and acted as an interpreter when the couple went to Browning, Montana, in 1929. They rented an old Bureau of Indian Affairs building for a studio, and convinced the neighboring Indians to pose for sculpted portraits. Because of the Voisins' understanding and friendship, the Blackfeet Indians adopted the two into the tribe.

The cherished results of that productive year in Montana were twelve clay sculptural portraits. Too poor to have them cast into bronze in New York, the Voisins went to France, where bronzes could be cast at considerably less cost. He submitted the set of twelve for a formal showing at the Galleria Bernheim in Paris, which brought him much critical acclaim.

In 1931, a shipment of American sculptures destined for the Exposition Coloniale Internationale in France was lost en route. Consequently, Voisin was prevailed upon to represent the United States with his twelve Indian sculptures. The show received worldwide attention, and the French government awarded the artist the Diplôme d'Honeur for his work. The following year, his sculptures took the Gold Medal at the International Art Exhibit in Paris.

Returning home in 1934, Voisin traveled for years throughout Montana, Washington, Idaho, and Oregon seeking Indians as models. He completed dozens of sculptural portraits, as well as sculpting a number of animals native to the regions.

A humble and modest man, Voisin lived in relative obscurity after having received worldwide praise, his career cut short a second time by a second World War. He departed for the "Happy Hunting Ground" on May 7, 1979, at the age of 88. His sculptures live on, however, as powerful, poignant reminders of his art and his dedication to preserving the image of the American Indian.

HAPPY HUNTING GROUND

In 1929, Voisin sculpted the portrait head of Nina-Stuko, Mountain Chief of the Blackfeet, shown to the right. This monumental work carries the imagery of the American Indian to its finest expression in sculpture.

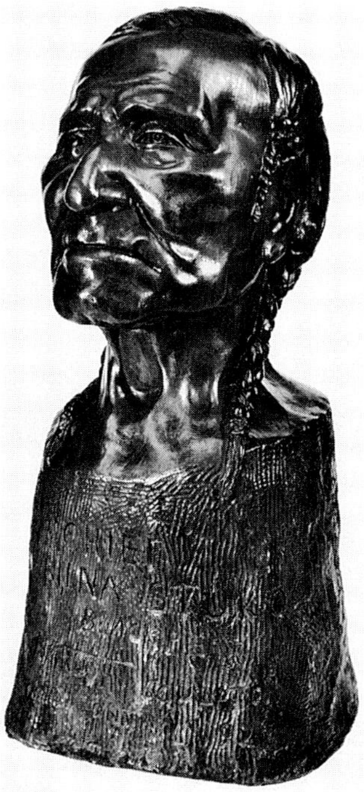

Adrien Voisin

Portrait bust of Nina-Stuko modeled in 1929. Height 21", bronze.

Known as a wise and honest man, Nina-Stuko had been the leader and hereditary Chief of the Confederation of the Five Nations. There had been three Mountain Chiefs named Nina-Stuko—each the father of the next.

Already ninety years old when he modeled for Voisin, the Indian's failing eyesight did not allow him to see the finished project, so he inspected it through the sense of touch. He insisted that Voisin sculpt him showing his eyes open, stating, "Me not always blind—want children to see me with eyes always open."

While modeling for the portrait head, Nina-Stuko was asked by Voisin about his thoughts of the future world. The Blackfeet chief answered that his wish was to go to the Happy Hunting Ground, "and ride a great stallion over a herd of charging buffalos."

Voisin was so moved by Nina-Stuko's dignity, he was inspired to create "Happy Hunting Ground" as a tribute to a great friend and honorable chief, showing him forever young and strong riding his swift stallion through eternity. Nina-Stuko died in 1942 at the age of 103.

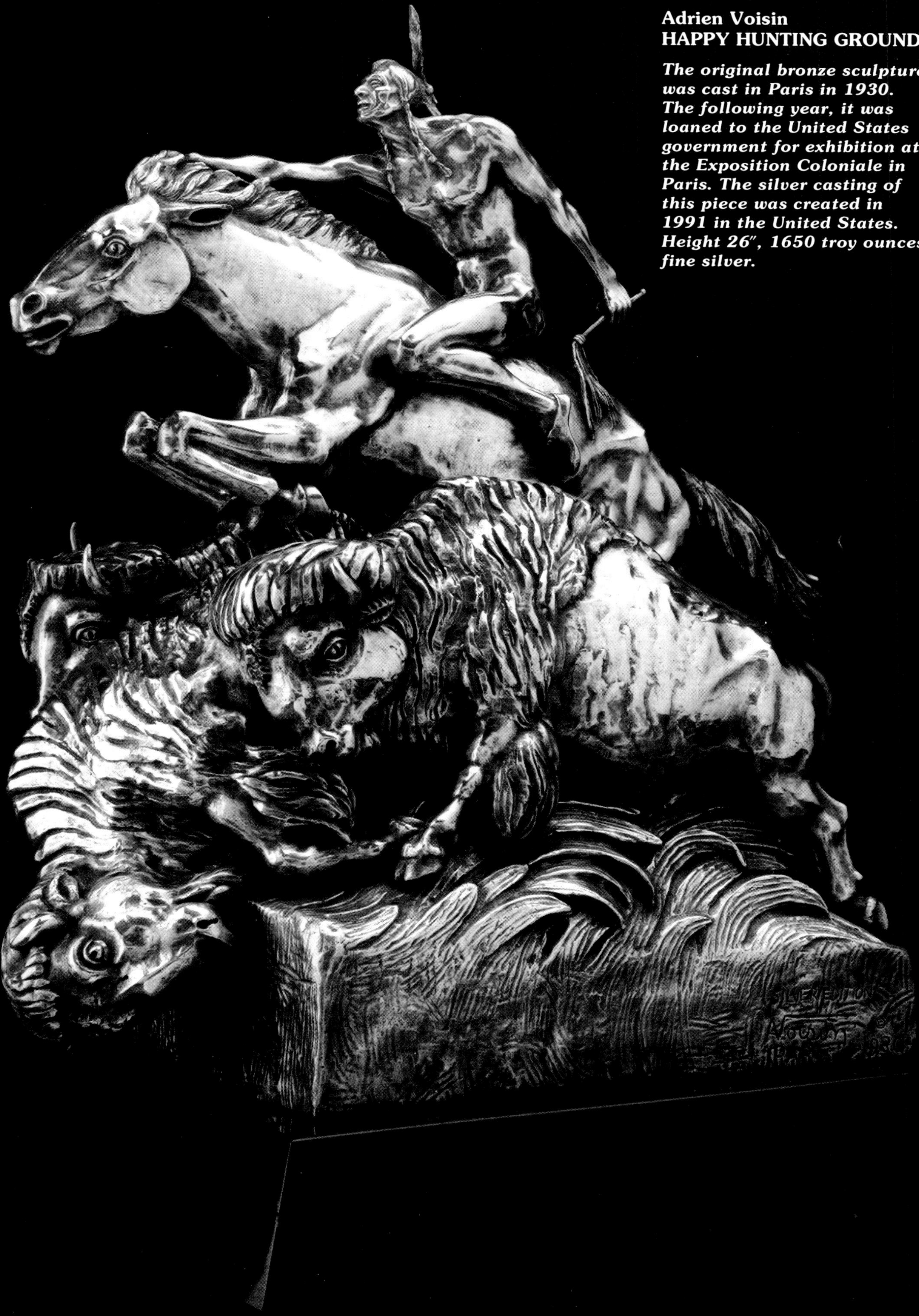

Adrien Voisin
HAPPY HUNTING GROUND

The original bronze sculpture was cast in Paris in 1930. The following year, it was loaned to the United States government for exhibition at the Exposition Coloniale in Paris. The silver casting of this piece was created in 1991 in the United States. Height 26″, 1650 troy ounces fine silver.

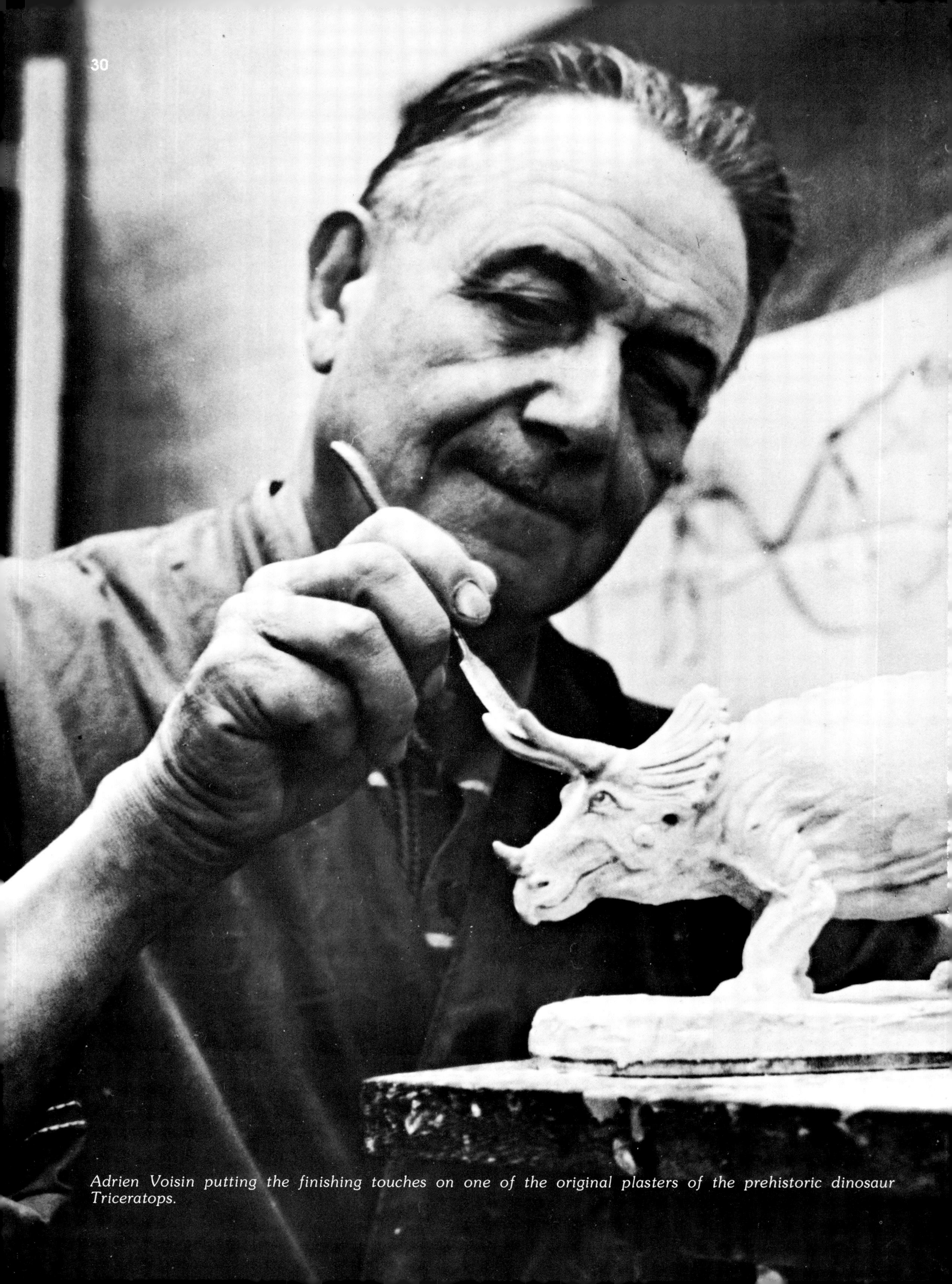

Adrien Voisin putting the finishing touches on one of the original plasters of the prehistoric dinosaur Triceratops.

PREHISTORIC SERIES —

DINOSAURS

Adrien Voisin
TRICERATOPS

Fossils of Triceratops (referring to three-horned face) have been found in Wyoming and Montana. This dinosaur matured to 20 feet in length, and may have traveled in herds. The horns, which were grown by both sexes, were probably used in fighting and courting. Dated 1958. Height 5″, length 9½″, 92 troy ounces fine silver.

In 1955, Adrien Voisin donated his time and efforts to the Steinhart Aquarium at Golden Gate Park in San Francisco. The city hoped to add on an Anthropology section, and Voisin spent his time preparing specimens for exhibit.

During this same time, government scientists had been assembling full-scale dinosaurs in the Old Mint Building from fossil bones gathered at the Dinosaur National Monument in Utah. Based on this work, the Smithsonian Institute sent four of their men armed with detailed drawings and plans to work with Voisin in creating six miniature dinosaurs, exactly and naturally proportioned, to be used as the models for life-size sculptures at the exhibit.

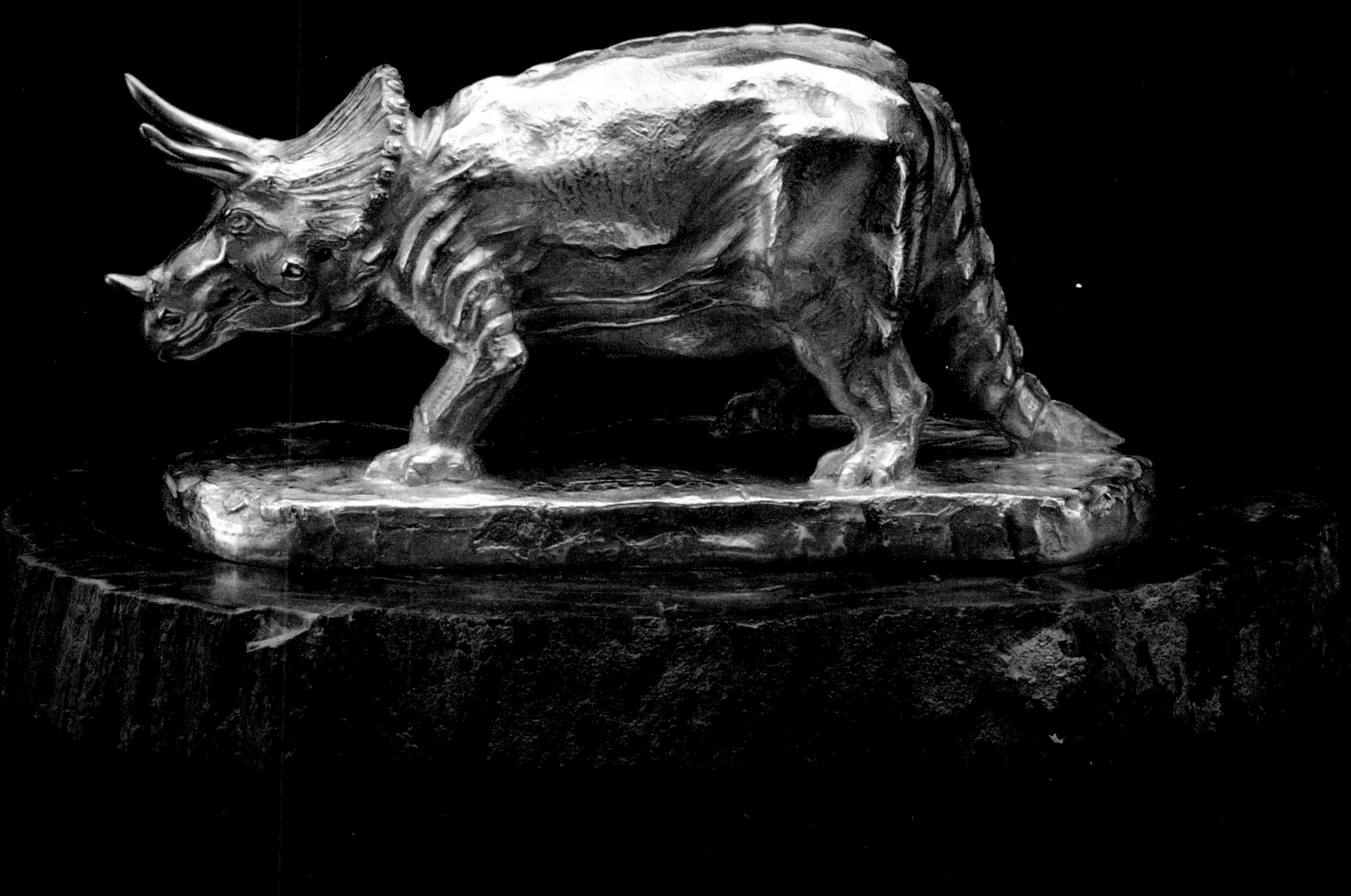

The six dinosaurs shown here are from the original plasters made by Voisin, never cast into metal until commissioned by the Harmsens. It was Voisin's hope that the set would be preserved as a unit and be displayed someday in a museum.

The name "dinosaur" comes from two Greek words meaning "terrible" and "lizard," although dinosaurs are reptiles, not lizards. Dinosaurs existed on this planet more than 100 million years ago. The last of them were extinct millions of years before our earliest ancestors were known to exist.

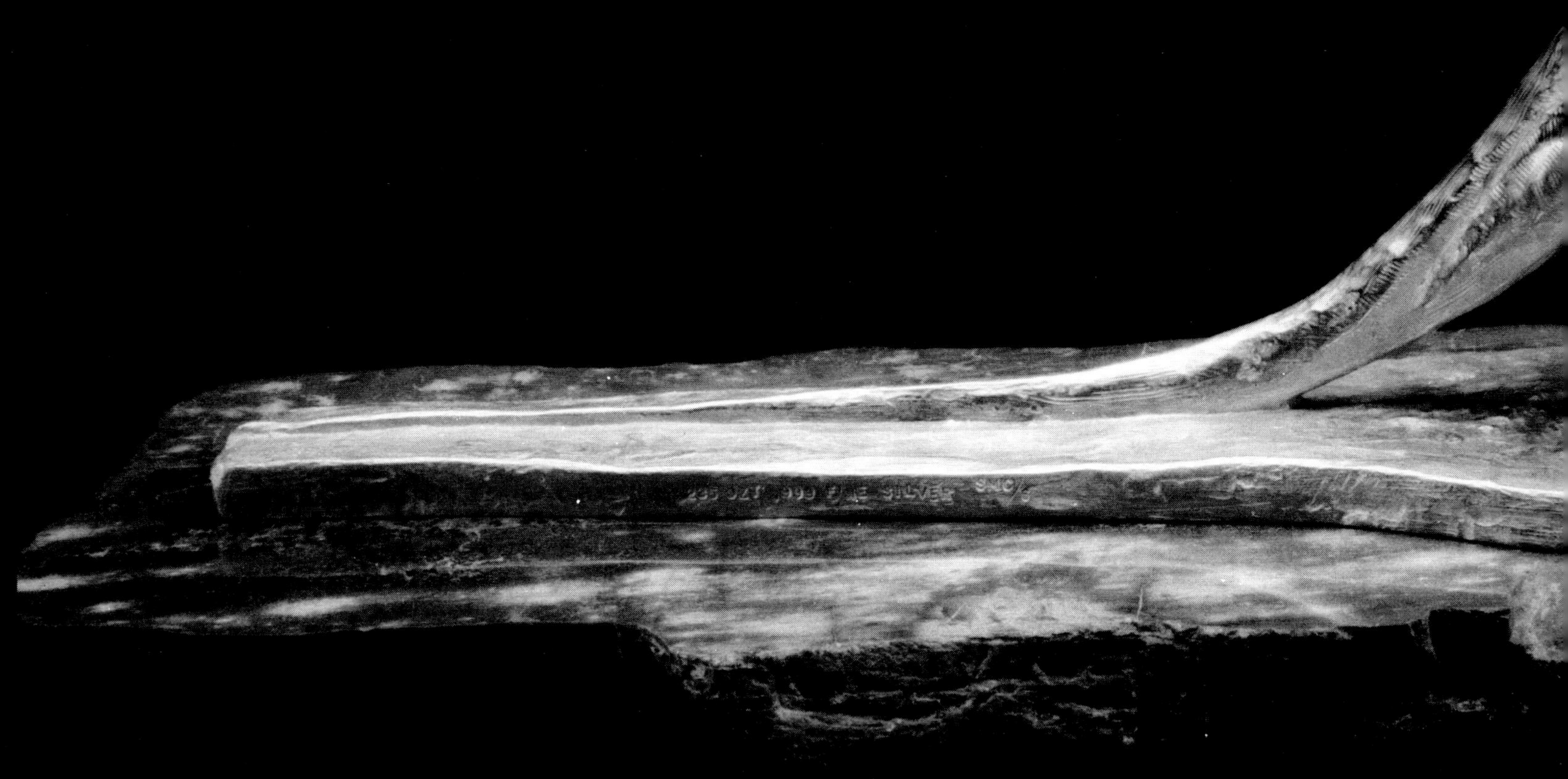

Scientists first discovered dinosaur fossils about 1820, so the science of paleontology is a relatively new pursuit. Since then, exhaustive studies of rock formations and discoveries of new fossil sites have added tremendously to our knowledge of these ancient gigantic beasts.

Dinosaurs existed in all shapes and sizes; some were carnivorous, others ate only plants; some lived on land, some in water; and still others flew through the air. Although many theories have been presented for their extinction, no conclusive evidence has yet been discovered to explain the mystery of their disappearance. The current scientific consensus holds that climatic changes dramatically altered plant and animal life and are probably to blame.

Adrien Voisin
BRONTOSAURUS

The fossils of this "thunder lizard" are found in Wyoming, Montana, and other Western states. Brontosaurus was one of the largest reptiles, measuring some 68 feet long and weighing about 20 tons. It roamed the lakes and upland terrain covering much of the West some 100 to 60 million years ago. Dated 1958. Height 6½", length 28", 235 troy ounces fine silver.

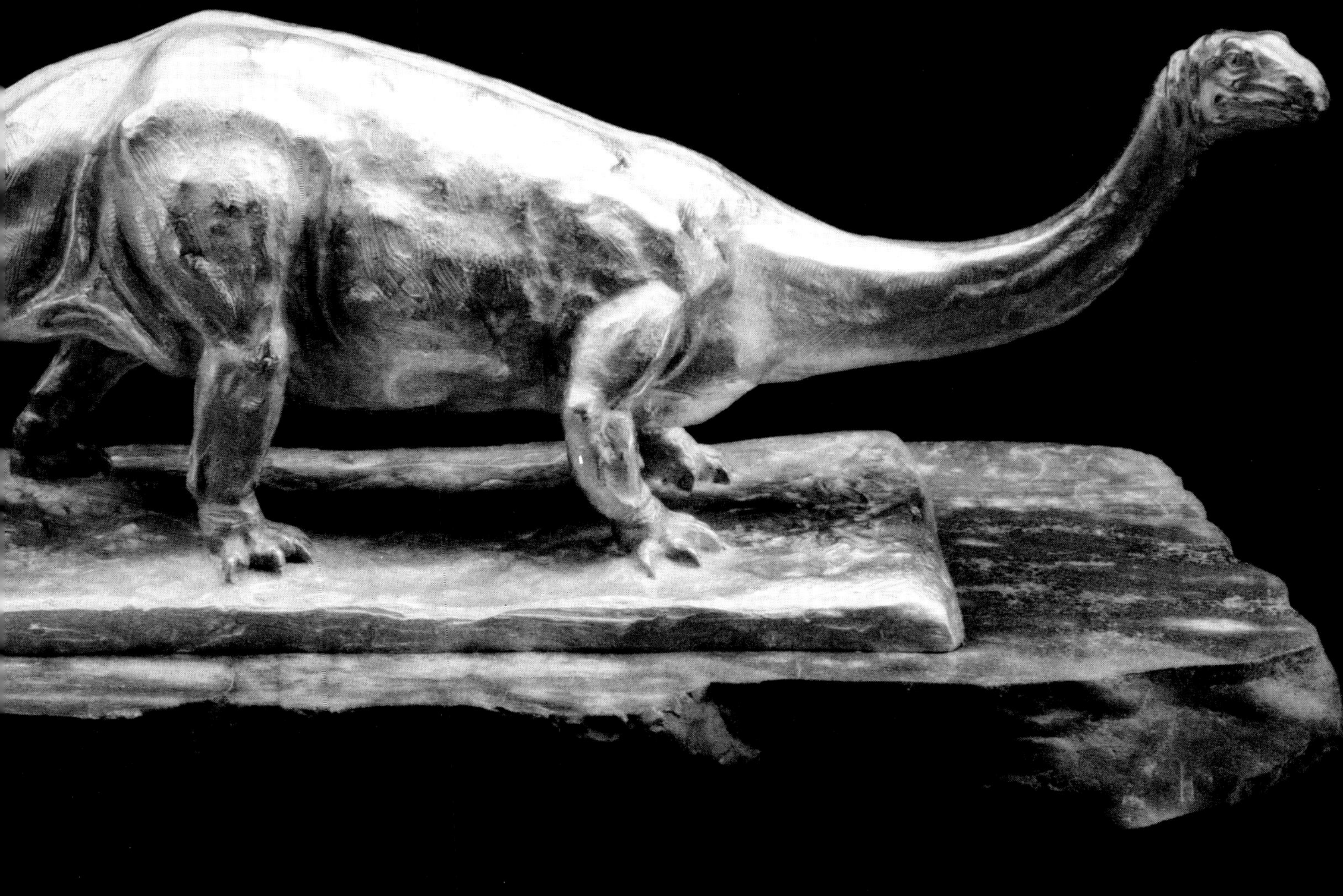

Adrien Voisin
TYRANNOSAURUS REX

The "tyrant lizard king" was a fierce predatory reptile towering 20 feet tall and measuring 47 feet long. Sites in South Dakota and in Hell Creek, Montana, have yielded fossil remains of this dinosaur, whose four-foot head displayed three- to six-inch teeth. Dated 1958. Height $11\frac{1}{4}$", length $10\frac{1}{4}$", 133 troy ounces fine silver.

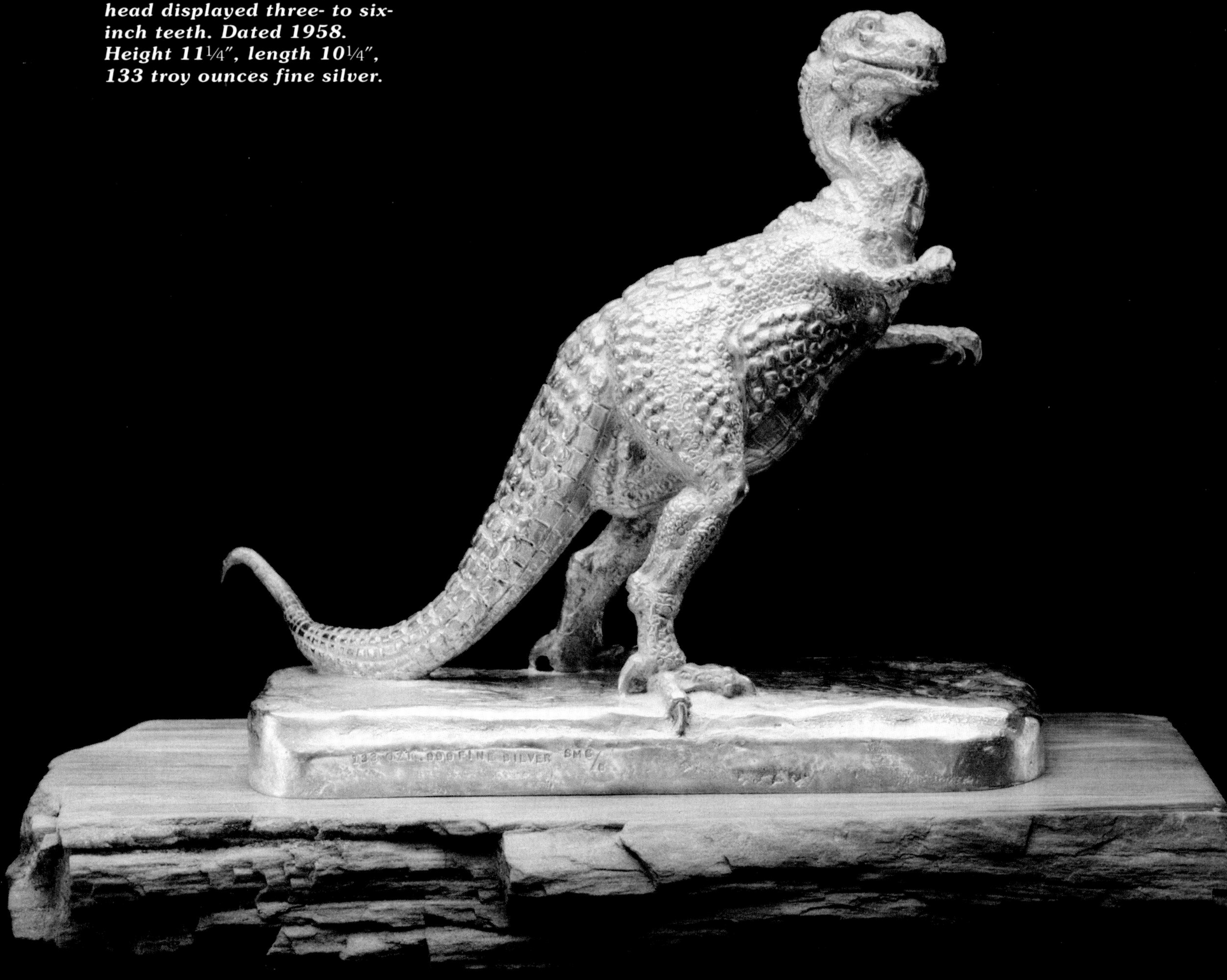

Adrieǹ Voisin
ANATOSAURUS

The "rough tooth lizard" had a soft skin which made it a favorite of predatory dinosaurs. Anatosaurus was most abundant during the Cretaceous period some 100 million years ago. Dated 1958. Height 11¼", length 12", 140 troy ounces fine silver.

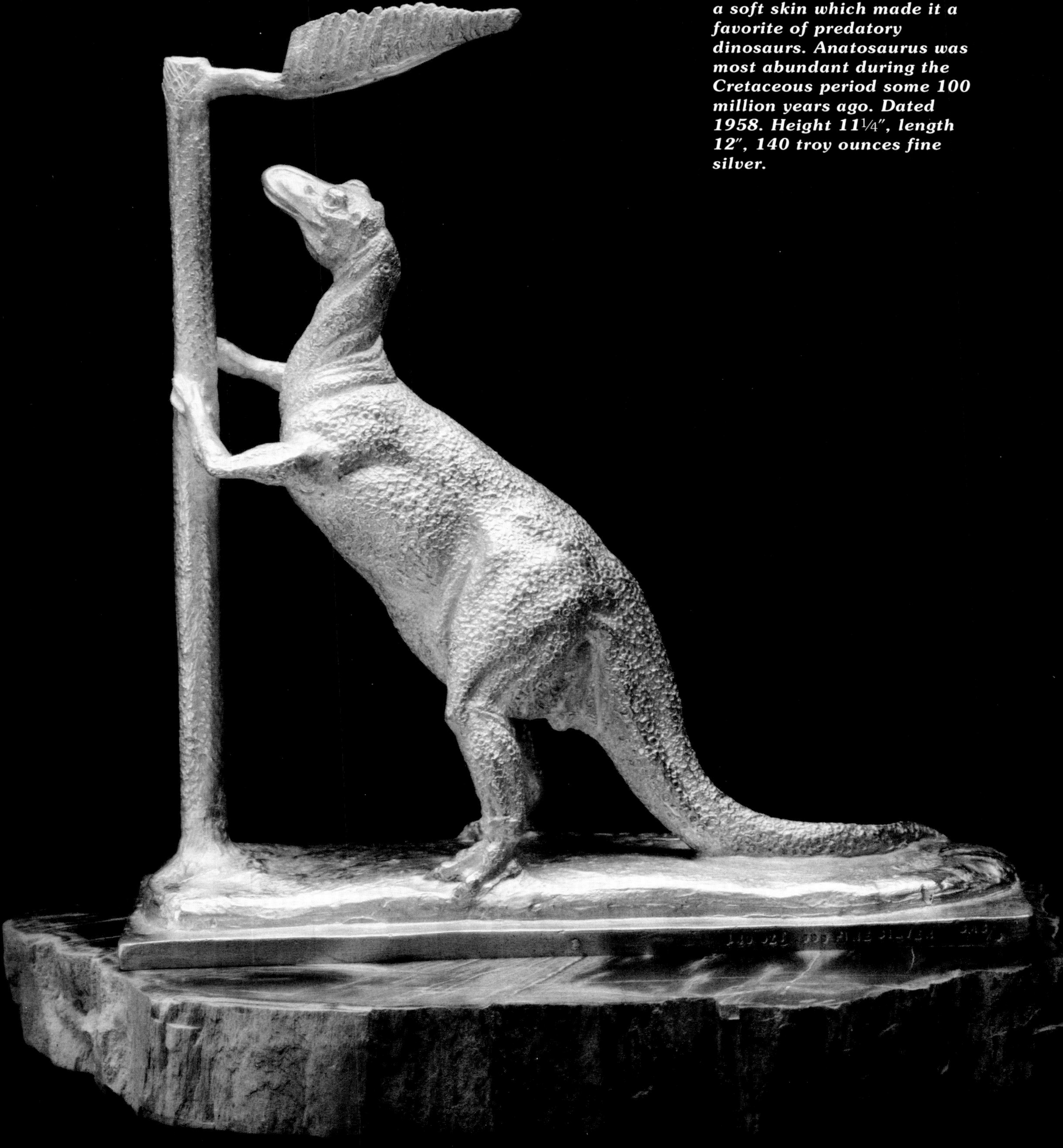

Adrien Voisin
ANKYLOSAURUS

This armor-plated reptile lived 80 to 63 million years ago. With the exception of turtles, Ankylosaurus' carapace made it the most fully armored reptile of all time. Dated 1958. Height 8", length 4", 72 troy ounces fine silver.

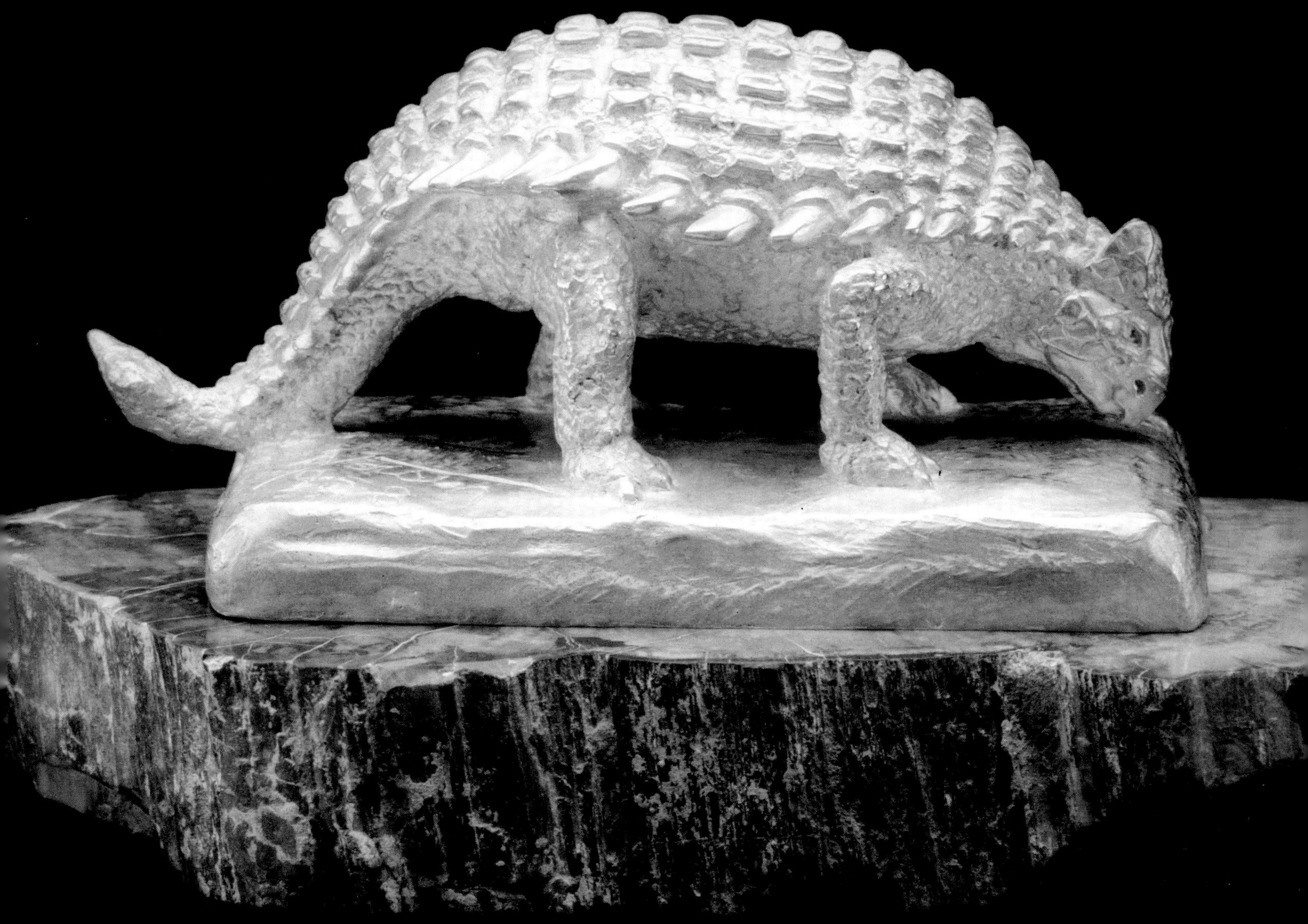

Adrien Voisin
STEGOSAURUS

Thriving 158 to 110 million years before the present, Stegosaurus seems to have been the first dinosaur to disappear, during the early Cretaceous period. This "covered lizard" measured 14 to 20 feet long, and its spikes and plates served both as protection and for thermal regulation. Dated 1958. Height 8½", length 5", 62 troy ounces fine silver.

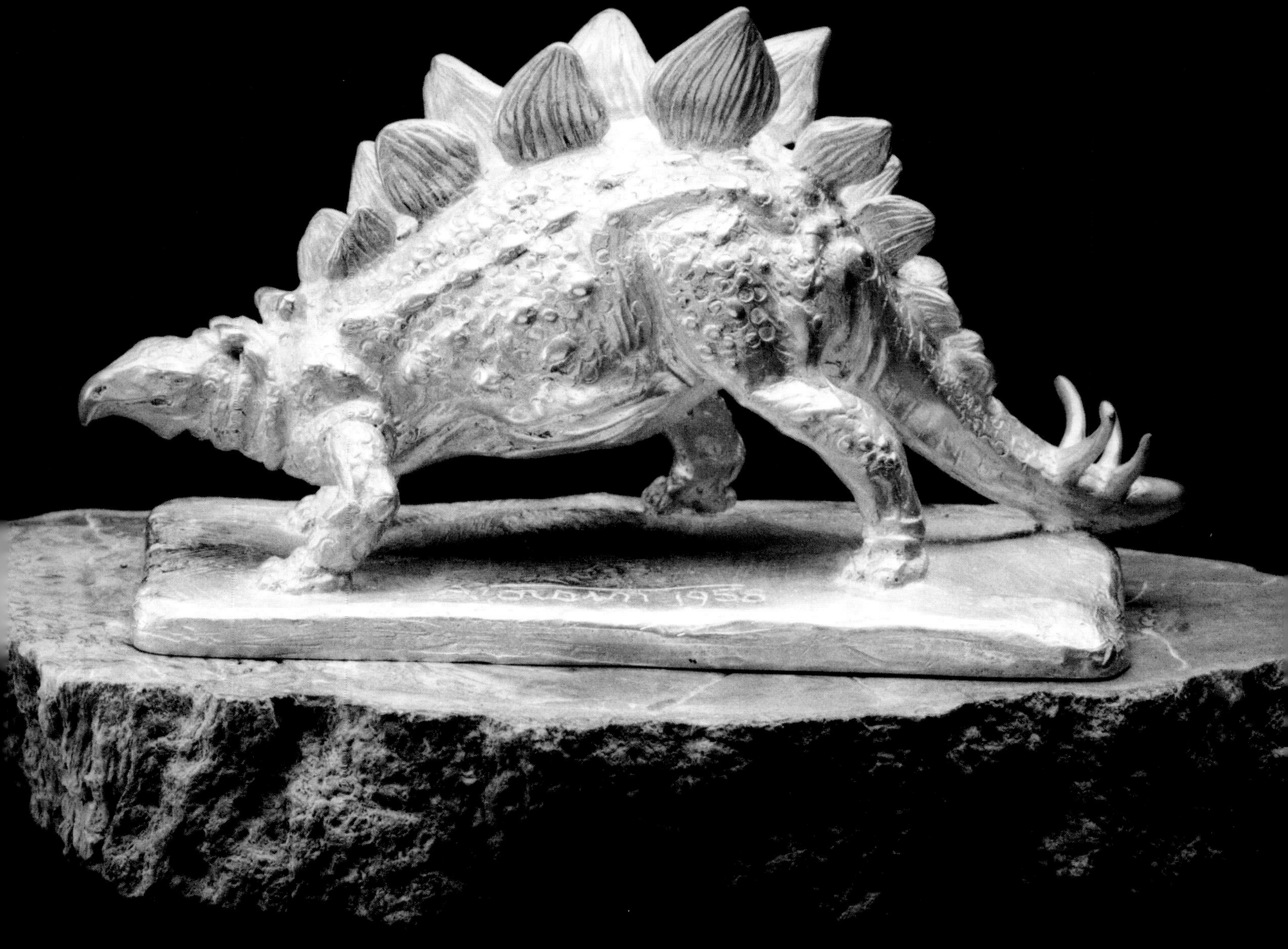

Adrien Voisin
CAYUSE HORSE

The native range horse or Indian pony used by the Cayuse and Blackfeet Indians in Oregon, Washington, and Montana, this horse is thought to be an extinct breed today. The sculpture shows the DJ brand on the right flank. Dated 1936. Height 9″, length 11″, 107 troy ounces fine silver.

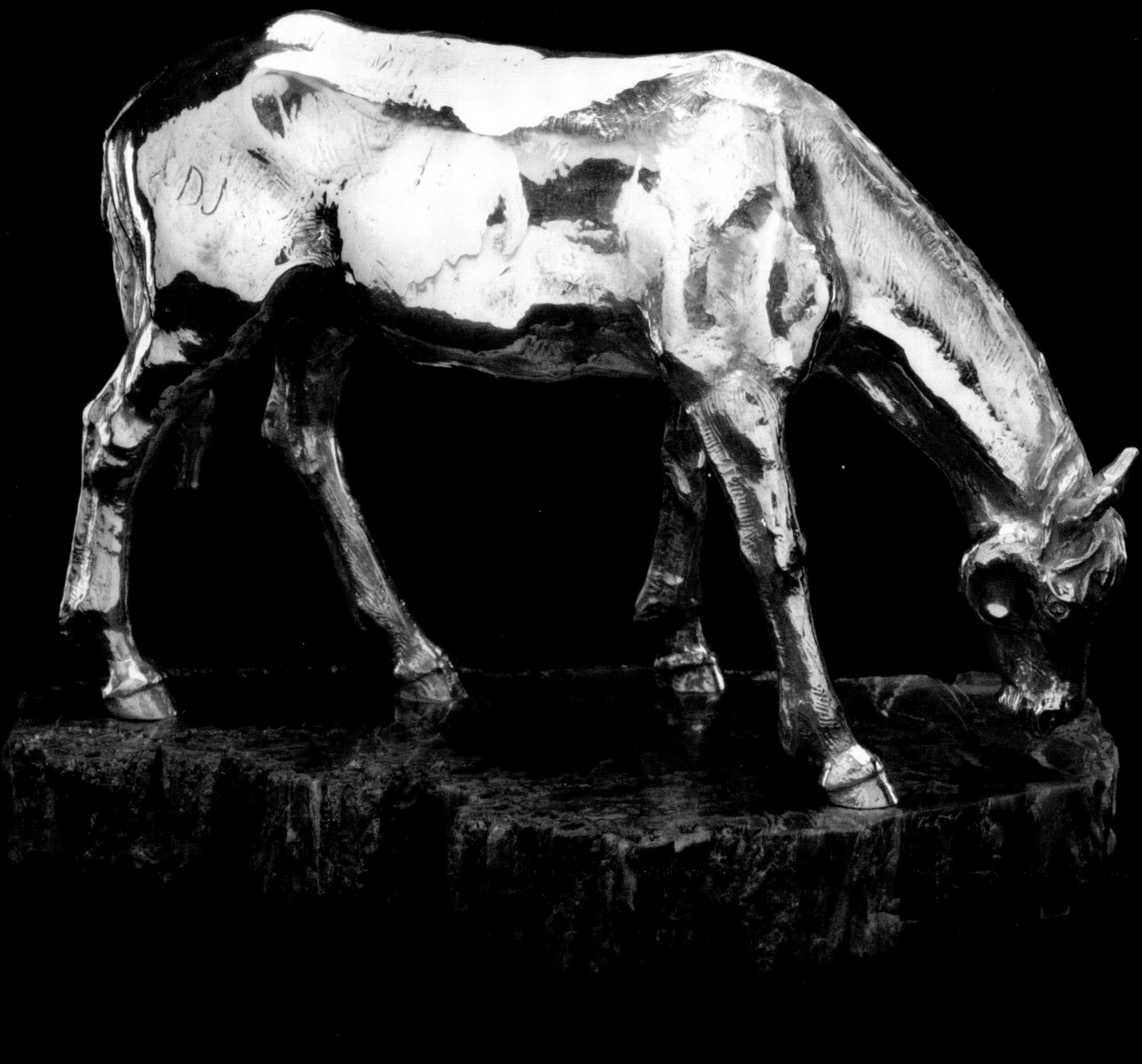

Adrien Voisin
CROUCHING INDIAN WITH WOLF CAMOUFLAGE

An Indian wearing a wolf skin on his head and back was a favorite subject of early frontier painters such as Carl Bodmer and George Catlin. Dated 1936. Height 6″, length 5½″, 60 troy ounces fine silver.

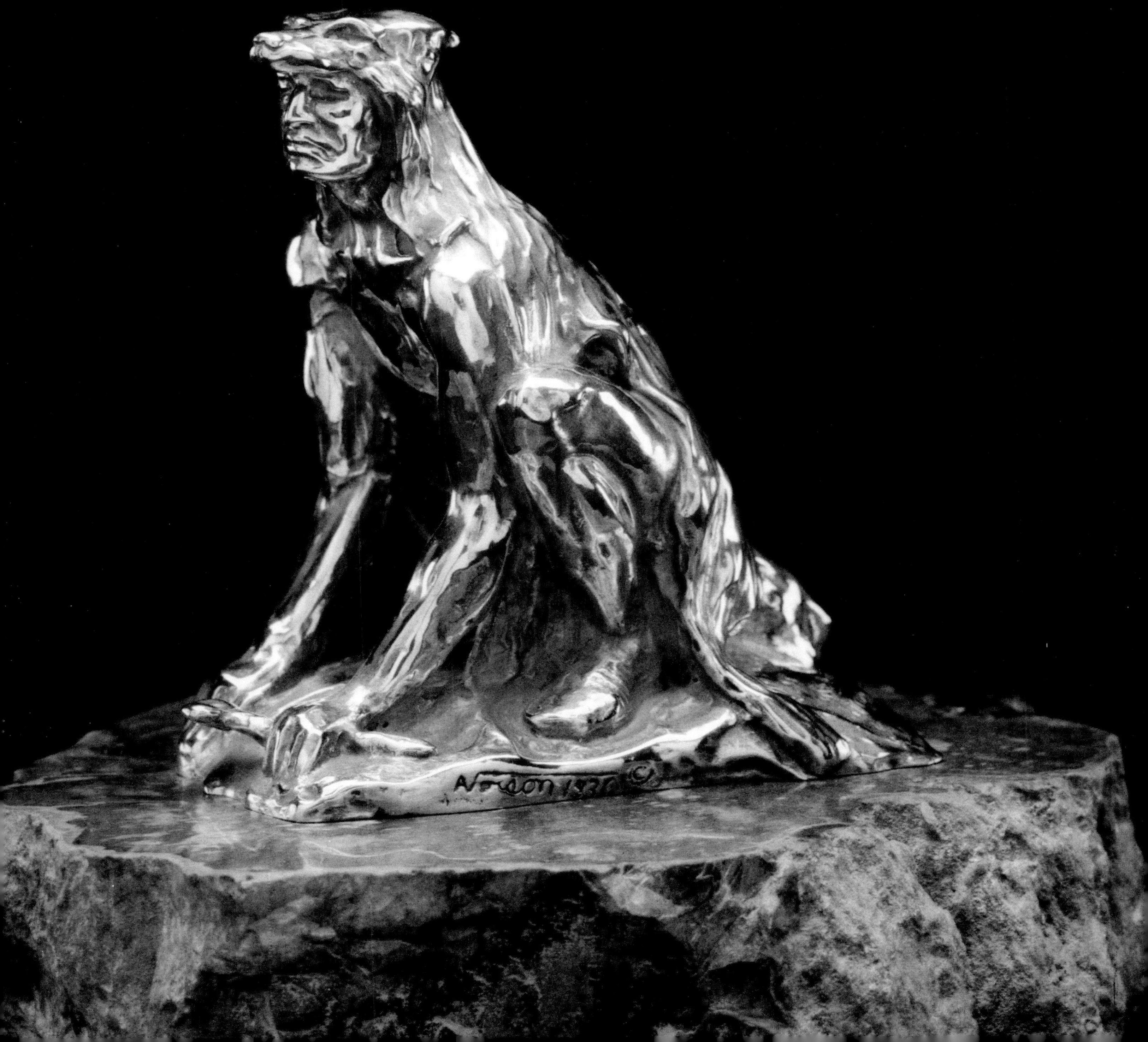

Adrien Voisin
SACAJAWEA AND SON

A Shoshone woman who served as guide for the Lewis and Clark expedition of 1805-06, Sacajawea accompanied the trader/guide Charbonneau, by whom she had a son, Baptiste (Nate-Sta-O-Ta-Pa-Ke). She interpreted for the explorers and led them to the camps of her own people, where they procured supplies and horses. Little is known of her ultimate end, although one story indicates that she returned to the Dakota territory, where she died in 1880 at the age of 100. Dated 1936. Height 21", length 7", 386 troy ounces fine silver.

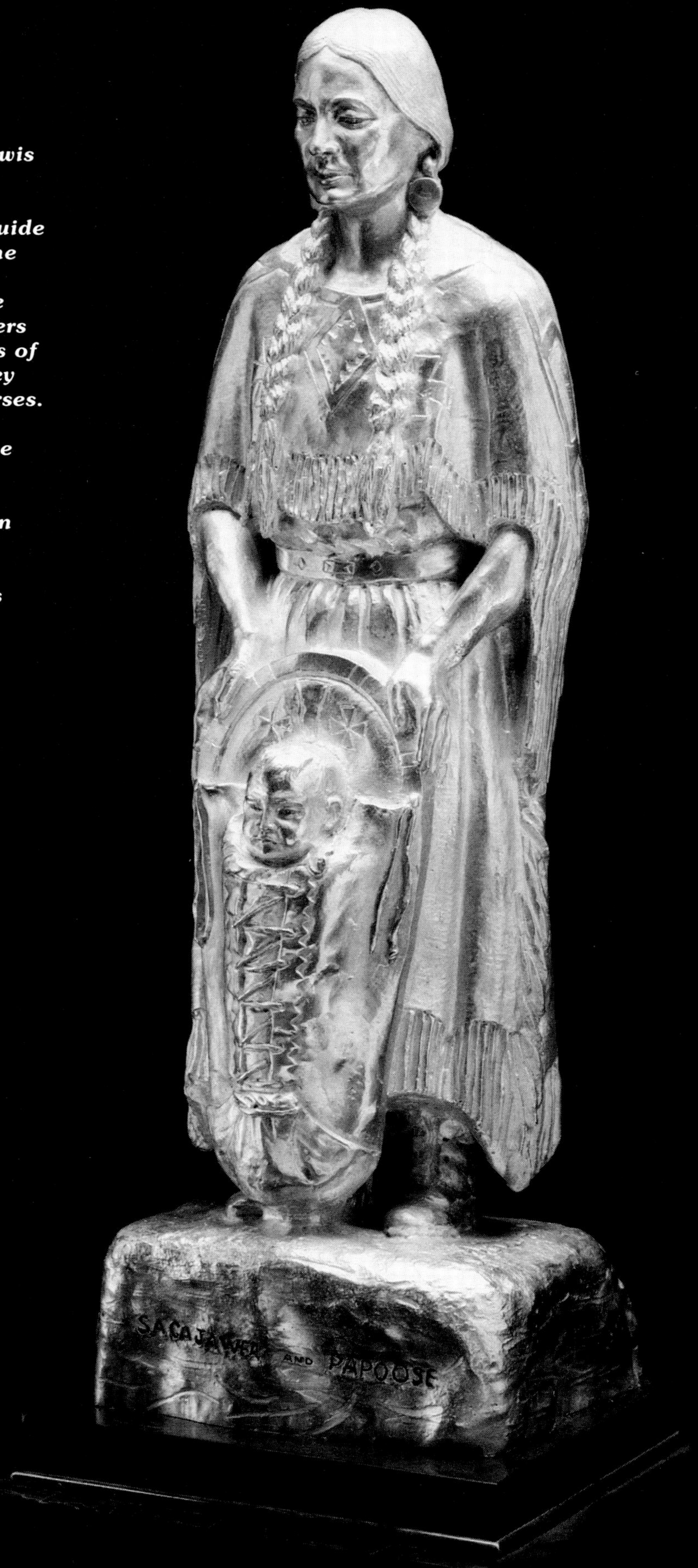

PETRIFIED WOOD

Indian legend says that a tired goddess who had been walking all day came upon a group of logs. She killed a rabbit for her dinner, then tried to make a fire to cook it, but found the logs were wet. Hungry and frustrated, she turned the wood to stone and created the Petrified Forest of northern Arizona.

Petrified wood is extremely hard and polishes beautifully, making it an excellent material for sculpture bases. All of the bases under Voisin's silver dinosaurs are of petrified wood, an appropriate choice, since petrified wood dates from the time of the dinosaurs. The Hopi silver kachina collection documented later in this book is also mounted on this fossilized wood, which is indigenous to the lands of the Hopi Indians of northern Arizona.

Once mined and removed by the ton, petrified wood was crushed into industrial grinding powder as late as 1890. By 1906, however, a park was established to preserve what was left of the Petrified Forest. This park was enlarged later to add a portion of the Painted Desert, and, in 1962, the site was designated a national park.

Some 220 to 225 million years ago during the Triassic Period (a subdivision of the Mesozoic Era, which most of us know as the "age of dinosaurs"), northern Arizona was part of an enormous valley, now covering parts of four states, that sloped all the way to the Pacific Ocean. At its higher elevations, the valley was covered with trees that were similar in appearance to today's Norfolk Island pines and that grew as much as 200 feet tall. In between slow-flowing streams, the valley terrain consisted of plains punctuated by marshes, ponds, lakes, and swamps.

At some point, the streams flooded and washed tree trunks and vast quantities of sediment down from the nearby highlands. In a short time, the sediment layer covered the uprooted forest trees to a depth of 3000 feet. It all happened

so quickly, the trees had no time to decay before they were completely buried in the oxygen-depleted muck.

Sediment-rich water seeped into the trunks of these buried trees, replacing the water found naturally in the wood. Over time, the sediment solidified into stone, retaining the shape and textures of the original trees.

This stone forest was under a shallow ocean until sixty million years ago. The ocean waters dried when the bottom was pushed up 5000 feet above sea level during the geologic upthrusting that created the surrounding Rocky Mountain ranges. Since then, natural erosion has exposed these petrified trees, and more are uncovered each year.

The silica found in petrified wood has been transformed into opal, a semiprecious gem, and chalcedony, a waxy-looking, translucent form of quartz. Traces of other elements deposited in the wood along with silica produce the palette of colors for which petrified wood is famous. Iron produces red, yellow, brown, and occasionally blue hues. Carbon may produce black, while manganese causes pinks as well as black. Rarely, chromium and cobalt create blue and green tones.

Petrified wood resembles glass because it lacks a crystalline or granular texture. It flakes easily into stone tools and ornaments, and is found frequently by archaeologists studying the prehistoric peoples of the Colorado Plateau.

A Folsom spear point of petrified wood found in what is now northern Arizona had been used by big game hunters approximately 9000 B.C. The Anasazi who farmed and hunted much of the area from A.D. 300 to 1450 chipped and flaked the rock into tools and arrow points. They also traded high quality petrified wood with other peoples for pottery, shells, turquoise, and other ornaments not locally available.

When the Puerco River valley around the Petrified Forest was abandoned after A.D. 1400, the Anasazi inhabitants most likely settled in Hopi villages and became the ancestors of the modern Hopi people.The Petrified Forest region seems always to have been a prehistoric crossroads between east and west, north and south. Even today, roads, highways, and railroads crisscross the area.

Driving back to Tucson after one of his trips to the Hopi area, Bill Harmsen happened to visit the Petrified Forest for his first look at petrified wood. Intrigued by the material, he joined a rock club after returning home. There he sought out craftspeople who could work with petrified wood, since the

hardness and density of the rock dictate the use of special equipment, patience, and time to cut and polish it.

His friend, Everett Fry, an experienced lapidarist, arranged to acquire chunks of petrified wood from ranches near the Petrified Forest, on land that is also contiguous with the Hopi Reservation. He cut and polished the material, then converted the pieces into sculpture bases for the Hopi silver kachina collection and for Voisin's cast silver sculpture.

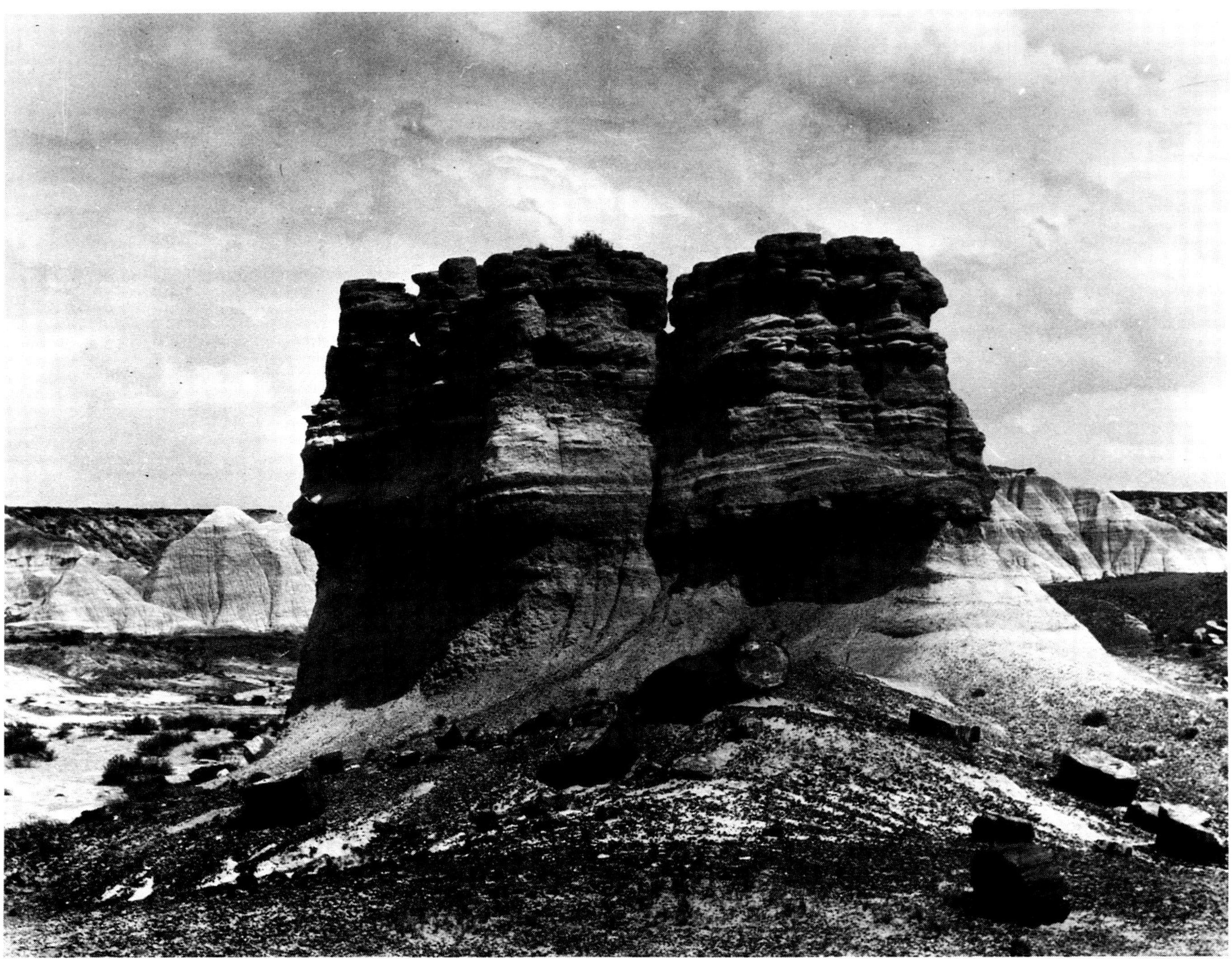

Petrified wood eroding from the Chinle Formation in the badlands of the Petrified Forest. Petrified trees naturally fracture into sections, as shown in the photograph. (Photo by Forman Hanna, 1922, courtesy of Arizona Historical Society.)

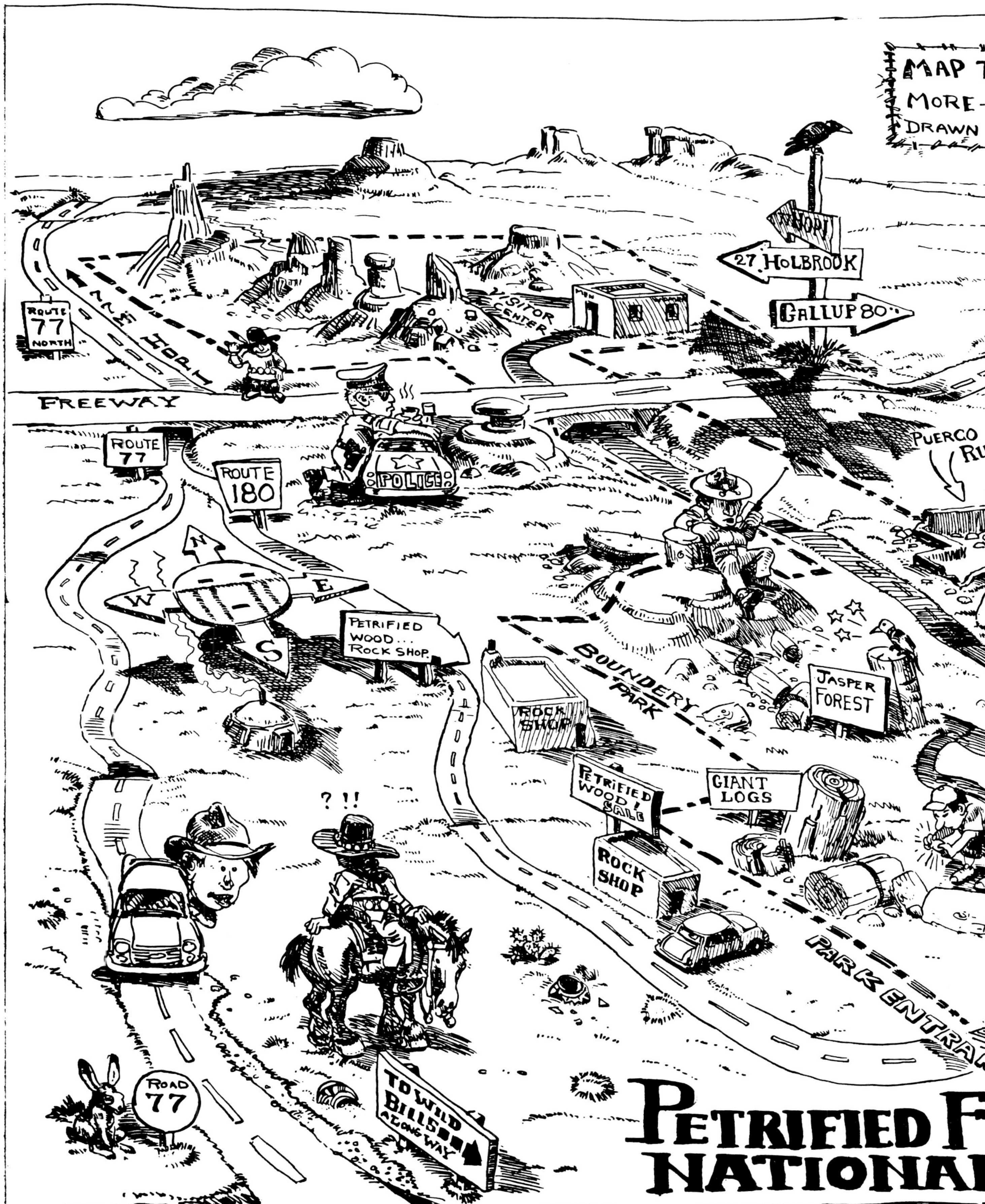
27 HOLBROOK
GALLUP 80
ROUTE 77 NORTH
FREEWAY
ROUTE 77
ROUTE 180
POLICE
N
E
W
S
PETRIFIED WOOD... ROCK SHOP.
ROCK SHOP
BOUNDERY PARK
PUERCO
JASPER FOREST
PETRIFIED WOOD! SALE
GIANT LOGS
ROCK SHOP
? !!
ROAD 77
TO WILD BILLS
PETRIFIED

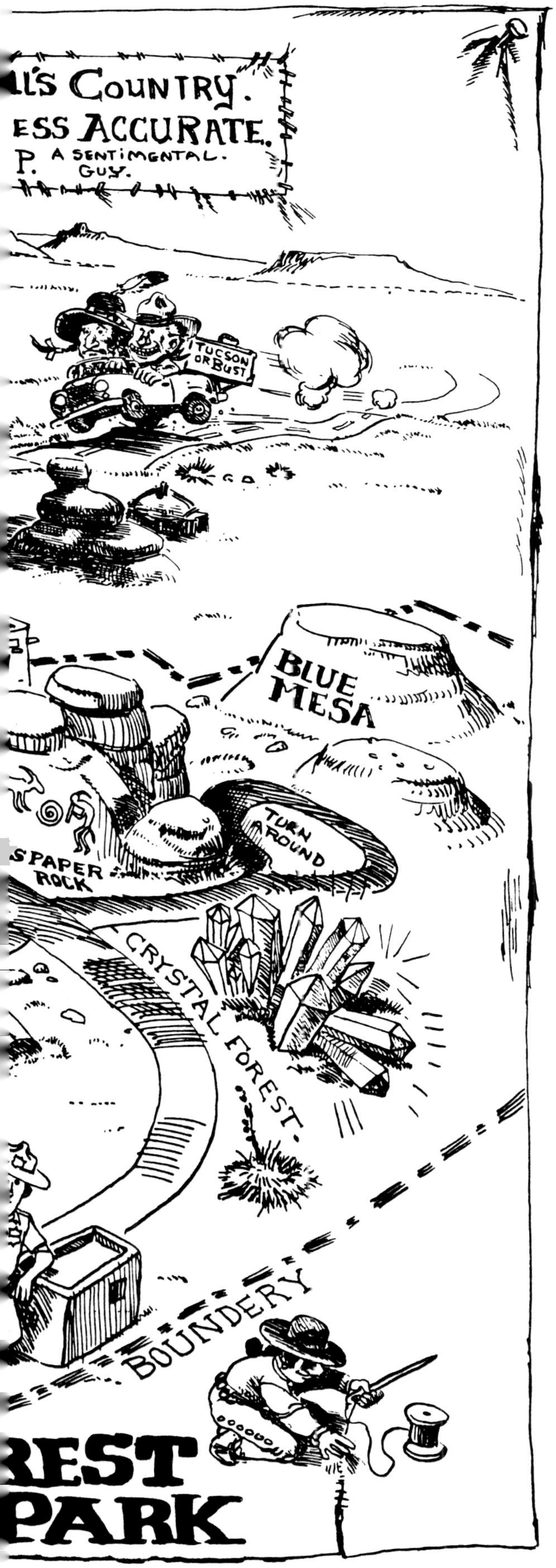

A Day in the Life of an Artist

On a recent ride in the Huachuca Mountains of southern Arizona with 165 members of Los Charros del Desierto, we returned from a long day in the saddle, and went over to our tent where we were lucky to have two artists who entertained us day and night. If they weren't drawing cowboys and Indians and Western graffiti on our hats, chaps, and saddlebags, the two were telling jokes or recounting the history of the Wild West.

One of the artists, Dave Powell, was interested in this book, which I was working on at the time. After we talked about the Hopis, the Petrified Forest, and dinosaurs, he decided to drive home through the Petrified Forest area. I gave him a map to follow, and jokingly said that if he'd quit all his doodling and draw a proper map, I'd put it in the book.

About three weeks later, to my surprise and delight, this map arrived in the mail. I include it here to add some fun and zest, with thanks to a friend and great artist.

The son of artists Ace Powell and Nancy McLaughlin Powell, Dave was born and raised in Montana. The Powell household constantly hummed with artistic activity, and Indians, trappers, cowboys, and loggers made regular visits. Based on this colorful background, Dave seriously began to study art while in his teens, and has worked as a professional artist for most of his adult life.

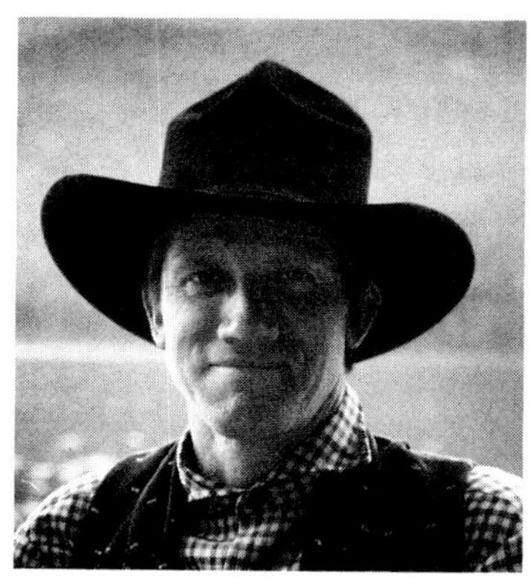

Dave Powell

Possessing a vast knowledge of the dress and habits of pioneers, cowboys, and Native Americans, Dave is often called upon to provide costumes and props, and offer technical advice on authenticity for film and television, including productions such as *The Life and Times of Grizzly Adams, Silverado,* and *Lonesome Dove.* He has participated in historic reenactments and group rides all across the West as inspiration for his sculptures, paintings, and illustrations.

Bill Harmsen

CONTEMPORARY MASTERS OF

CAST SILVER SCULPTURE

Of the twenty-four fine-silver cast sculptures currently in the Harmsen Collection, the following fourteen are works by contemporary masters. These pieces were chosen for the Harmsen Foundation Collection because of their diversity of subject, excellence of design, and artistic merit. Each of these contemporary sculptors is an artist in the truest sense of the word, combining talent, training, and hard work with vision, imagination, and expression.

James Turpen, Jr.

Buck McCain

Buckeye Blake

Tom Knapp

James A. Gruzalski

Alexander Moyle

Robert E. Barber

Ralph Crawford

James C. Turpen, Jr.

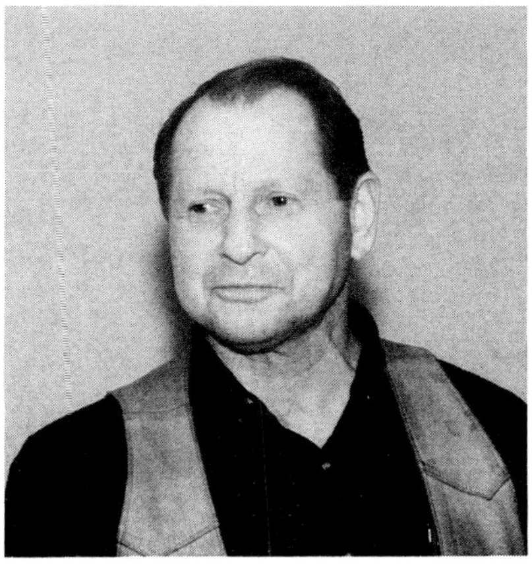

Jim Turpen was born in Winslow, Arizona, into a family of Indian traders. As a boy, he frequently visited areas of the Navajo Reservation isolated from all but the Navajo people. The family later moved to the Grand Canyon, maintaining close business ties with all of Arizona's reservations.

He attended high school and university in Tucson, earning a degree in Wildlife Management. While working in Colorado with Martin Marietta and IBM, his spare time was spent studying Western and Indian history.

After visiting a foundry in Taos, Turpen tried his hand at sculpting, completing his first bronze in 1969. He cast his earliest pieces in his own foundry, personally taking each sculpture from idea, to clay model, to finished bronze. Because of his long and close association with Indian people, he concentrates on depicting their dances, ceremonies, and customs in his sculptures and drawings.

James C. Turpen, Jr.
SHALAKO

A reenactment of the creation and migration of the Zuni people to Heptina, the "Middle Place," the Shalako ceremony has persisted throughout centuries. Its dance steps, motions and sounds all have their own significance, and are prescribed through the heritage of a matrilineal society comprised of ten clans. Each of six different kivas has a Shalako representative. These spectacular figures stand approximately ten feet tall because the mask and costume are carried on a pole. Dated 1974. Height 21", length 9", 263 troy ounces fine silver.

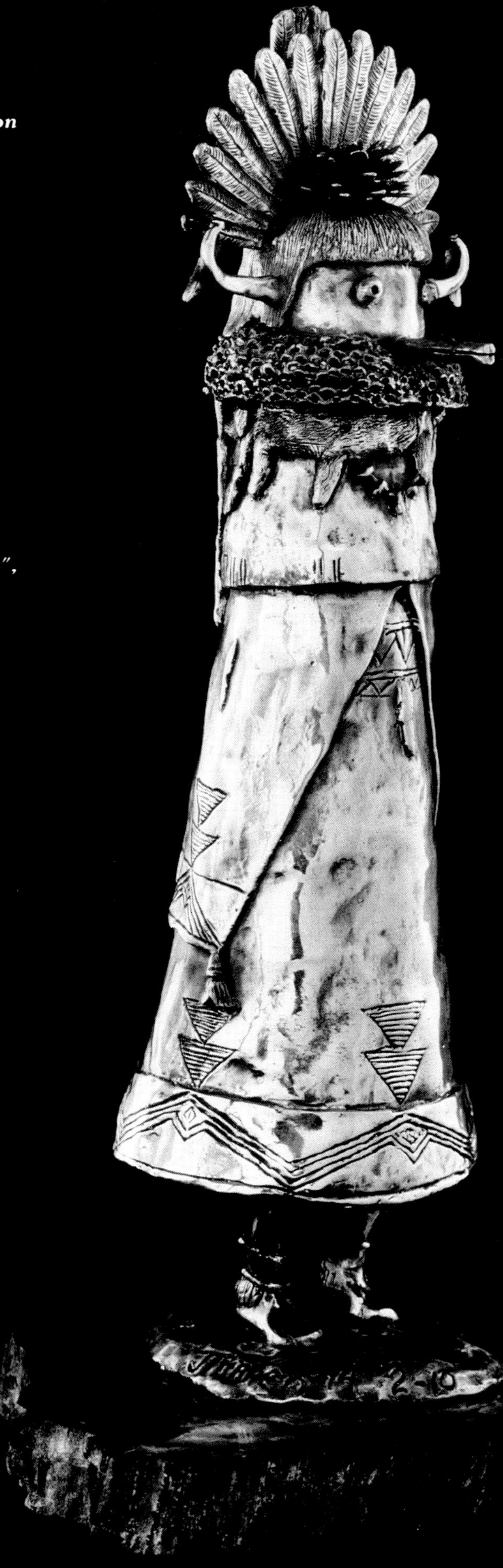

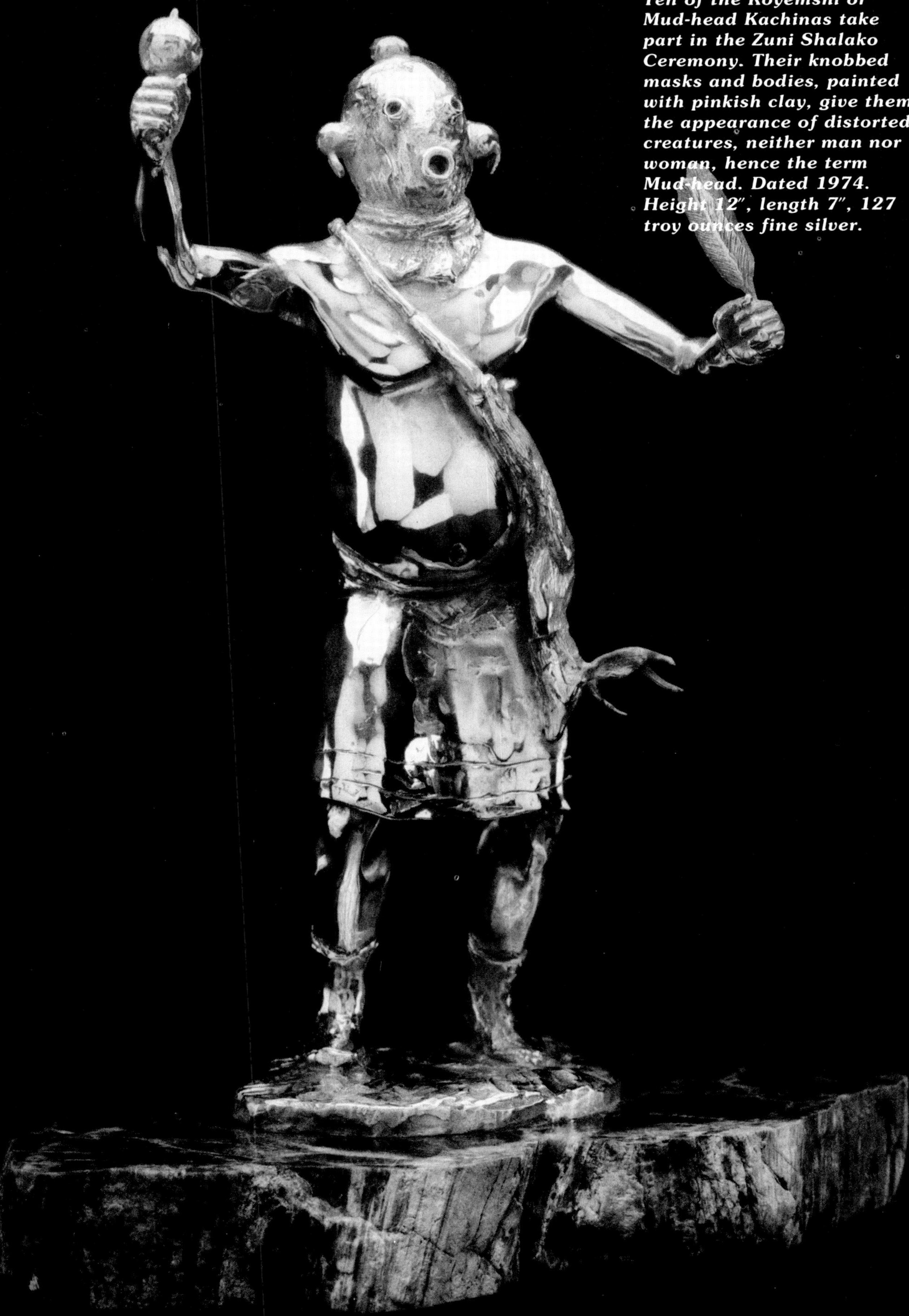

James C. Turpen, Jr.
KOYEMSHI

Ten of the Koyemshi or Mud-head Kachinas take part in the Zuni Shalako Ceremony. Their knobbed masks and bodies, painted with pinkish clay, give them the appearance of distorted creatures, neither man nor woman, hence the term Mud-head. Dated 1974. Height 12″, length 7″, 127 troy ounces fine silver.

Buck McCain

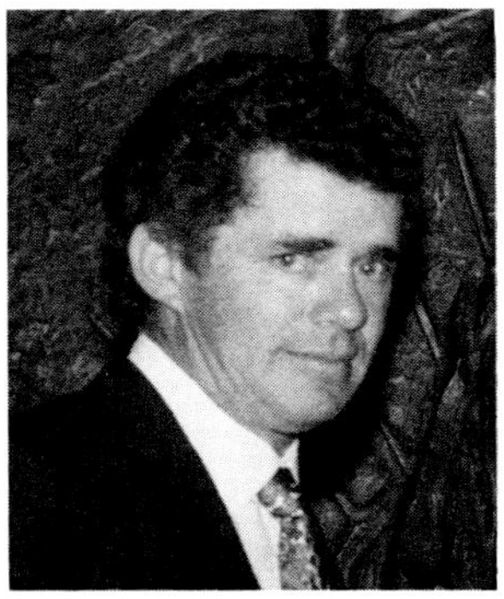

Growing up on a cattle ranch in southern California, it was during his college days that Buck McCain awakened to the notion that art could be a life's work. At twenty-five, he plunged into art on a full-time basis and since then he has won awards and commissions as both a painter and a sculptor.

In painting, he quickly earned a reputation as an authority on color, producing richly glazed oils of Western scenes and Indian life. He went on to master an impressionistic style of painting, and through continual research and experimentation, he has forged his own individualistic painting style and identity.

His first bronze was completed only fifteen years ago, yet the artist's credits now include seven major monuments and dozens of smaller sculptures. All of McCain's sculptures are strong and vital images expressing eternal themes and emotions. His monumental bronzes include historical portrait figures of the founder of Albuquerque, the founder of Scottsdale, and silver screen cowboy star, Rex Allen.

Buck McCain
THE CHALLENGE

The life of a warrior tested all the resources of a Plains Indian, from courage to determination to horsemanship. In "The Challenge," Buck McCain depicts the natural grace of a mounted Plains warrior; he is alert, clear-sighted, and prepared to meet whatever will rise to challenge him. Height 15", length 27", 245 troy ounces fine silver.

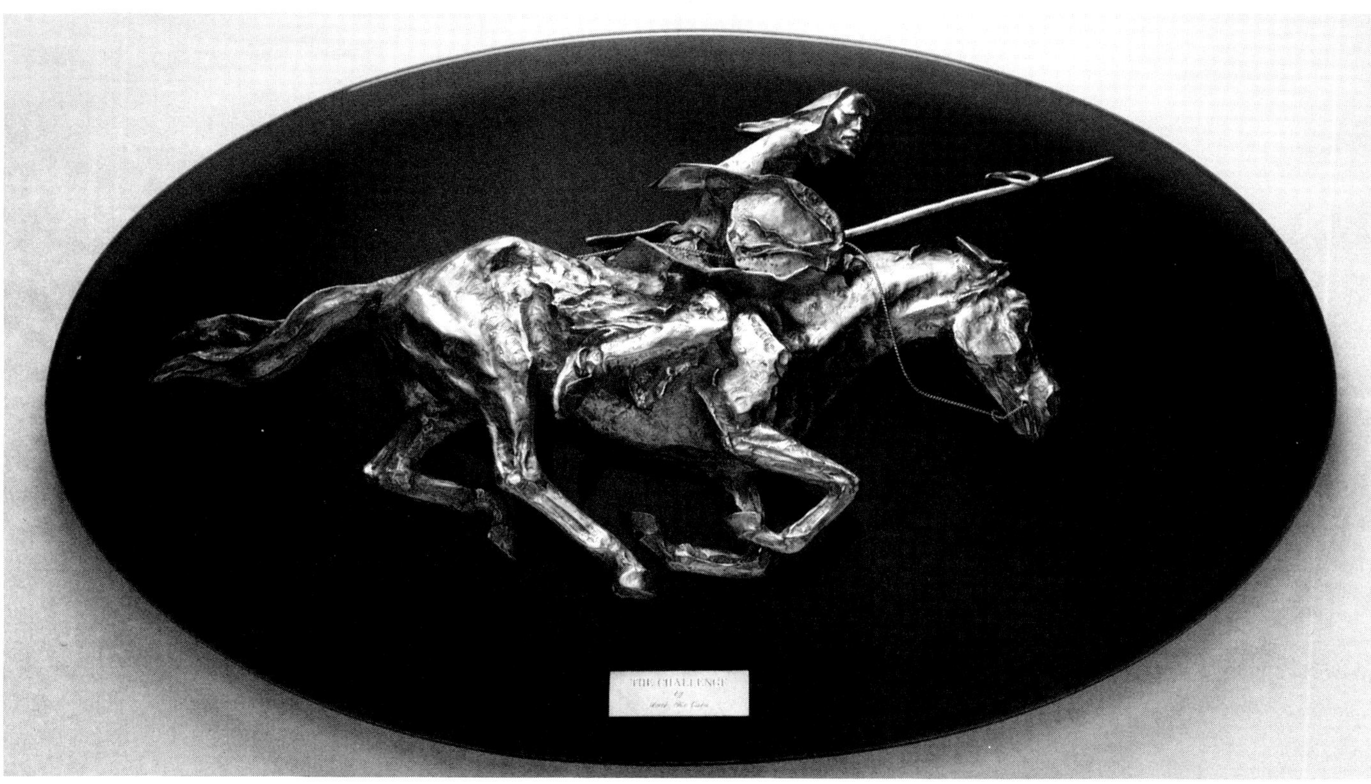

Buck McCain
REQUIEM

"Requiem" has been produced as both a smaller work, as shown here in silver, and as a 14′9″monumental bronze, retitled "Invocation." In addition, the Franklin Mint commissioned a small bronze version of this image which was named "Prayer to the Healing Spirit." On a literal level, the sculpture depicts a Plains Indian who invokes a power greater than himself. He foreshadows the end of an era, and the passage of a people and a way of life into the pages of history. In the figurative sense, the image represents the commonality of humanity's deepest aspirations—a universal prayer for love, peace, and security. Height 16½″, length 10½″, 191 troy ounces fine silver.

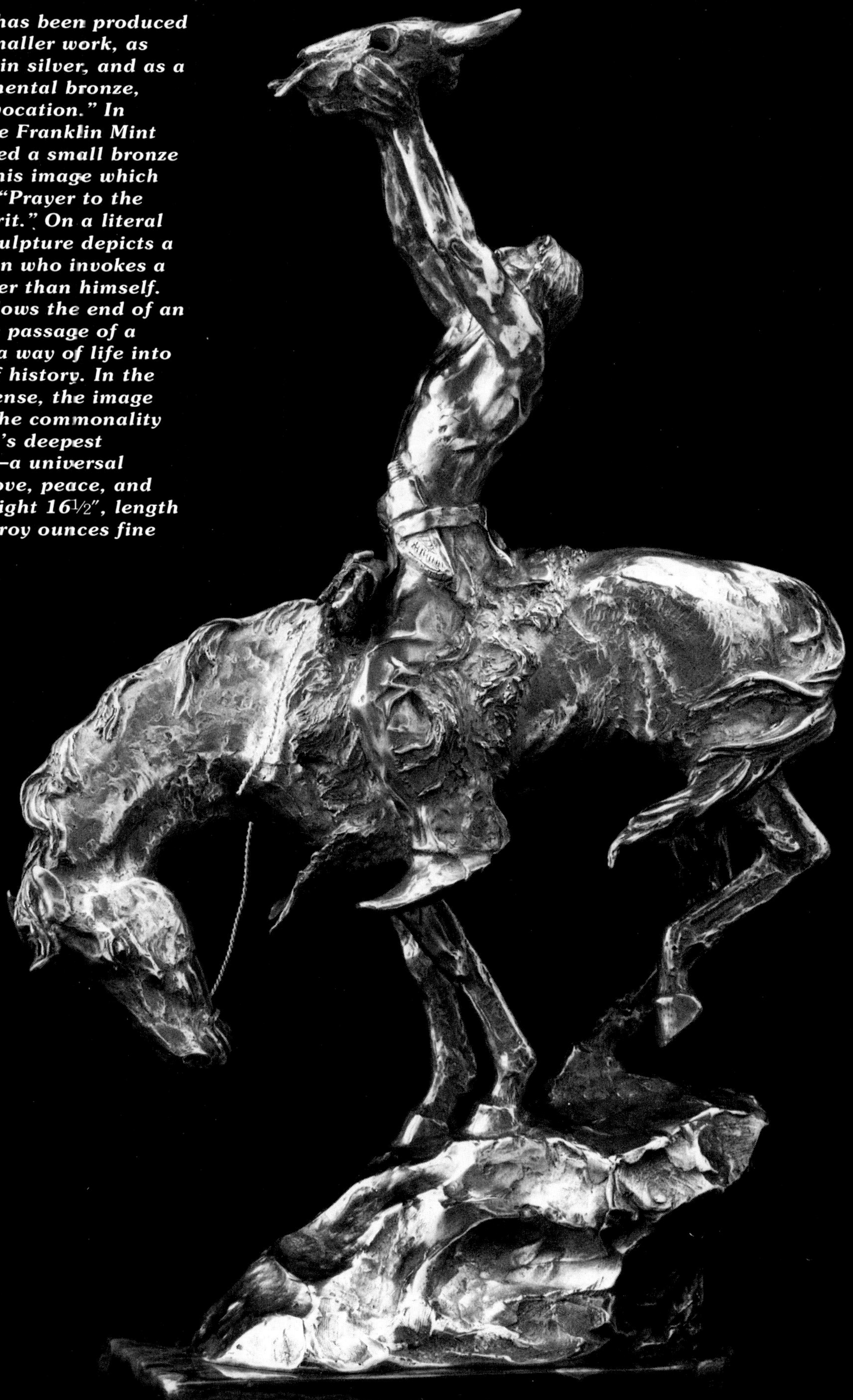

Buckeye Blake

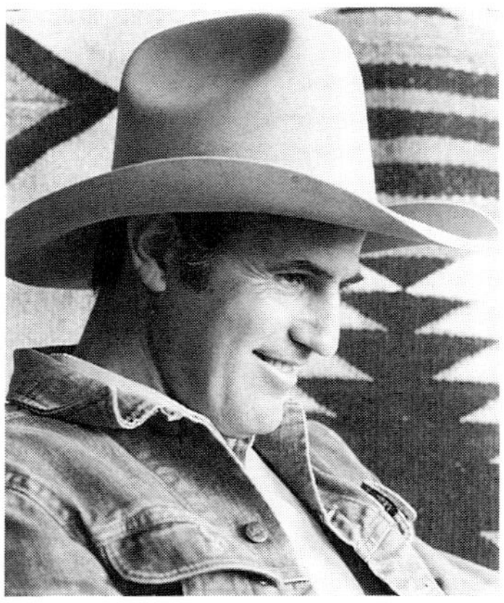

As a young man, Buckeye Blake traveled from rodeo to rodeo with his father, a roper and bull-rider, and his mother, an artist. Their influence is evident in Blake's artwork, which expresses a deep interest in his Western heritage.

After the family settled down in Carson City, Nevada, Blake started his art career by winning art competitions in school. He left for Los Angeles after graduation to work as an illustrator, then began to show his own paintings in galleries following his return to Nevada.

In 1978, he completed his first bronze, an ambitious six-foot-long replica of Charlie Russell's funeral procession. Since then, he has explored his fascination with Native American people and Western culture in both paint and bronze.

Blake continually strives for authenticity when he works, drawing from research as well as his own experience. He has received many honors and awards and his artworks are included in major museum collections, such as the National Cowboy Hall of Fame and the C.M. Russell Museum.

The Birth of a Sculpture

Artists are often caricatured as goateed individuals wearing smocks and berets, and poised to paint whatever they "feel." Real artists are quite different, however.

Most professional artists work many hours on a sculpture idea before even setting thumb to clay. They may start with library research, then execute a series of drawings. These precede the many quick thumbnail sketches a sculptor makes in clay or wax, all designed to help define the form and gesture the sculpture must take to convey the mood, emotion, or concept desired. When the essence has been pinned down, details are tackled, again with library research and drawings.

It may take weeks or months of such preparatory work before a sculpture is born. Producing a work of art is more than a happy accident—it takes time, thought, and a lot of hard work.

The drawing on the opposite page is Buckeye Blake's preliminary sketch for his silver sculpture of Will Rogers, depicted on page 55.

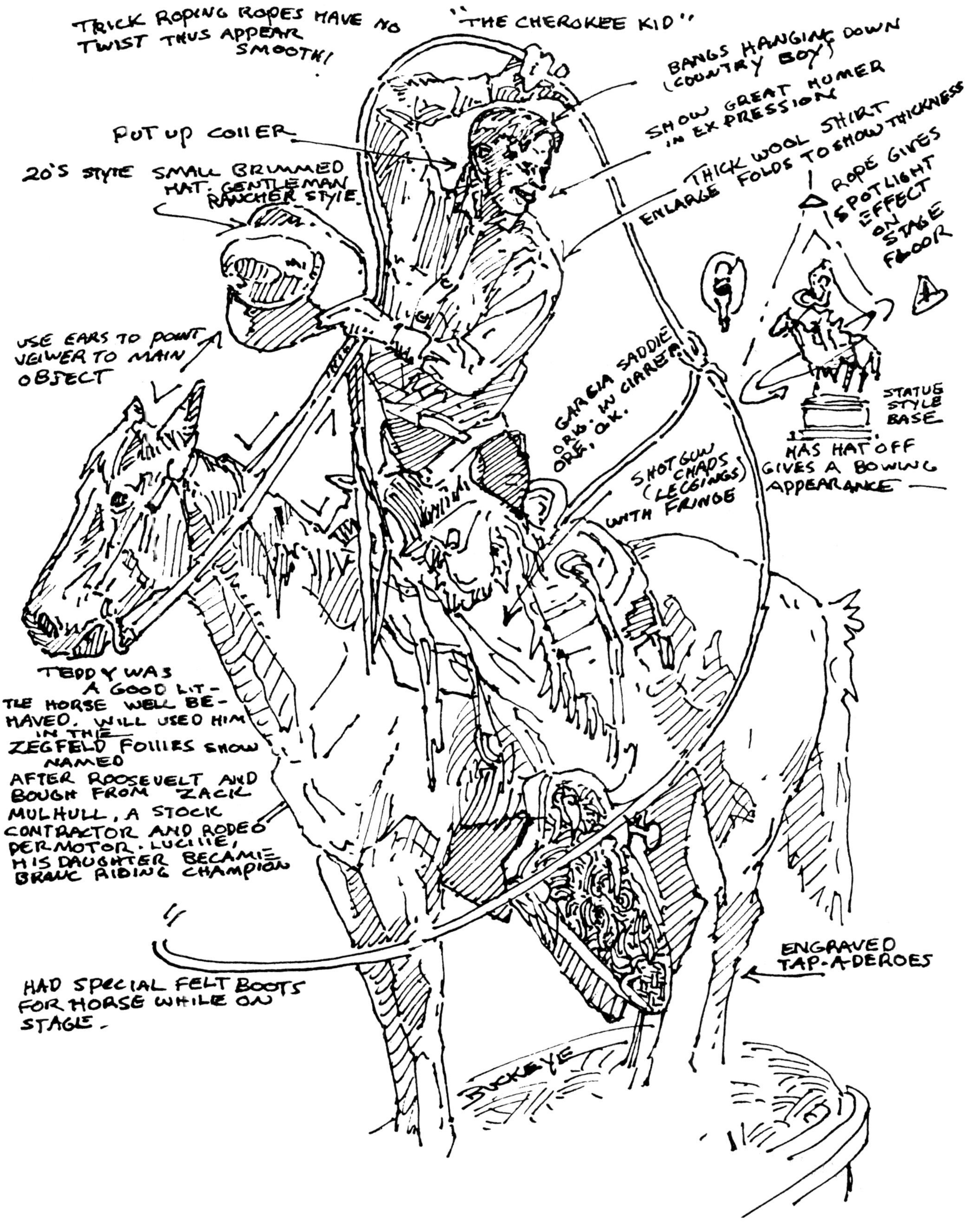
TRICK ROPING ROPES HAVE NO TWIST THUS APPEAR SMOOTH!
"THE CHEROKEE KID"
BANGS HANGING DOWN (COUNTRY BOY)
SHOW GREAT HUMER IN EXPRESSION
PUT UP COLLER
THICK WOOL SHIRT ENLARGE FOLDS TO SHOW THICKNESS
20'S STYLE SMALL BRIMMED HAT. GENTLEMAN RANCHER STYLE
ROPE GIVES SPOTLIGHT EFFECT ON STAGE FLOOR
USE EARS TO POINT VEIWER TO MAIN OBJECT
GARCIA SADDLE ORIG. IN CLAREMORE, OK.
STATUE STYLE BASE
HAS HAT OFF GIVES A BOWING APPEARANCE
SHOTGUN CHAPS (LEGGINGS) WITH FRINGE
TEDDY WAS A GOOD LITTLE HORSE WELL BEHAVED. WILL USED HIM IN THE ZEGFELD FOLLIES SHOW NAMED AFTER ROOSEVELT AND BOUGH FROM ZACK MULHULL, A STOCK CONTRACTOR AND RODEO PERMOTOR. LUCILLE, HIS DAUGHTER BECAME BRONC RIDING CHAMPION
ENGRAVED TAP-A-DEROES
HAD SPECIAL FELT BOOTS FOR HORSE WHILE ON STAGE.
BUCKEYE

Buckeye Blake
KID RUSSELL AND MONTE

Charles Russell's favorite horse was called Monte. This is the model used for a life-size sculpture unveiled in Great Falls, Montana, at the home of the Russell studio and museum. Height 10½″, length 10″, 190 troy ounces fine silver.

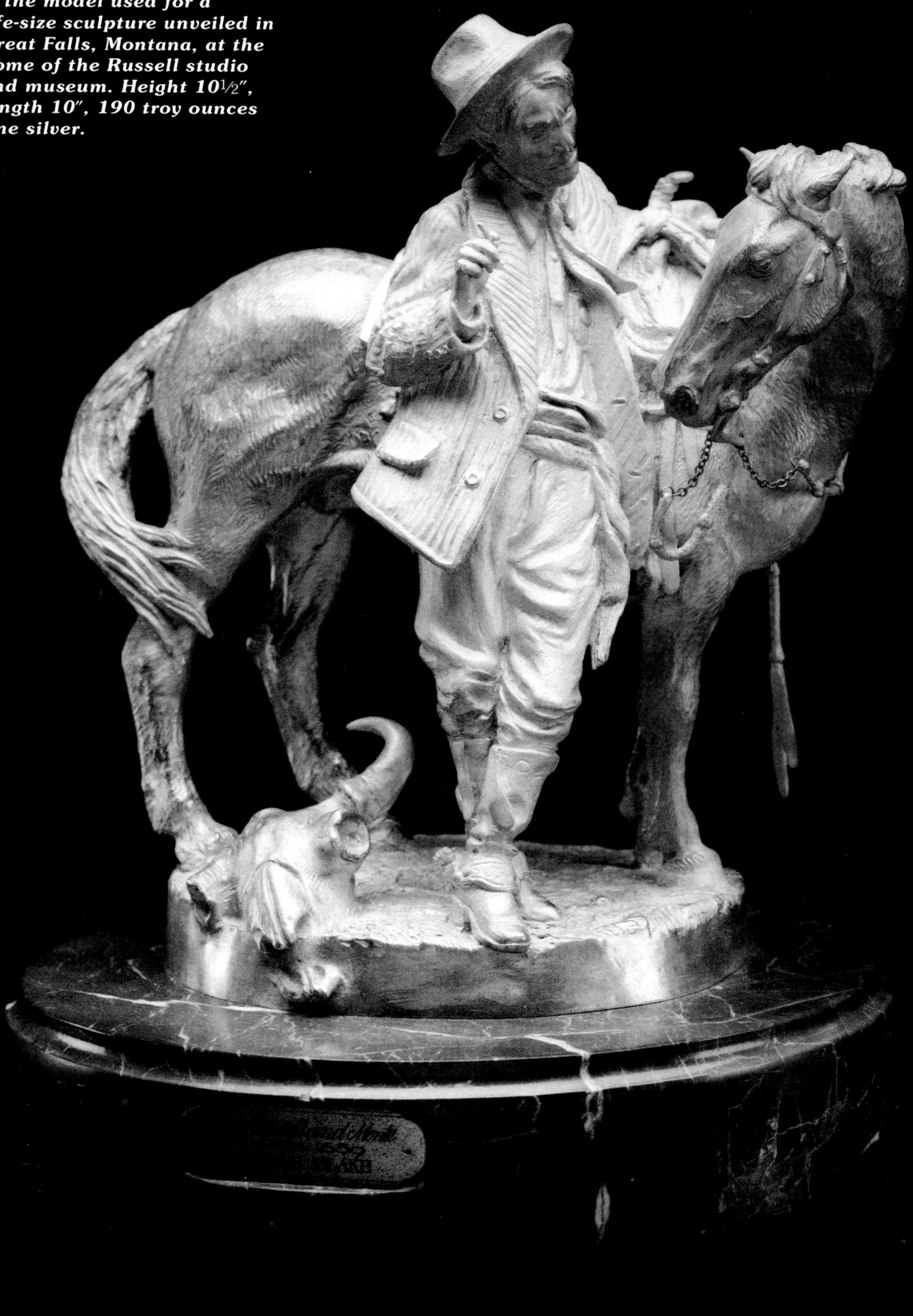

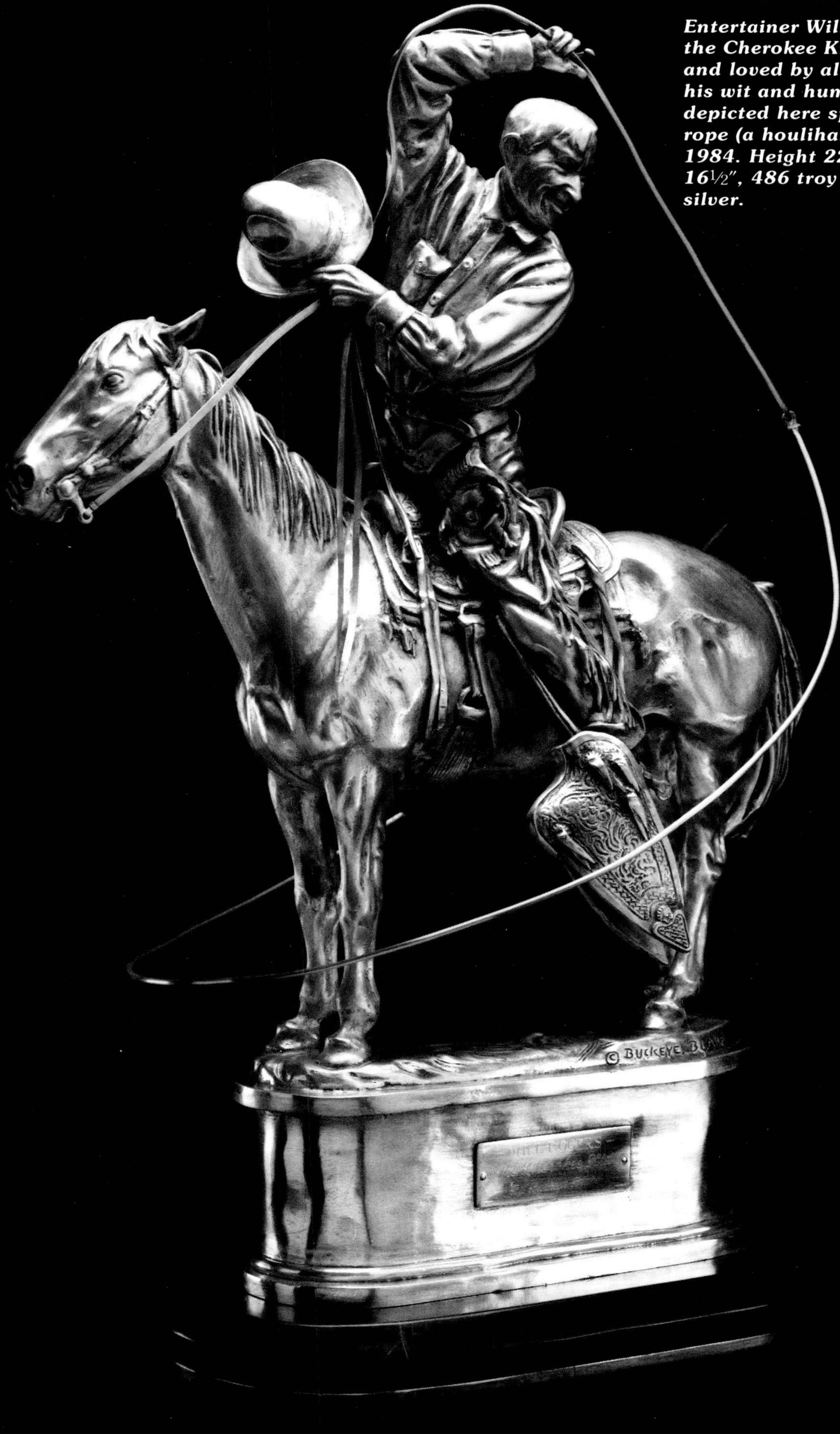

Buckeye Blake
THE CHEROKEE KID

Entertainer Will Rogers, called the Cherokee Kid, was known and loved by all Americans for his wit and humor. He is depicted here spinning his rope (a houlihan). Dated 1984. Height 22″, length 16½″, 486 troy ounces fine silver.

Tom Knapp

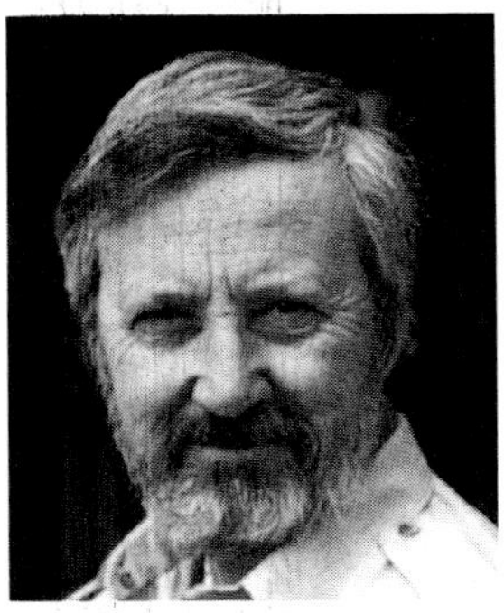

With a background as diverse as liquid rocket technician at White Sands Missile Range and animator for Walt Disney Studios, Tom Knapp brings a fascinating spectrum of experience to his life as a sculptor.

He received his formal art training from the California College of Arts and Crafts in Oakland, and at Art Center School in Los Angeles. A member of American Mensa, he is listed in *Who's Who in American Art, Who's Who in the West, Who's Who in America,* and the *Dictionary of American Sculptors.*

Knapp spent his boyhood on a ranch homesteaded by his father in northeast Wyoming. The experience formed the basis for his lifelong interest in wildlife, the West, and the American Indian, all subjects that are well represented in his bronze and silver sculptures.

A stickler for accuracy, Knapp researches extensively before sculpting each new work, although he admits that detail cannot be an end in itself. From the start, he searches for the essence of his subject, and works to capture a sense of vitality and movement in whatever he sculpts.

Tom Knapp
BIGHORN RAM

Renowned for its sure-footed mastery of rugged, mountainous terrain, the bighorn mountain sheep readily climbs what seem to be impassible vertical cliffs. The ram's dense, heavy horns often grow more than a yard in length along their outside curve. Height 8″, length 10½″, 90 troy ounces fine silver.

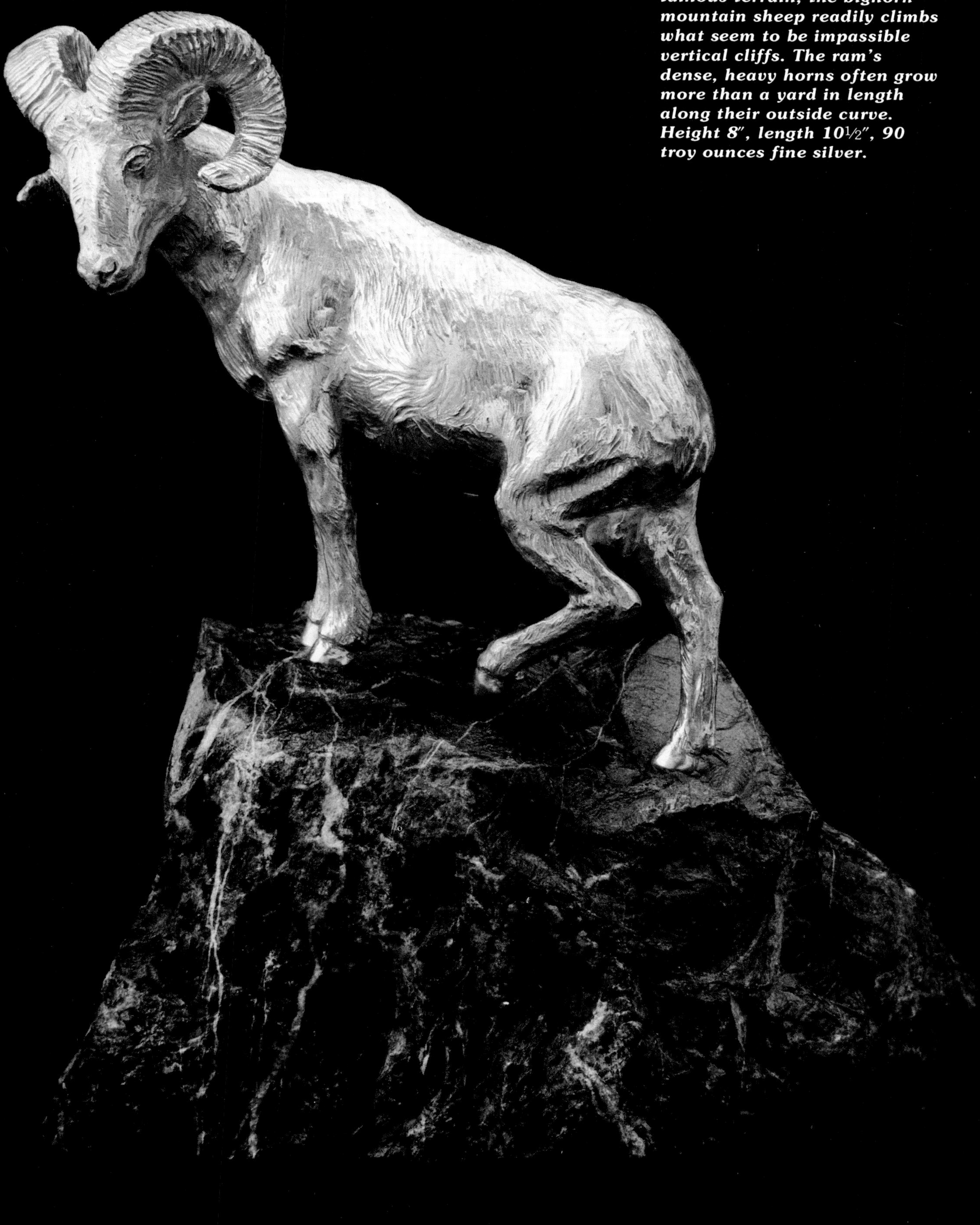

Tom Knapp
CHEETAH

The cheetah is an African (formerly Asiatic) cat the size of a small leopard. Its great speed is assisted by blunt, nonretractable claws which provide traction while running. The cheetah is often tamed and trained to run down antelope and other game. Height 14½", length 8½", 145 troy ounces fine silver.

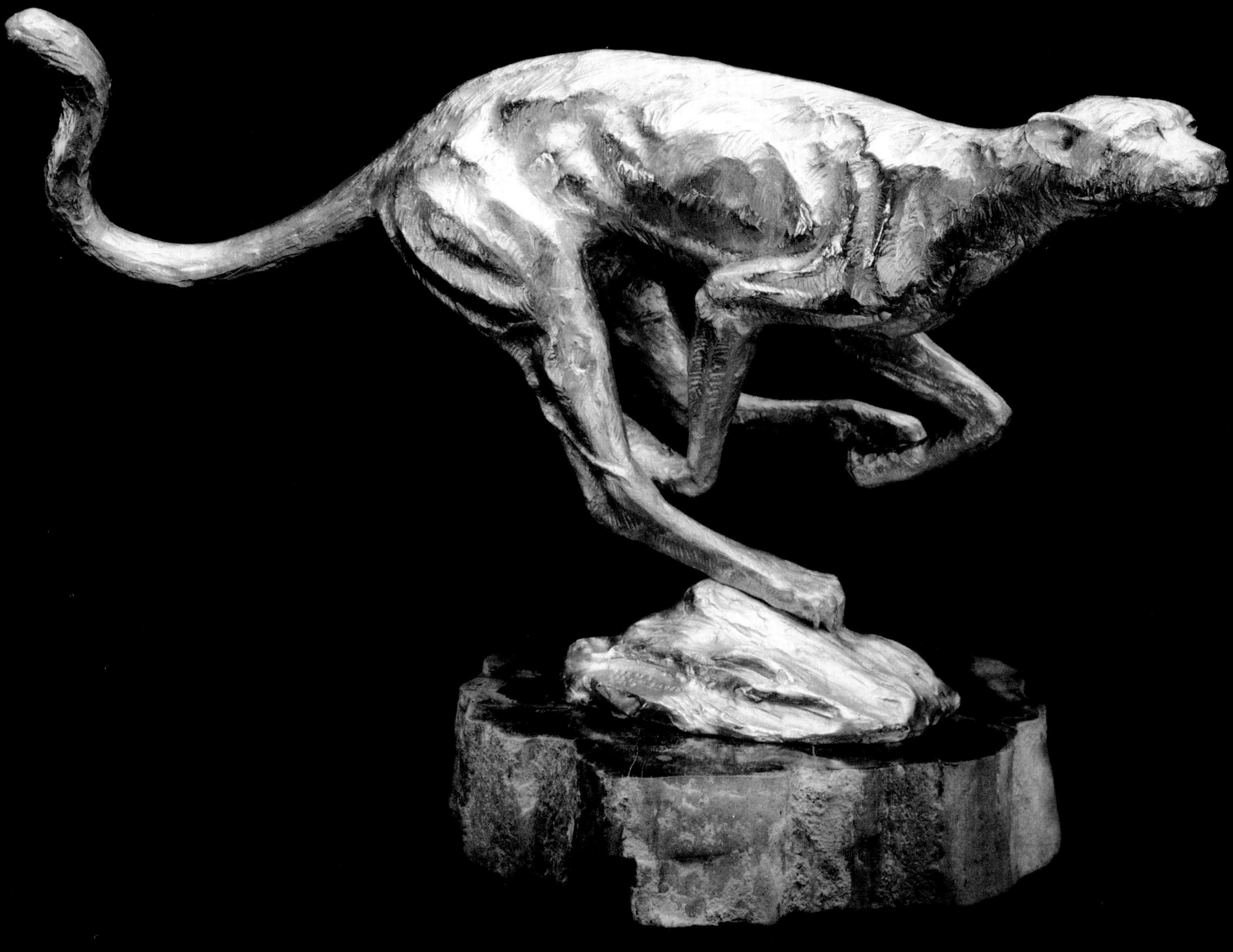

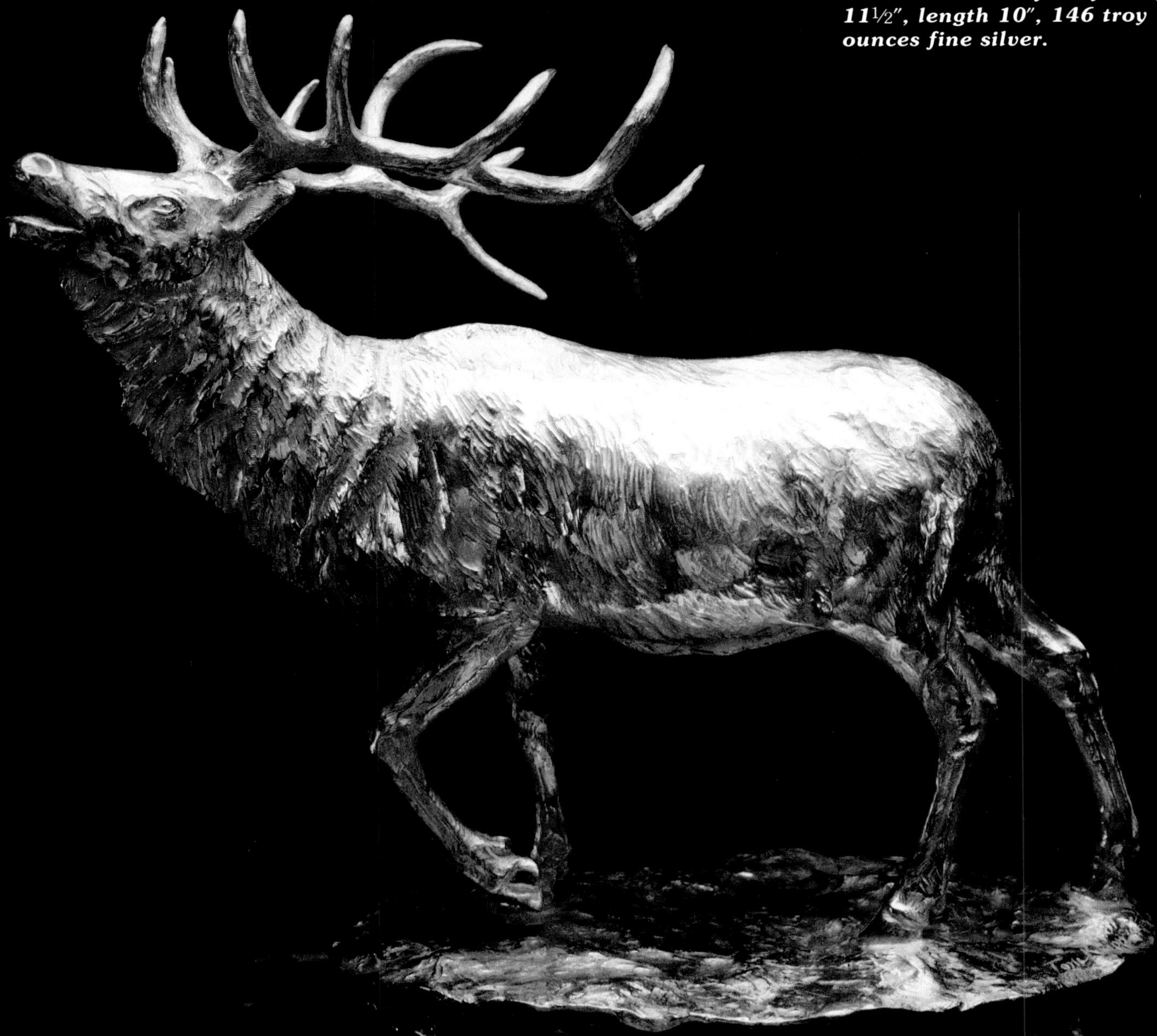

Tom Knapp
THE BUGLER

Confined to high, mountainous areas, the elk is one of the most sought-after trophies for American hunters. Like the deer, his massive antlers are shed yearly. Height 11½″, length 10″, 146 troy ounces fine silver.

James A. Gruzalski

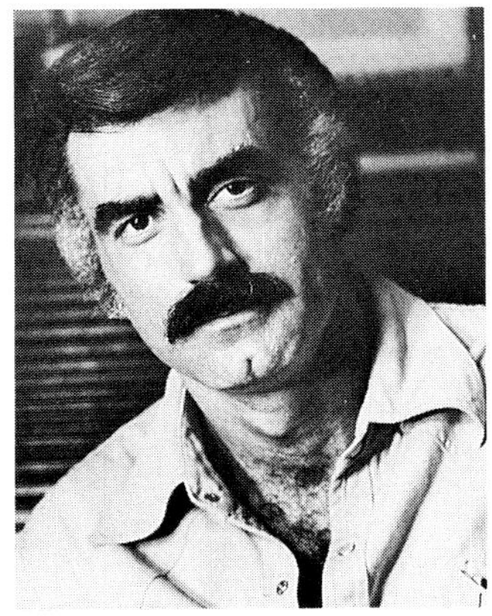

Tucson sculptor James Gruzalski has devoted his talents to portraying historic figures and the American Indian, showing the strength, pride, and spirit inherent in them. He studied at the Art Institute of Chicago, then further honed his skills with classes in sculpture and industrial design at the University of Illinois. He has also studied privately with many prominent painters and sculptors.

His sensitivity in sculpting faces was recognized early by medical professionals working with medical prosthetics. He has executed models from which surgeons have performed facial reconstructive surgery, and holds patents for several medical inventions and orthopedic devices.

Gruzalski also designs fine jewelry although the primary fascination in his own work remains the Old West.

CHARGE

A formidable animal when aroused, the bull lowers his head and charges horns first, whether his foe be another bull, a cowboy, or a bullfighter. Height 17½", length 29½", 930 troy ounces fine silver.

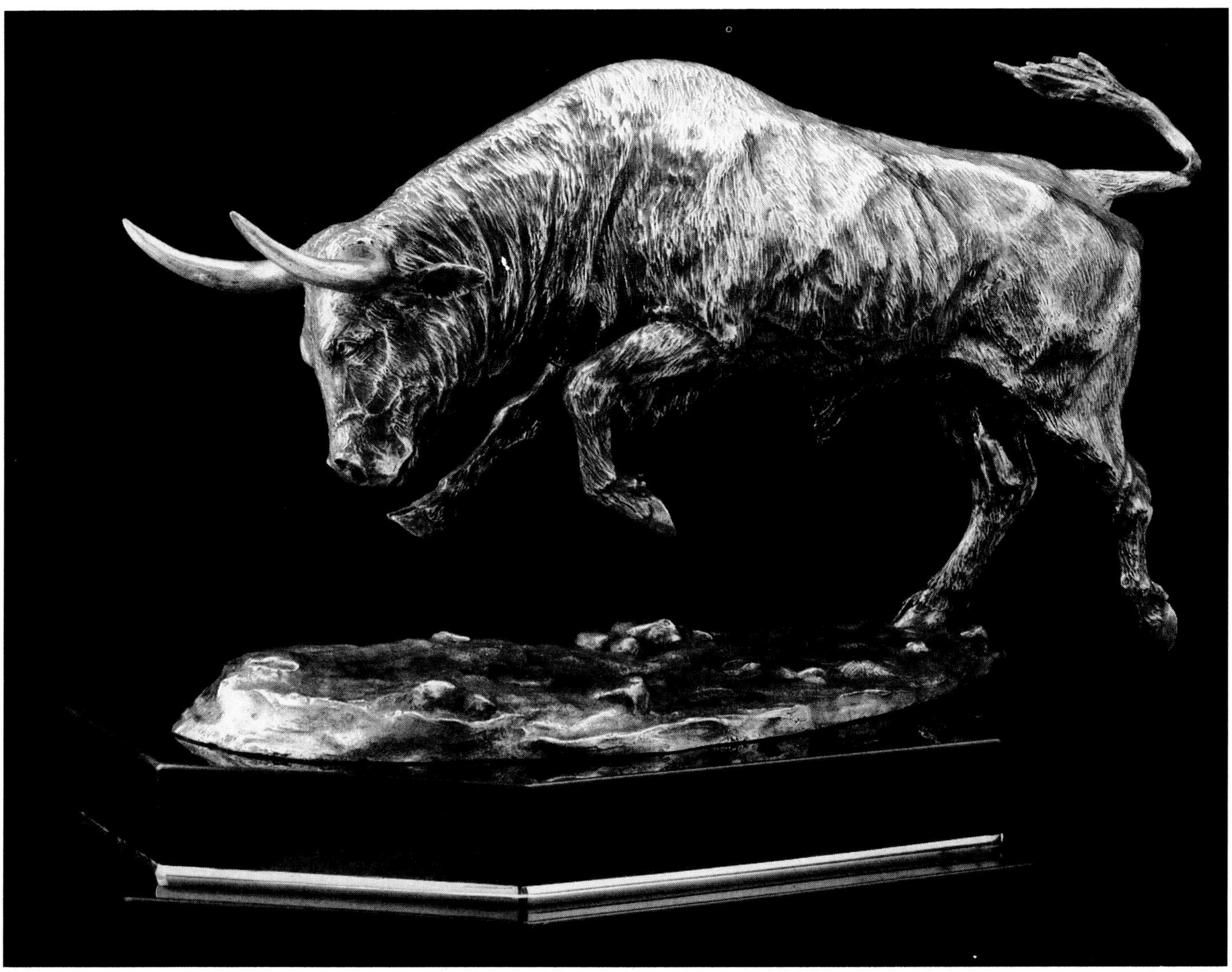

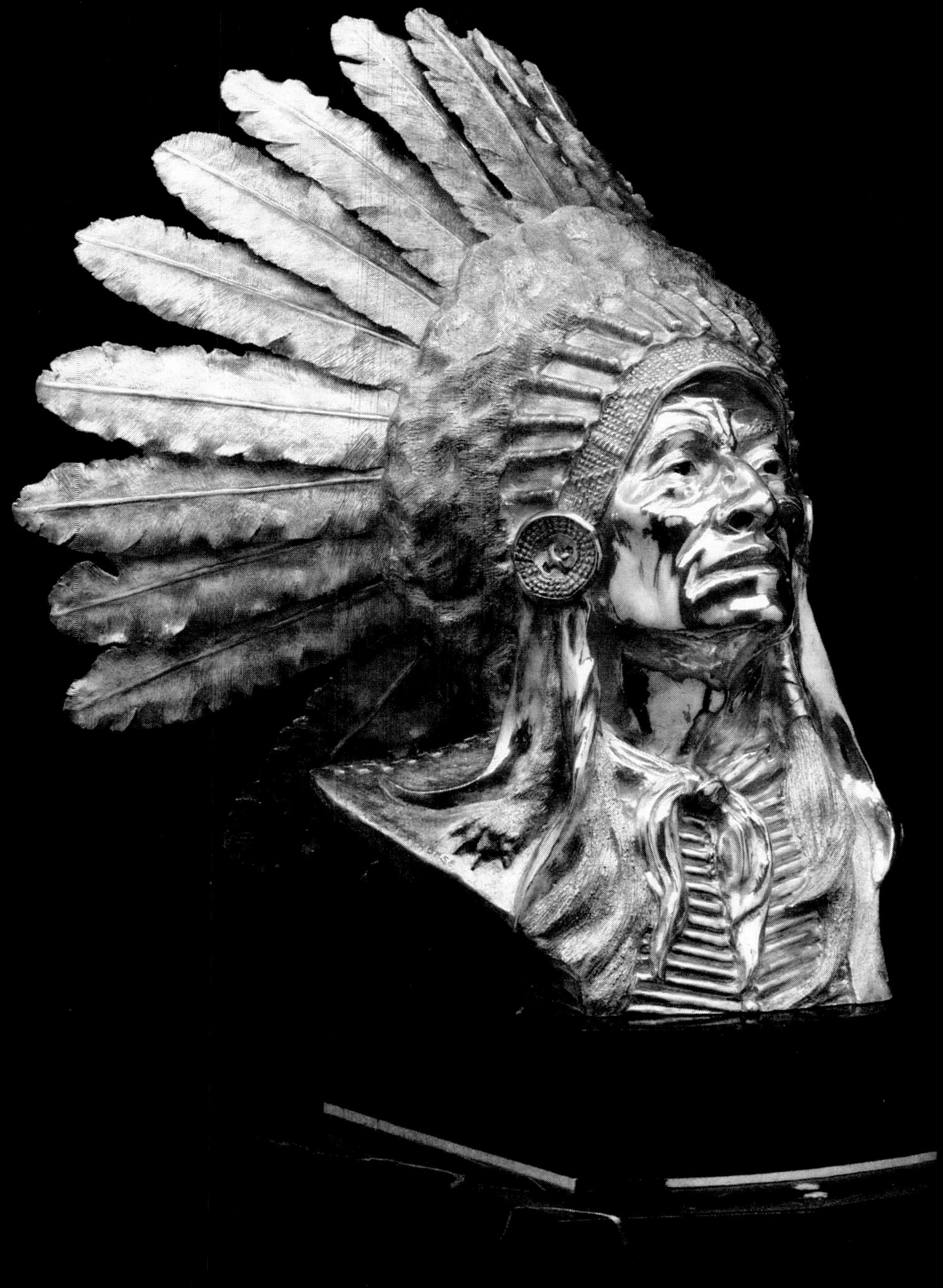

James A. Gruzalski
CHIEF CRAZY HORSE (1844?–1877)

Skillful war strategy combined with an unshakable defiance against American occupation of the Northern Plains catapulted "Tashunca-Uitco," or "Crazy Horse," into leading his people as a great warchief as early as 1865.

Uniting his Sioux warriors with Cheyenne Indian forces, Crazy Horse helped launch a surprise attack on General George Crook along the Rosebud River on June 17, 1876. Just eight days later, they went on to annihilate Custer and the 7th Cavalry at the Little Bighorn.

Crazy Horse and his band of men returned to the hill country to resume their old ways, but cold and hunger forced their surrender less than a year later to General Crook in Nebraska. Confined to Fort Robinson, Crazy Horse was mortally stabbed in the back while supposedly trying to escape.

Height 24½″, length 17″, 1300 troy ounces fine silver.

Alexander Moyle

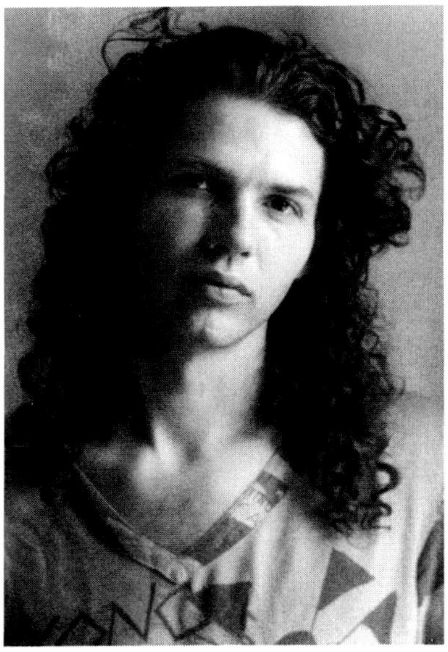

Artist Alexander Moyle graduated from the Philadelphia College of Art in 1981 with a degree in sculpting. Since then, he has pursued an abiding interest in the classics by depicting classical and mythological subjects with an eye toward contemporary line and form.

Moyle's background includes extensive practical experience related to the field of sculpture. Skilled in every facet of fine art metal casting, he has worked professionally in fine art foundries. He served as sculptor's assistant on several monumental bronze projects in Arizona, then refurbished statuary while working as an art conservator in New York City, at West Point, and at the Pennsylvania State Capitol. This wealth of technical expertise has served to enhance his understanding of composition, structure, shape, and surface in his own sculptures and bas-reliefs.

Currently living in Toronto, Canada, Moyle has exhibited his sculptures in shows both in the United States and Canada. His work is characterized by the rich, almost baroque, application of texture, and a metaphysical world view.

Alexander Moyle
ISIS

"Isis" is Alexander Moyle's interpretation in silver of the Egyptian goddess of fertility and divine motherhood. Considered a mourning goddess as well, Isis was one of four who protect the dead body. She was born out of the union of earth and sky, thus she is often depicted as a winged figure. Height 12", length 4½", 122 troy ounces fine silver.

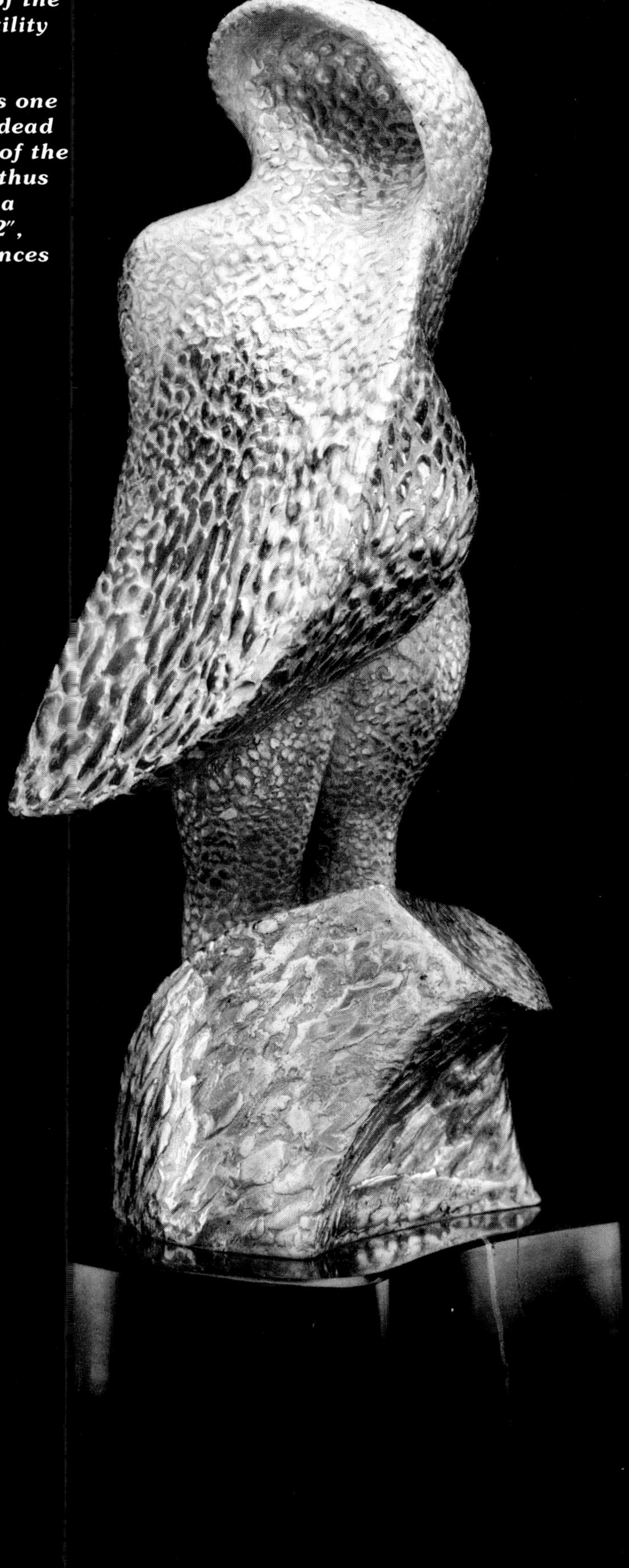

Robert E. Barber

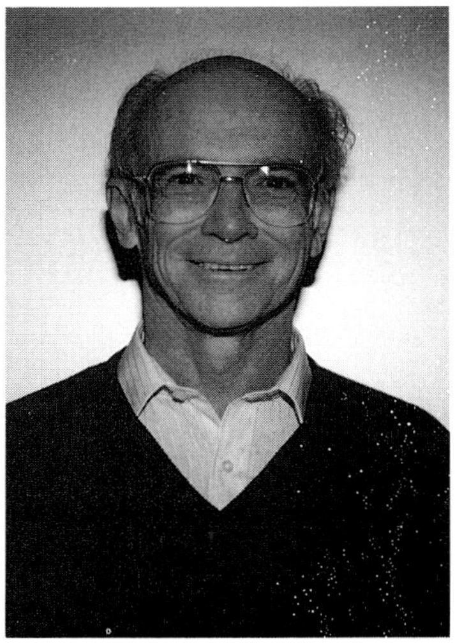

The founder of an engineering and manufacturing company in Arvada, Colorado, Bob Barber has maintained a lifetime interest in wildlife and the out-of-doors. An avid fisherman, he worked as a guide for fly fishermen on Oregon's McKenzie River before he even finished high school.

In the 1970s, he began to experiment with various types of art forms, settling on sculpting in wax. This led to the sculpturing of more than thirty wildlife pieces, from birds to fish to mammals.

Barber's work has been exhibited primarily in Colorado. It is included in the collections of the National Soaring Museum in New York State, and the Petro-Lewis Corporation in Denver, which commissioned a six-foot-high modernistic eagle head for the lobby of its skyscraper headquarters.

Besides sculpting, Barber spends as much time as he can spare photographing nature.

Robert E. Barber
PROUD SPIRIT—EAGLE

Emblem of the United States of America, the eagle is noted for its strength, size, grace, keenness of vision, and powers of flight. Height 15″, length 10″, 72 troy ounces fine silver.

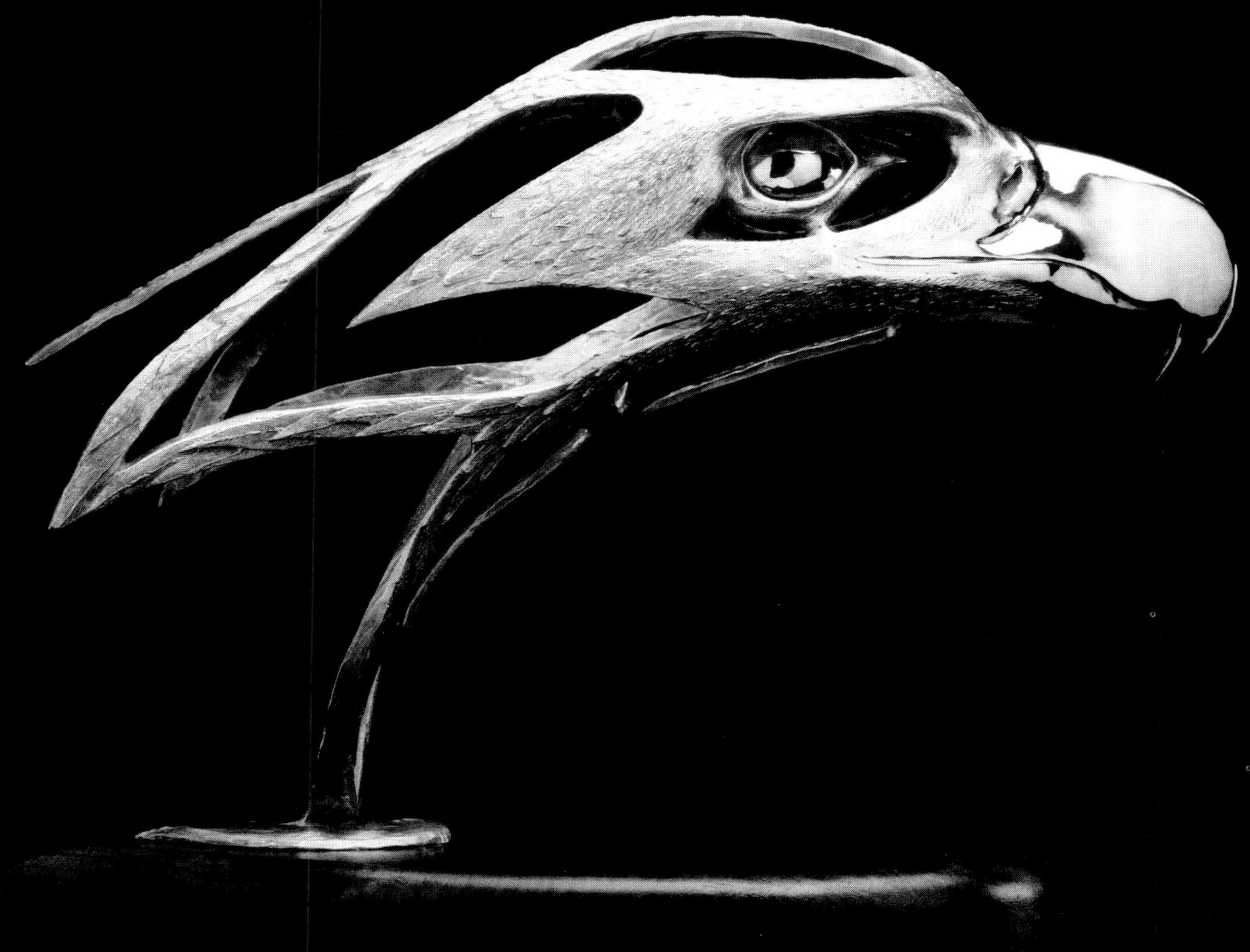

Ralph Crawford

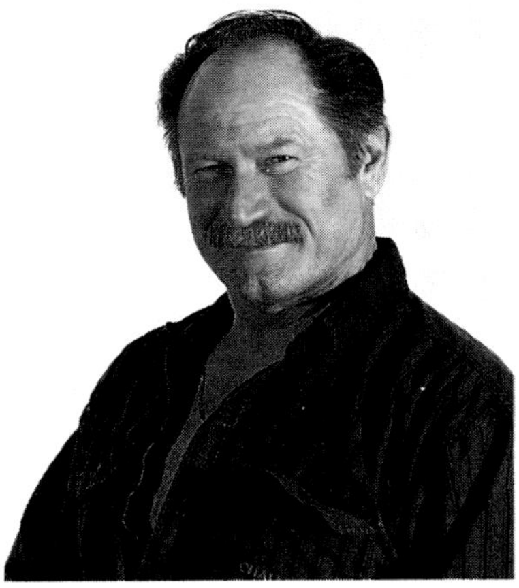

Showing an interest in art since childhood, Ralph Crawford was often found drawing instead of studying. After finishing school in Los Angeles, he supported his family by working as a roofing contractor. Out of necessity, art was relegated to hobby status, yet during this period, he filled dozens of sketch books with drawings of family and friends.

In 1970, he quit the roofing business to devote all his time to art, discovering a penchant for working clay. He claimed the "three Rs" (Russell, Remington, and Rodin) as his role models, describing his art as classic western.

Although early pieces reflected a passionate interest in frontier history, he has since expanded his subject matter dramatically. Later sculptures include African wildlife, the Greek mythological winged horse Pegasus, and contemporary body builder Arnold Schwarzenegger, who is a close friend. Crawford attempts to record emotion in the forms he creates, while assuring that everything is anatomically correct and accurately detailed.

Recently, he has returned to painting in oils, acrylics, and watercolors. A versatile artist, he also works in pastels and has successfully experimented with paper sculpture.

Ralph Crawford
THE ROGUE

When separated from the herd, an elephant can become a fierce and dangerous animal, thus Crawford's title, "The Rogue." Height 6¼", length 7½", 100 troy ounces fine silver.

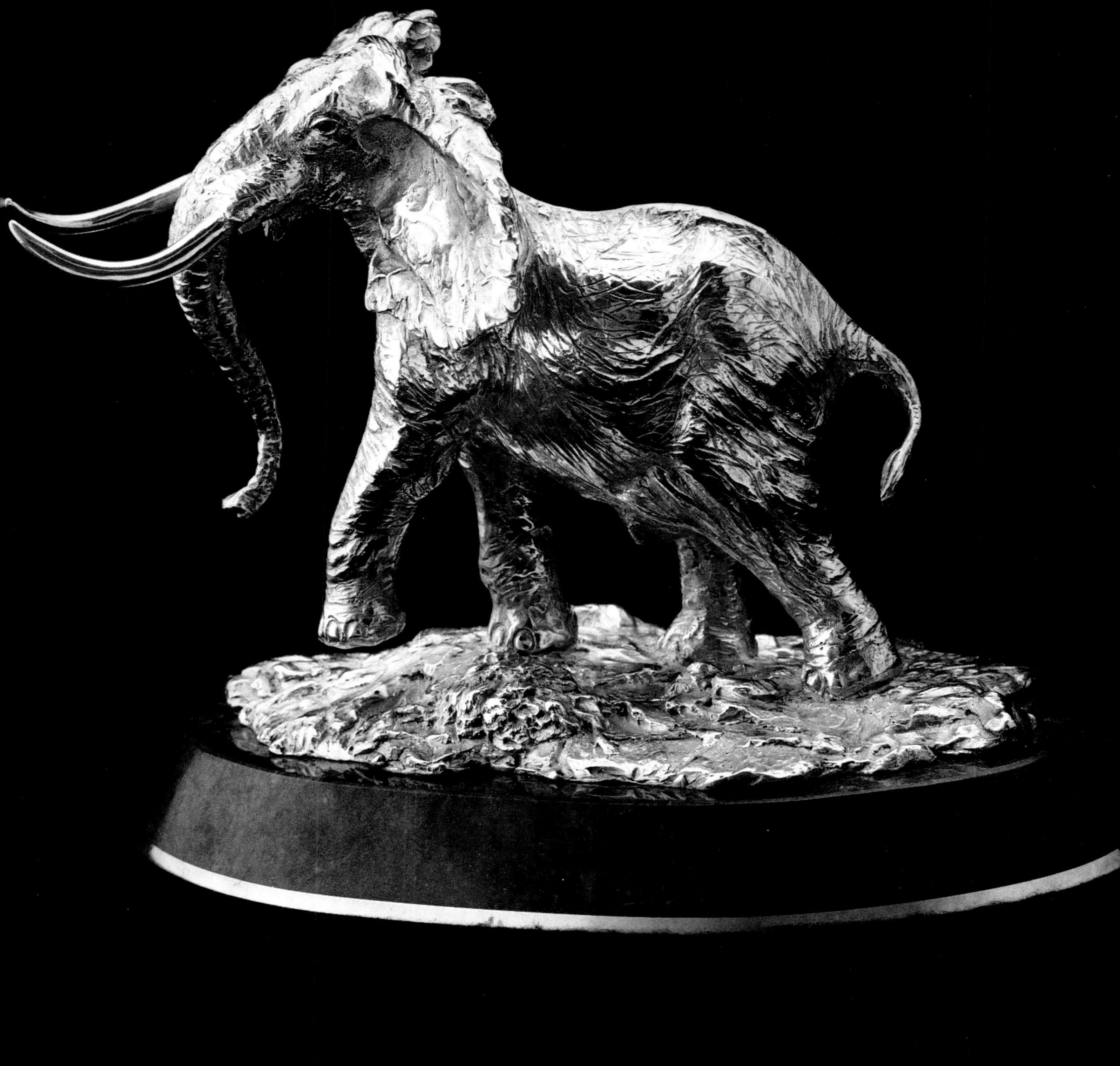

THE HOPI

SILVER KACHINA COLLECTION

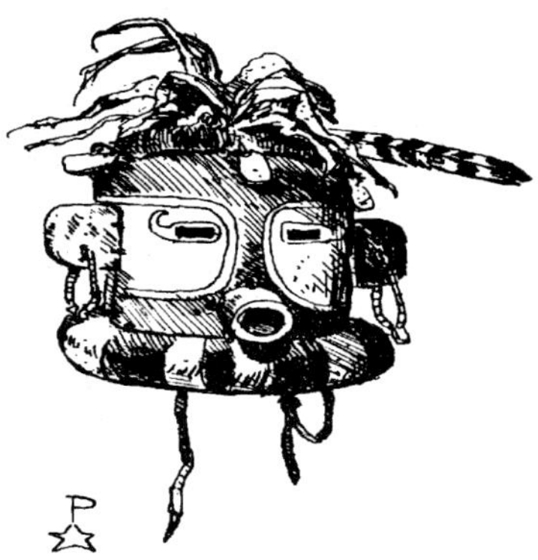

A few years ago, after completing his book on Zuni kachinas, Bill Harmsen visited Third Mesa in Hopiland, where he noticed and admired some jewelry made with the Hopi silver overlay technique. He saw this same type of work on display at the Hopi Cultural Center, and was struck by the thought that the myriad Hopi kachinas would be beautiful depicted in sterling silver with silver overlay. The idea challenged him to begin a silver Hopi kachina collection.

He identified several fine Native American silversmiths, and spent three years working with them on the collection. Harmsen provided the artists with silver sheet and photos or drawings of the kachinas he was most interested in. The silversmiths then created personal interpretations of the kachinas, working in silver overlay dressed with stamped, embossed, and appliqued details.

Harmsen had envisioned creating just a few of the more important kachinas, but with encouragement from his friend Barton Wright, an author of books about Hopi kachinas and kachina dolls, he went on to commission 118 kachinas in silver standing six to twelve inches tall. To Harmsen's knowledge, this is the only collection of its kind in the world.

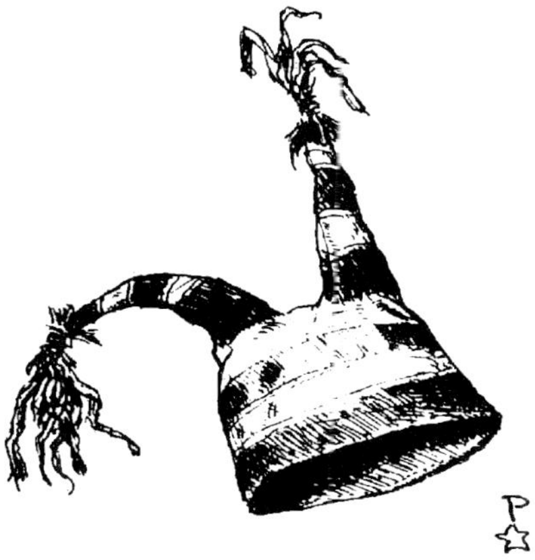

HOPI SILVER OVERLAY

Hopi silver overlay was developed as a distinctive Hopi technique around 1947, when an eighteen-month silversmithing course was established for veteran Hopis at New Oraibi. As employed in Hopi silverwork, the overlay technique basically consists of sheet silver with designs cut out of it to create negative shapes as the primary design element.

Designs are first carefully and precisely cut out of sheet silver using a jeweler's saw. The "leftover" piece of silver—the one with a hole where the design was cut out—is then soldered onto another sheet of plain silver, and all edges are trimmed and filed. In this way, the cut-out area becomes a recessed area of negative design. This area is sometimes textured, then oxidized a black color with acid, to contrast against the surrounding upraised polished silver.

Many of the Hopi kachinas in the Harmsen collection have up to four layers of silver overlay. This extra layering creates great depth and detail even before the final tooling and engraving is added.

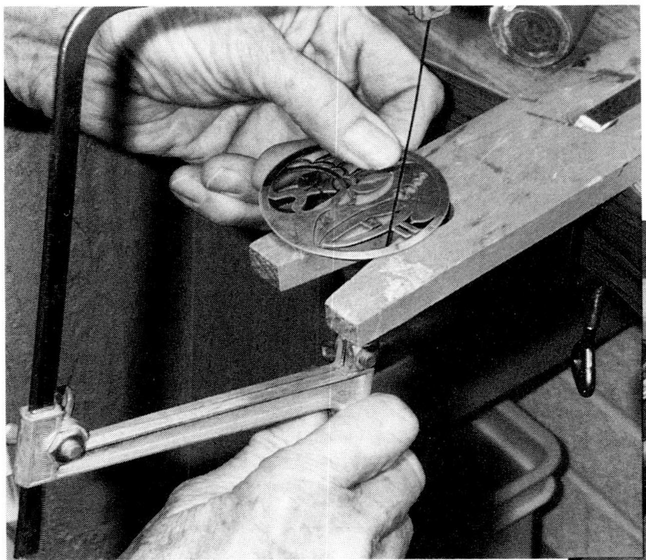

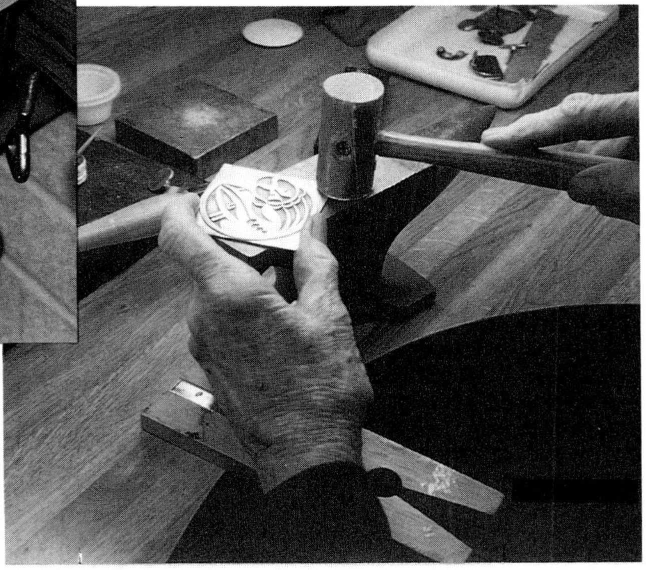

THE HOPIS AND THEIR RELIGION

The Hopis of northeastern Arizona are the westernmost of a group of indigenous peoples categorized as "Pueblo Indians." Extending from Arizona to New Mexico and south along the Rio Grande, the Pueblo peoples live in distinctive flat-roofed, compact villages built of rock or adobe, much like their prehistoric ancestors. Most practice complex religions which feature masked dancers in various ceremonies.

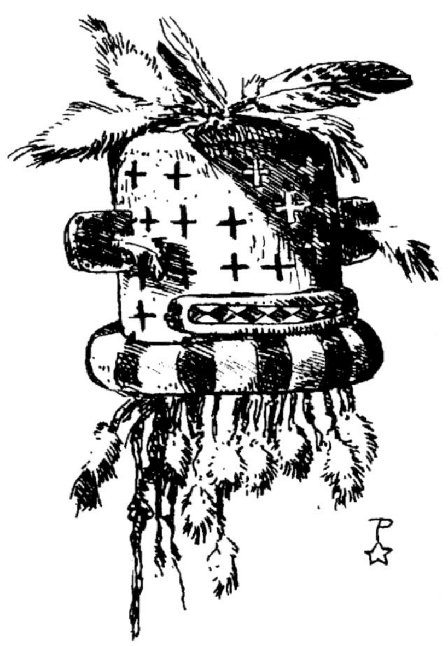

Hopi villages are located on three large mesas or plateaus that project southward like fingers extending from the immense Black Mesa. Oraibi on Third Mesa is considered America's oldest continuously inhabited town, located at the same site since about A.D. 1150.

For the Hopis, all things in life have two forms: the form that is visible to people, and a form that is spiritual or supernatural. The kachinas are the supernatural form of things in the real world.

Kachinas are given shape and personality through masks, paint, and costumes so that the Hopi people can interact with them. When a Hopi man dons the mask and costume of a kachina, he believes he loses his personal identity and receives the spirit of the kachina he represents.

There are hundreds of kachinas. Perhaps 200 to 300 kachinas appear in current ceremonies, while as many as 200 others appear only occasionally. Although most kachinas appear in ceremonies on all three mesas, there are some esoteric local differences in costuming and masks, and occasionally a kachina exists that is specific to only one village.

Kachinas are named in several ways. Some are descriptive and translatable (Motsin, the Disheveled Kachina), some originate from the distinctive cries made by the kachina (Aholi), and some have no English equivalents, making translation impossible. Several kachinas are named after birds, animals, or plants (Tumoala, the Devil's Claw Kachina), and various kachinas have been borrowed from other Pueblo groups (Hututu, from Zuni).

Every Hopi child past the age of ten is initiated into the Kachina Cult. Children are frequently given carved and painted cottonwood root kachina dolls as "lessons" in a sense, rather than as toys. The dolls are revered as important possessions and serve to teach young Hopis about the kachinas as part of their religious training.

The kachinas help to renew the Hopi world, readying it for the growing season and bringing rain. They are not worshipped as idols, but rather considered friends of the Hopis who serve as mediators between the gods and human beings. They instruct people as to proper behavior, but primarily they bring the Hopis happiness, good health, and a long life.

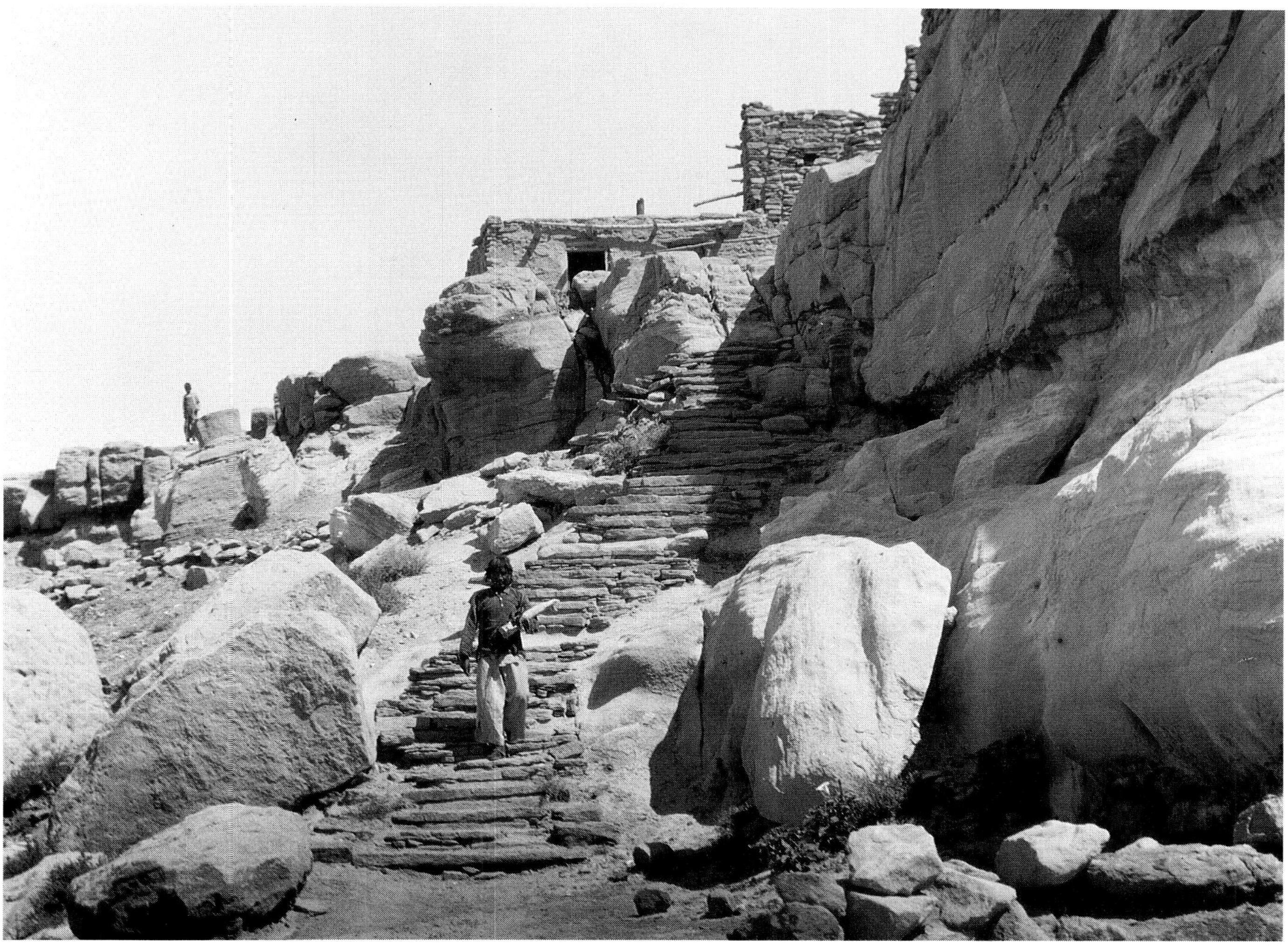

A stone stairway bridging Upper Supawlavi to Lower Supawlavi. The dwellings at the top of the stairs clearly show the roof support beams and masonry style typical of older Hopi villages. (Photo by Forman Hanna, 1922, courtesy of Arizona State Museum.)

The Hopi calendar is broken into two major ceremonial seasons with the Kachina Ceremonies comprising one part of the year, and the non-Kachina Ceremonies making up the remainder. Each major ceremony begins with an announcement at sunrise. Eight days of secret rituals follow, then a public dance is held on the ninth day.

Kachinas first appear near the winter solstice in December, emerging from underground kivas considered entryways to the underworld. In the first major ceremony, the Soyal kachinas perform rites to strengthen the individual, the clan, and the village in the coming year. The Powamu, or Bean Dance, follows as the next major ceremony. Throngs of kachinas pour out of the kivas during the Powamu to ready the world for the coming growing season. At this time, Hopi children are initiated into the Kachina Cult.

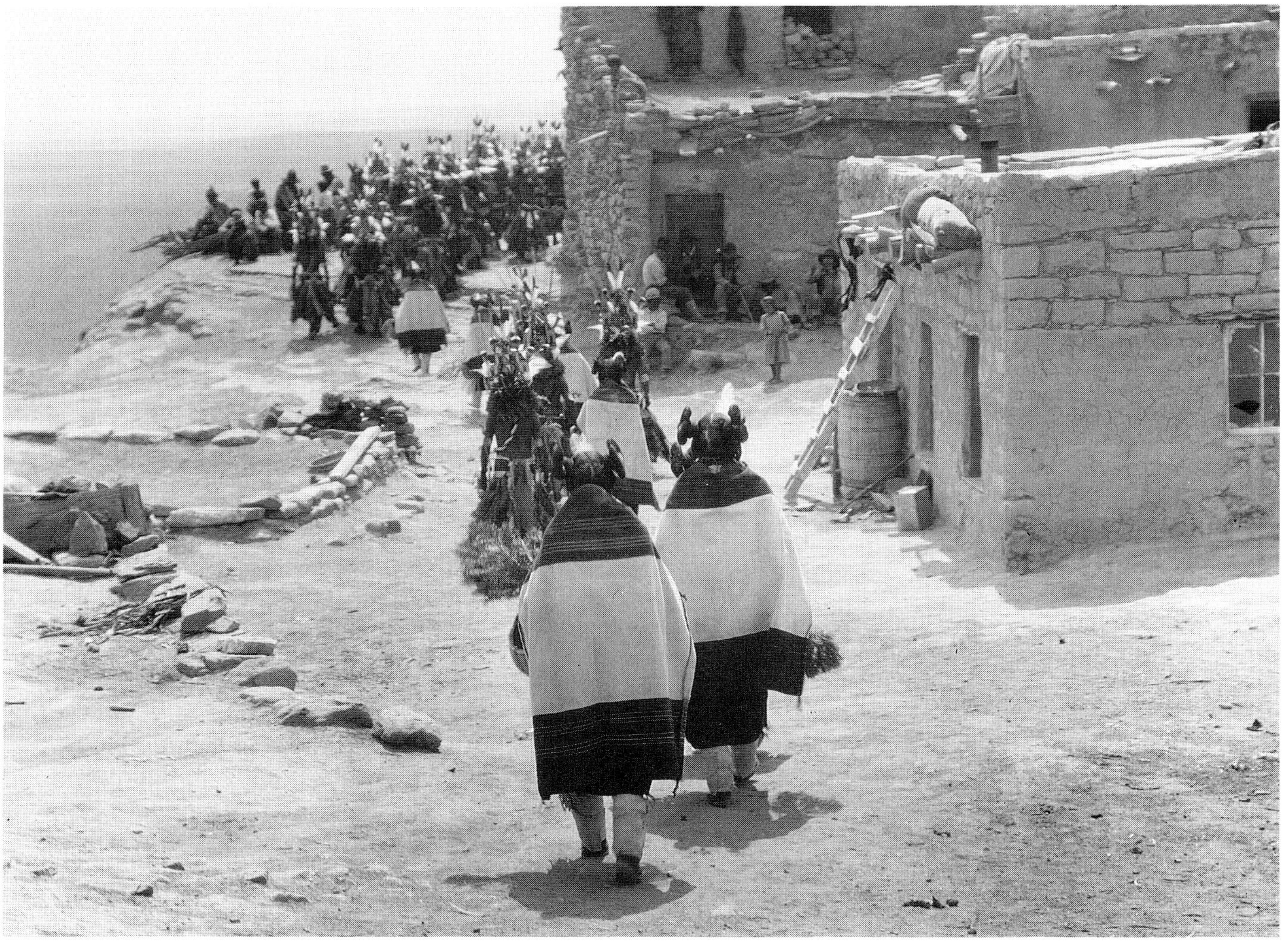

A procession of Hemis Kachinas and Kachin Manas winds through Mishongnovi toward the village plaza for the Niman Home Dance. The Niman ceremony in July closes the Kachina Season; it is the time when the kachinas are sent back to their home in the San Francisco peaks armed with requests for abundant summer rains. (Photo by Forman Hanna, 1922, courtesy of Arizona State Museum.)

The third major ceremony takes place in mid-summer, when the early corn has matured. This Niman Ceremony, or Home Dance, is a formal thanksgiving rite. Afterwards, the kachinas are symbolically sent home to their mountain peaks, disappearing into the kivas until the next winter solstice.

Between these ceremonies of the Kachina Season, many ritual dances take place inside the kivas while the weather is cold, then move out to the plazas when the weather improves. After the Niman Ceremony following the summer solstice, the remainder of the year's ceremonies are characterized by participants who may be painted, but who do not wear masks. The well-known Snake Dance is one such ritual.

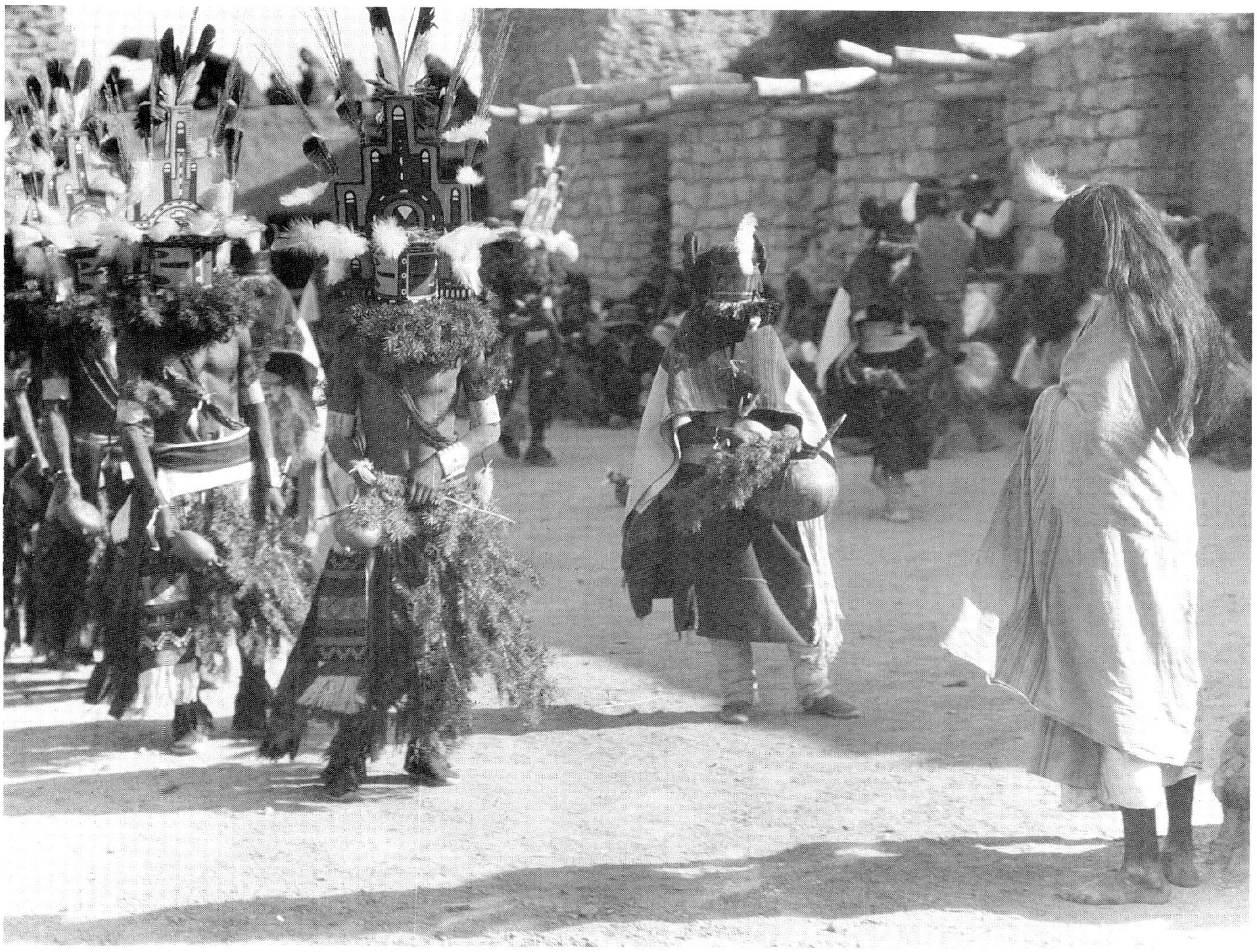

The line of dancers on the left are the splendid Hemis Kachinas whose towering tableta headdresses are painted with thundercloud symbols. Next to them stands one of their Manas, who carries a hollow gourd, sheep scapula, and notched stick to make a distinctive rasping music. (Photo by Forman Hanna, 1922, courtesy of Arizona State Museum.)

KACHINAS — THE HEART OF HOPI LIFE

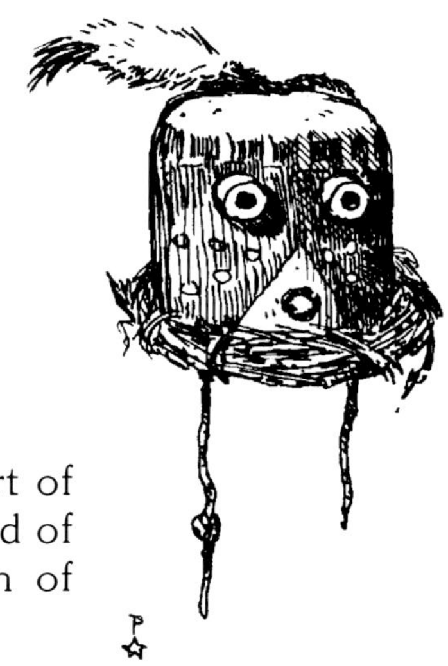

by Emory Sekaquaptewa

To the Hopi people, the kachinas (*katsinam*) are the heart of Hopi life. Almost every day of their lives, they are reminded of these kachinas by the things left behind after the season of kachina performances.

For example, the kachinas give children gifts of kachina dolls, painted rattles, and bows and arrows. These are usually hanging on walls in homes and are constant reminders of the kachinas. Performance songs are not easily forgotten by both young and old alike. These songs stimulate the aesthetic experience in individuals, provide poetic words of wisdom, and serve as reminders of the "good times" enjoyed during kachina appearances.

Today, carved kachina dolls are a craft item produced by the Hopi, as well as by some people who have no cultural affinity with kachinas or who find them irrelevant to their belief systems. This occurs because kachinas are a popular gift item in the market and are well-known around the world.

Kachinas (*katsinam*) are considered reverently by the Hopis and other Pueblo Indians because they represent the spirit beings. To the Hopi, kachinas are beings who once dwelled in this world; having passed through this one, they now dwell in the spirit world. Their transformation from this world of

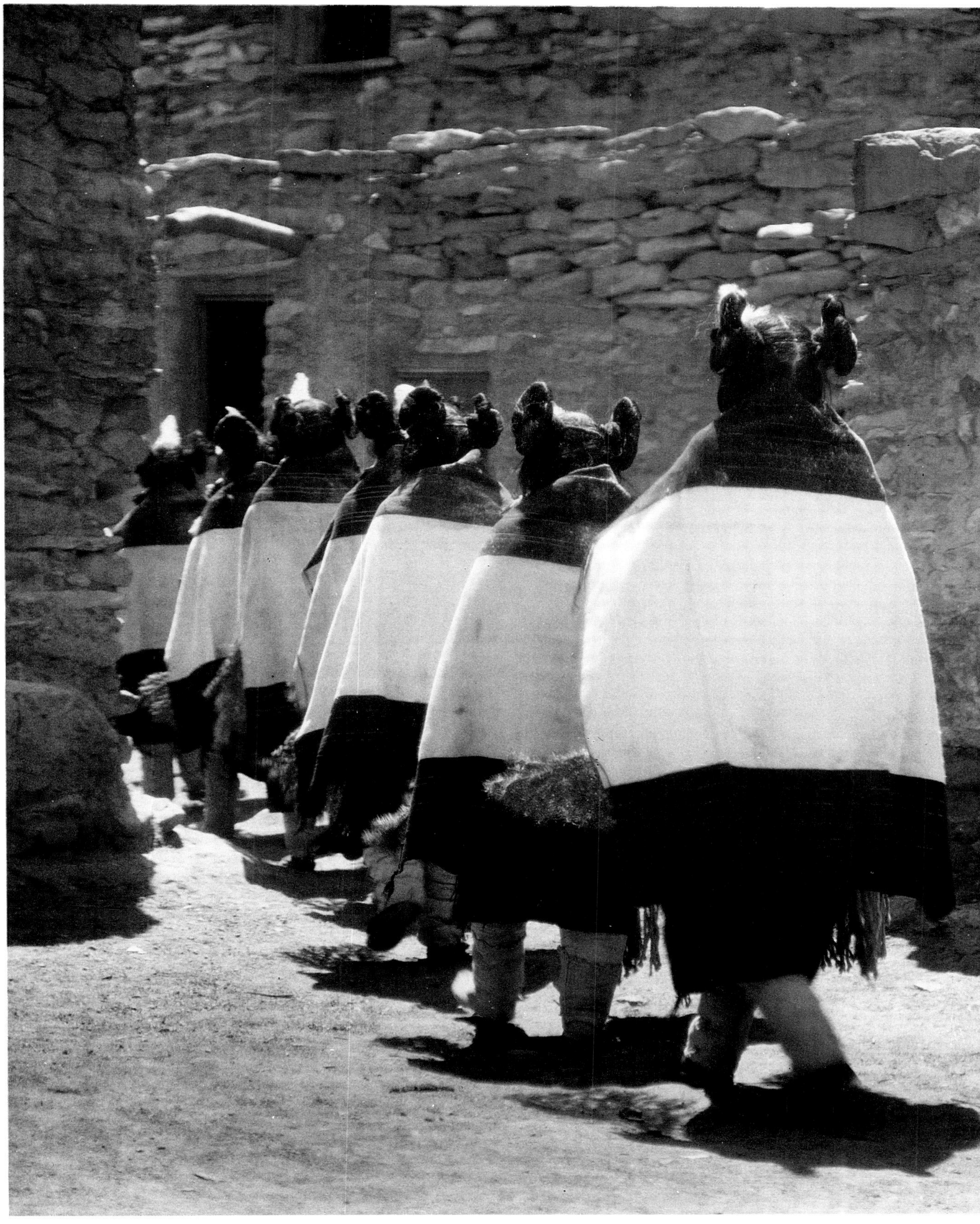

A line of Kachina Maidens enters the dance plaza at Mishongnovi. Distinguished as maidens by their butterfly hair whorls, they wear the woman's traditional cloak, dress, and white buckskin leggings, and each carries sprigs of douglas fir. (Photo by Forman Hanna, 1922, courtesy of Arizona State Museum.)

mortal life into immortality in the spirit world holds for the Hopi a belief in their own life and their ultimate destiny. Hopis are taught they, too, can go by way of the kachinas and become perfected beings with a gift of eternity.

The kachinas in this state of existence are said to possess the power of life and are benevolent in their concern for the life of the people who remain in this world. Based on a long oral tradition, their songs both admonish and remind the people about the teachings of the good world, and inspire them to rise up to the ways of good life that are taught.

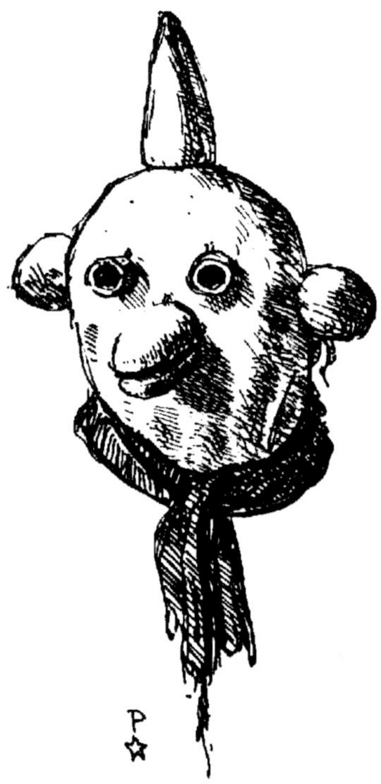

The gifts of food and the items such as kachina dolls that the kachinas bring symbolically demonstrate the gift of life, providing prosperity, longevity, and freedom from suffering. "Kachina gifts" are referred to in Hopi as *Na'mangwu*, or gifts burden. So, when kachinas come each time in a ceremony, they bring their gifts burden with them.

Although kachinas are endowed with a ritual symbolism as spirit beings and benevolent givers, they are looked on by Hopi people as real. The kachinas that Hopis see in the kivas and village dance arenas are not regarded as personations but are spiritually real beings and treated accordingly. There is no real-life personal identity attached to the kachinas, thus the kachinas are not seen as a disguise or a pretense. Children are taught that kachinas are real, in the same sense that Santa Claus is real for children of other cultures.

The kachina doll, or *tihu,* is a representation of the kachina, the spirit being. As spirit beings, the kachinas are said to make dolls in their image and to bring them for young girls. The young recipients are encouraged by their parents to play with and fondle them, so that the life force the dolls are endowed with as kachina creations will pass to them. In this way, they will become fertile for the reproduction of future generations.

Kachina dolls evolve in form through a development analogous to the development of the fetus in the womb until birth. The very first doll a child receives, usually at infancy, is flat and shows no third-dimensional shape with arms or legs. The head is distinguished from the body only by a small notch carved in from either side of the flat piece. There is a suggestion of arms that have been painted on, but no suggestion of legs yet.

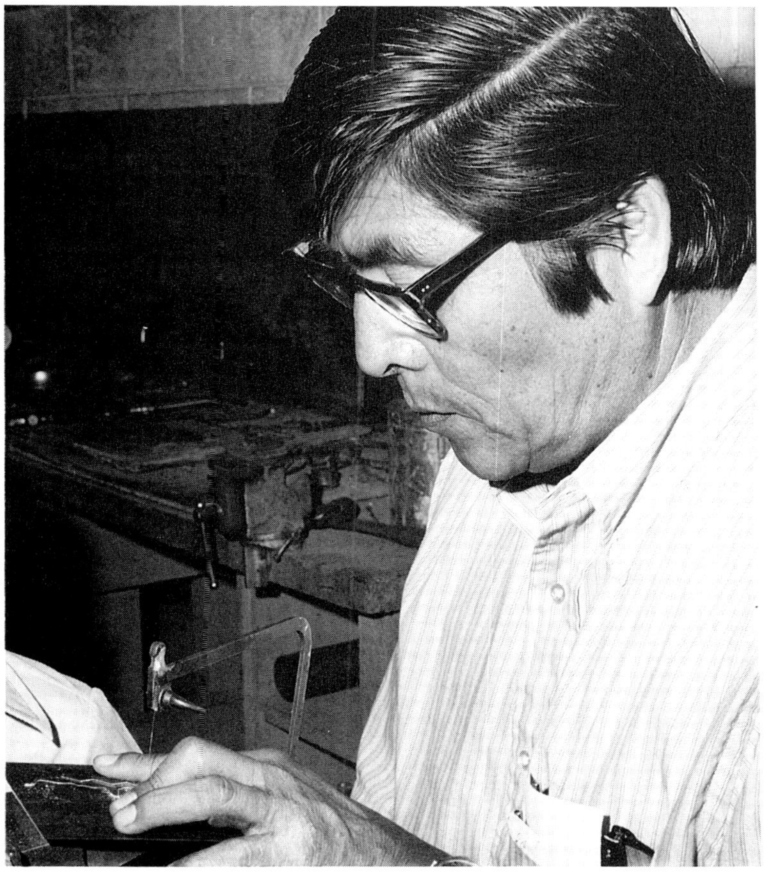

Emory Sekaquaptewa, Research Anthropologist with the Bureau of Applied Research in Anthropology, University of Arizona, Tucson.

As she grows up, the child receives dolls regularly, each doll being more developed in body detail than the last one. The doll reaches full body development at that age just before puberty when she is ready to be initiated into one of the two orders of the Kachina Society Priesthood.

This, then, completes the cycle for the kachina doll as a socializing tool in Hopi society. Today, kachina dolls may be given by Hopis to their non-Hopi friends with all the wishes for the things they stand for.

NATIVE AMERICAN SILVERSMITHS OF

KACHINAS IN SILVER OVERLAY

The following 118 sterling silver kachinas were created by Native American silversmiths using the traditional Hopi overlay technique. Each kachina is displayed on petrified wood, a semiprecious stone occurring naturally in the Petrified Forest and surrounding areas near the Hopi Reservation.

Victor Coohwytewa
Shannon Lamson
Mary Morgan
Jason Takala
Mark Tawahongva
Lee Wesley
Verna Wesley

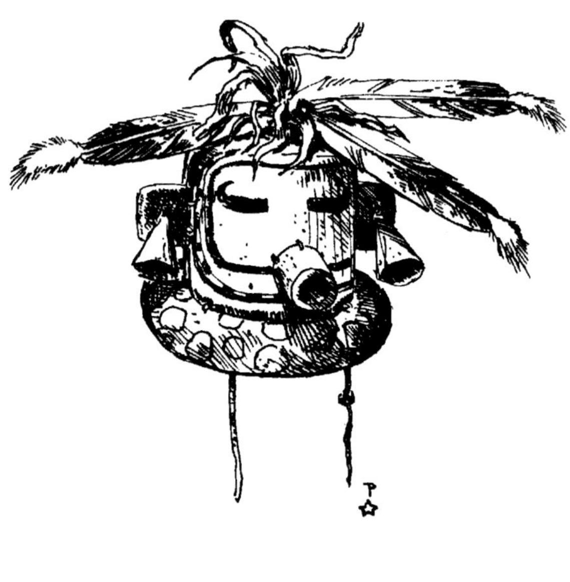

Winter Solstice and the Soyal Ceremony

The winter solstice marks the beginning of the Hopi year, the time when kachinas return to the Hopi mesas after a six-month absence. Their impending arrival is prepared in early December by the Solstice or Return Kachinas, who quietly appear, singing softly, to arrange prayer feathers and cornmeal in the kivas.

The Soyal is the winter solstice ceremony in which several kachinas dance to help turn the sun toward its summer path. During the Soyal, rituals are performed for the health and strength of the Hopi people. Corn is also consecrated at this time. The kivas are ritually opened on the final day of the ceremonies by kachinas who mark their entrances with cornmeal.

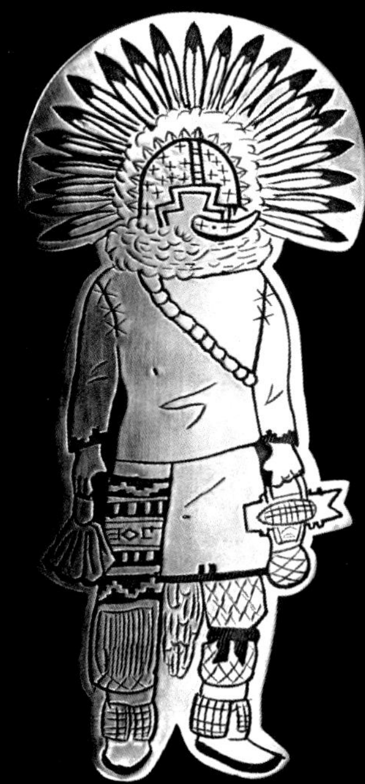

Ahöla

2. Ahöla is the ancient one of the Kachina Clan who led the people from the San Francisco peaks near Flagstaff to their homes on the mesas. He intercedes with the Sun to ask for long life, health, happiness, and abundant crops for his children, the Hopis.

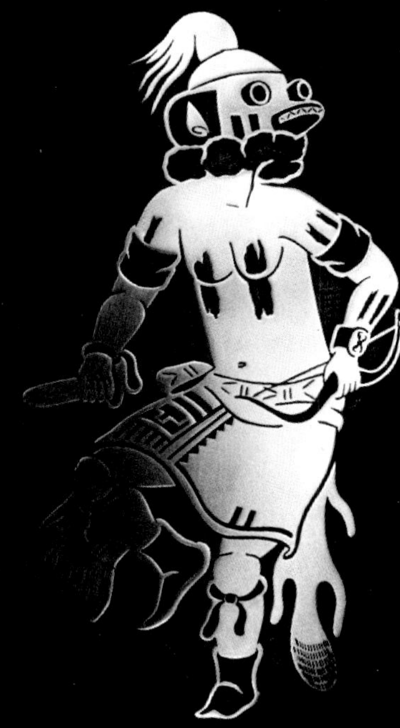

Kaletaka

4. Kaletaka accompanies Ahülani on First Mesa, carrying a bow and arrows. His body is painted black with white smears, and eagle feathers are inserted through his ears.

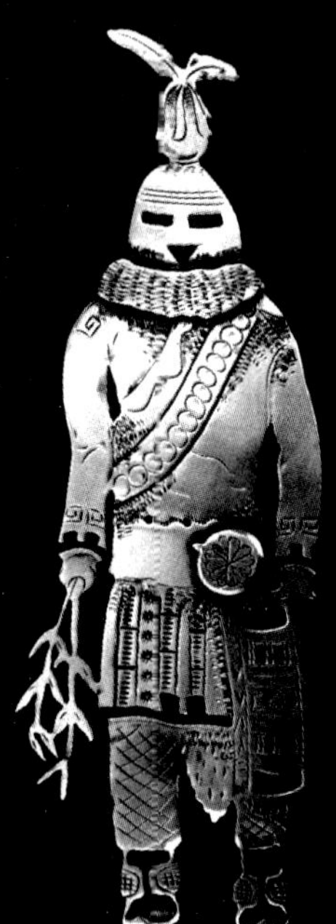

Soyal

1. The only Return Kachina who appears on Third Mesa, Soyal is old, feeble, and shabbily dressed. He leaves prayer feathers, or pahos, at each kiva, and is supposed to have taught the Hopis how to make their pahos.

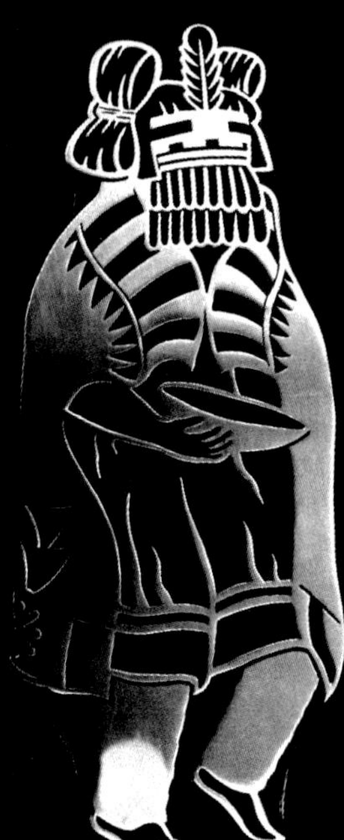

Ahöl Mana

3. Ahöl Mana appears only on Second Mesa, accompanying Ahöla as he visits the kivas and ceremonial houses. Her tray holds seeds from the fields of the Kachina Chief.

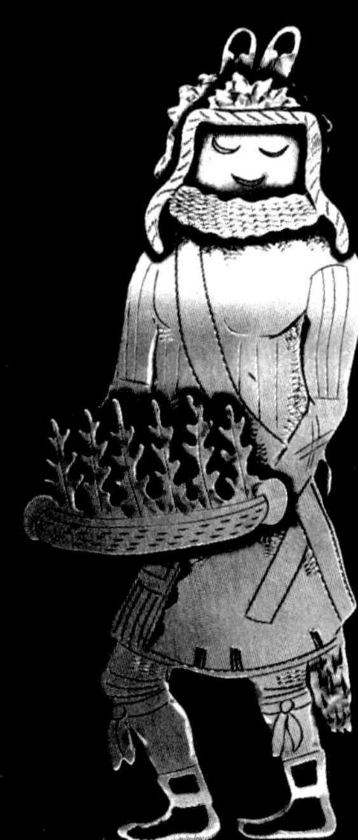

Ahülani

5. Just like Soyal on Third Mesa, Ahülani is the first kachina to appear on First Mesa. Accompanied by corn maidens, he announces the beginning of the kachina season.

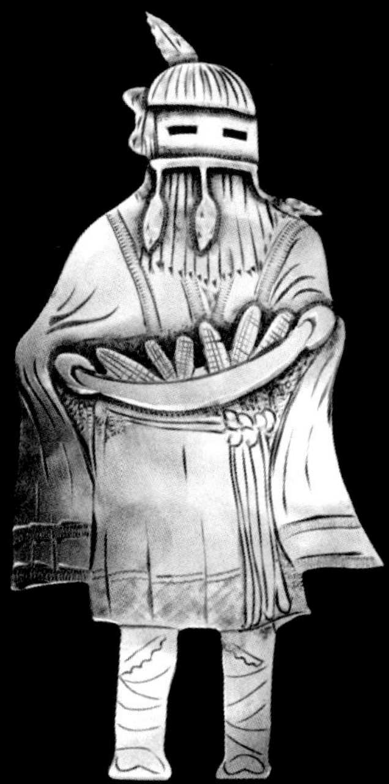

Sakwap Mana

6. Sakwap Mana is known as Blue Corn Girl because she carries a basket of blue corn. She is one of the corn maidens who escort Ahülani.

Powamu Ceremony

In expectation of the approaching season of growth, the February Powamu or Bean Dance Ceremony, encourages the fertility and germination of crops. All Hopi males who have been initiated into the Kachina Cult sprout beans inside their kivas. Ritual bundles of these sprouts are then presented to the women and children.

The Bean Dance Ceremonies include the initiation of children into the Kachina Society. It is a time to teach them about the kachinas, and an enormous number of these masked figures present themselves during the many events associated with the Powamu.

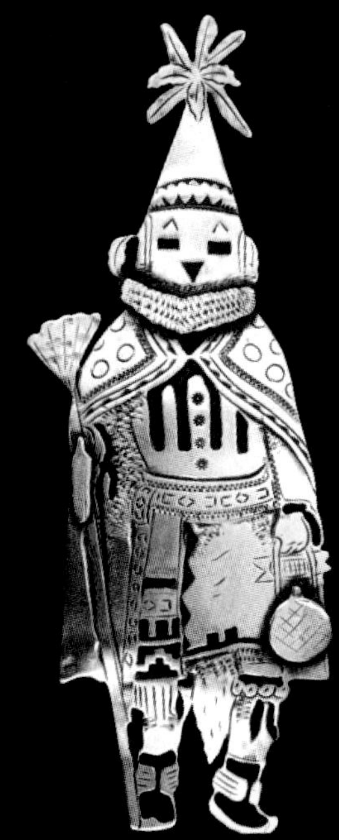

Aholi

9. Eototo's partner is called Aholi. This kachina places the tip of his staff on Eototo's cloud drawings and calls out "Ah-holi-i-i-i." He wears a multicolored cloak representing summer's flowers and an elongated helmet.

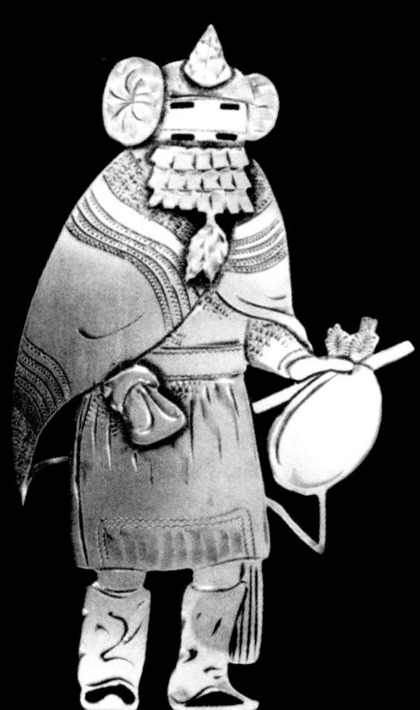

Kachin Mana

7. Kachin Mana carries a tray of corn just like Blue Corn Girl, except that it is filled with yellow corn. Known as Yellow Corn Girl, she serves as the second escort of Ahülani at the Soyal Ceremony.

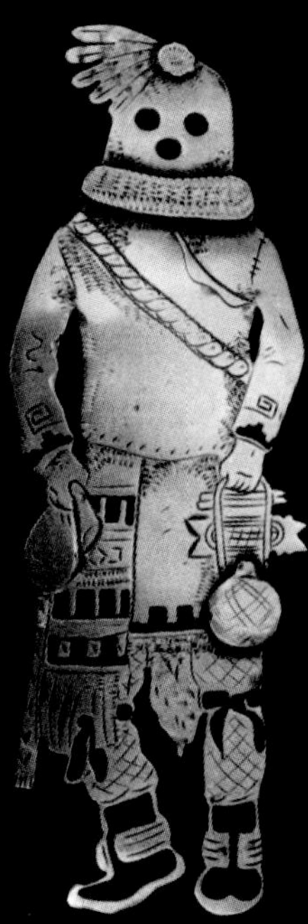

Eototo

8. Known as the "father" of the kachinas or the Kachina Chief, Eototo appears in all major ceremonies. One of his roles is to bring water to the village and its fields. In this capacity, Eototo draws symbols of clouds with cornmeal on the ground.

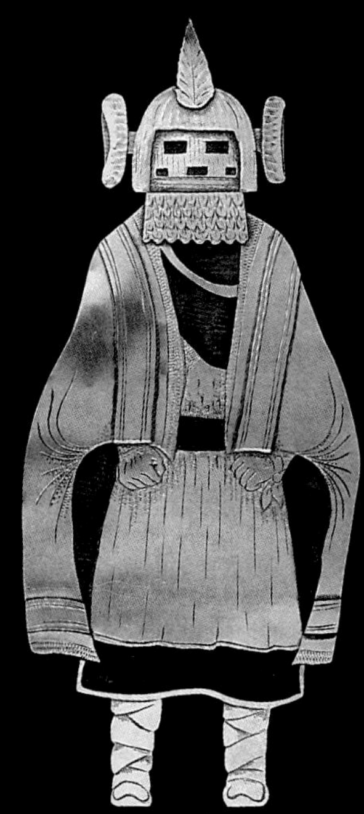

A-ha Kachin Mana

10. A-ha Kachin Mana is almost indistinguishable from Kachin Mana, except that she always appears in the company of one of the Chief Kachinas, known as A-ha, on Second Mesa.

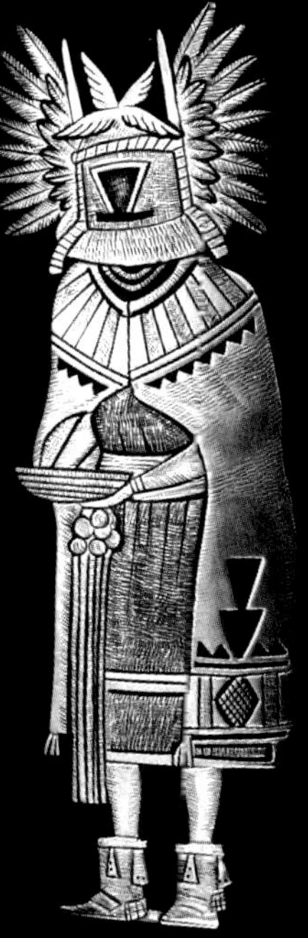

Angwushahai-i

11. The Crow Bride, Angwushahai-i, moves slowly through the village, stopping regularly to sing. When she stops, women come forward to take a corn sprout from her and to sprinkle her with cornmeal.

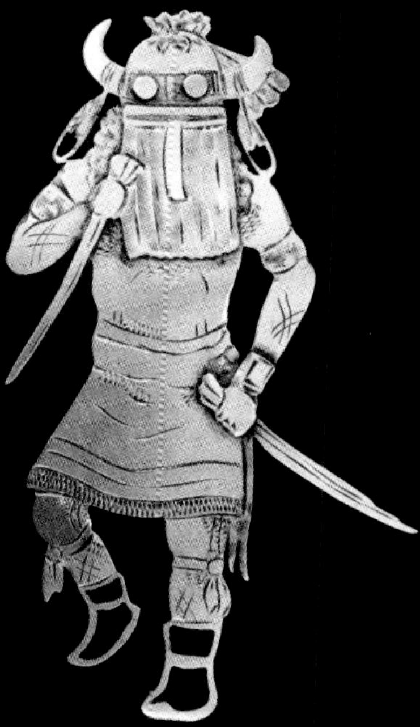

Tungwup Ta-amu

12. Tungwup Ta-amu, the Whipper's Uncle, carries a yucca whip in his role as guardian during the Bean Dance Procession. At times, he leads the procession.

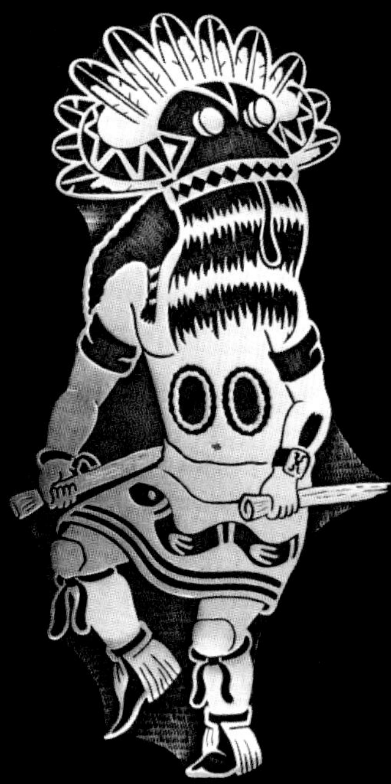

Wuyak-kuita

13. One of the Angry or Watching Kachinas, Wuyak-kuita can be seen at the end of the Bean Dance Procession, keeping everyone moving forward while terrifying the clowns. He is also a guard of the kiva.

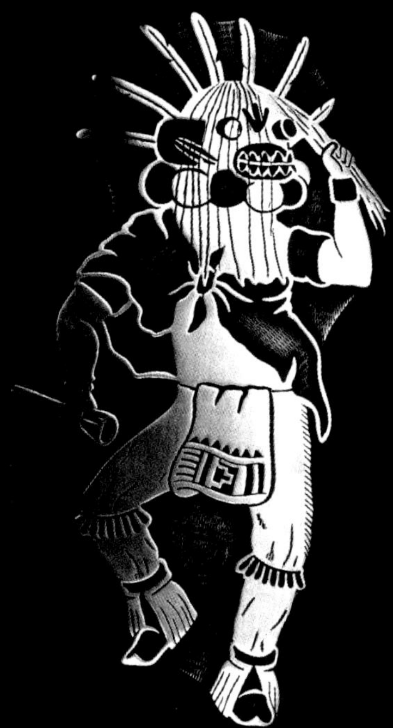

Chaveyo

14. The husband of Hahai-i Wuhti, Chaveyo is a giant kachina with hair covering his fierce eyes and face. He disciplines anyone, child or adult, who fails to live up to Hopi standards of work or conduct.

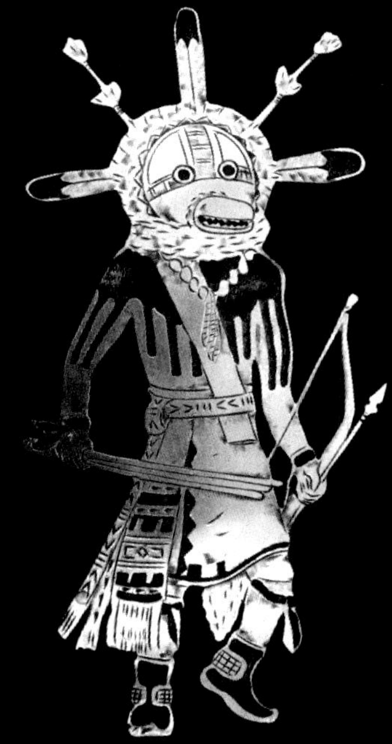

Wupamo

15. Wupamo is an important guard kachina whose yucca whips surprise incautious members of the audience, other kachinas, or even kiva priests. The strike of his whips is also known to cure rheumatism.

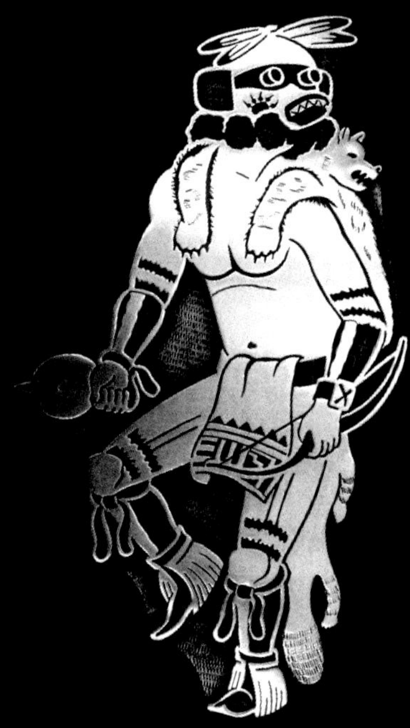

Tokoch Kachina

16. Tokoch Kachina is the Wildcat Kachina, one of the Angry Kachinas who appear when community work must be done. He wears a wildcat skin over his back and the pawprint of a wildcat is painted on either cheek of his mask.

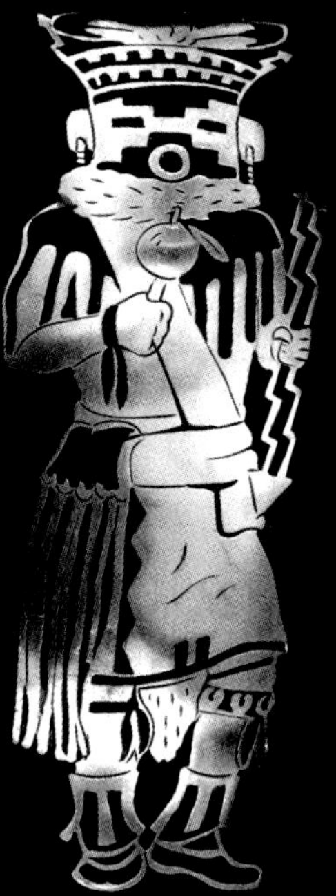

Nuvak'china

17. The Snow Kachina, or Nuvak'china, appears in many winter ceremonies because he brings cold and snow which will provide moisture for later crops. He frequently gives out presents on the morning of Powamu.

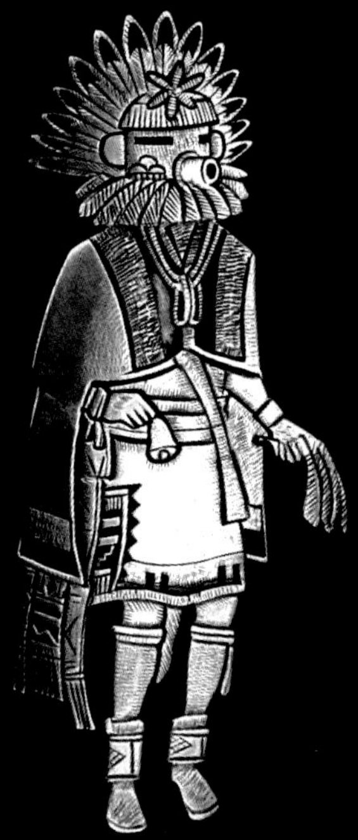

Talavai

18. Talavai Kachinas are known as Early Morning Singer Kachinas. They appear in pairs standing at one side of the main Powamu Procession, carrying a spruce tree, ringing bells, and occasionally singing.

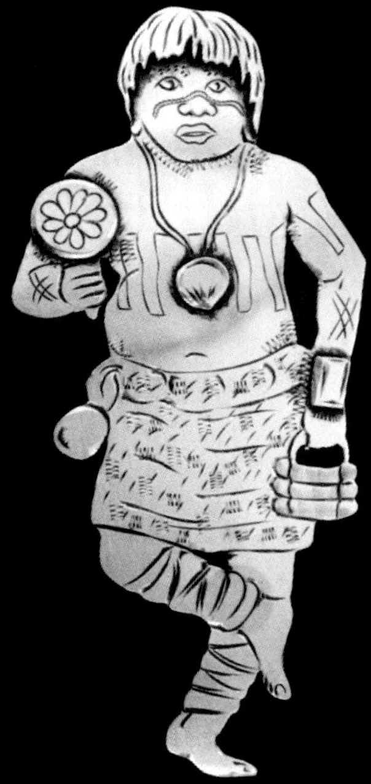

Choshuhuwa

19. Choshuhuwa, called the Bluebird Snare Kachina, represents the spirit of a mythical crippled man who was always cheerful and helpful. He is a much-loved, ragged looking, humorous kachina who often hands out gifts.

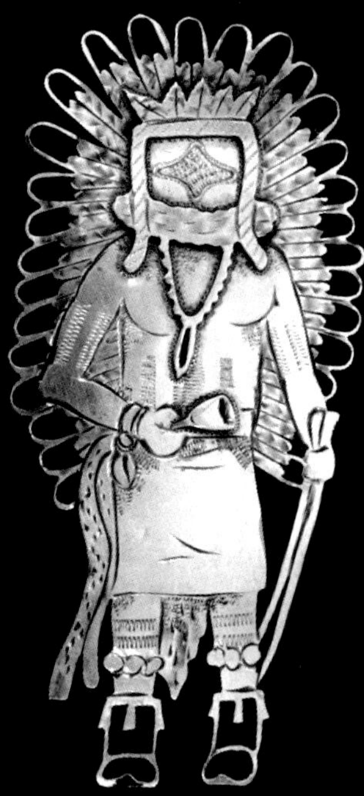

Na-ngasohu Kachina

20. Na-ngasohu Kachina is the Planet or Meteor Kachina, recognized by his beautifully fanned headdress of eagle feathers. He usually appears in pairs during the Bean Dance Procession.

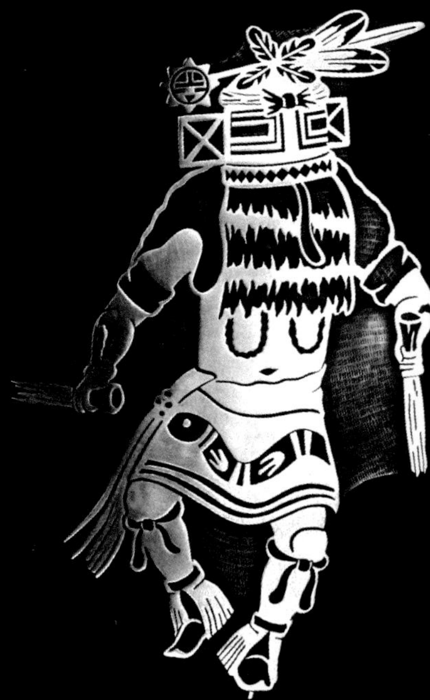

Hilili

21. Hilili is named for the call he makes. A guard kachina with a rapid dance, he was adapted at the end of the last century from an Acoma or Laguna kachina.

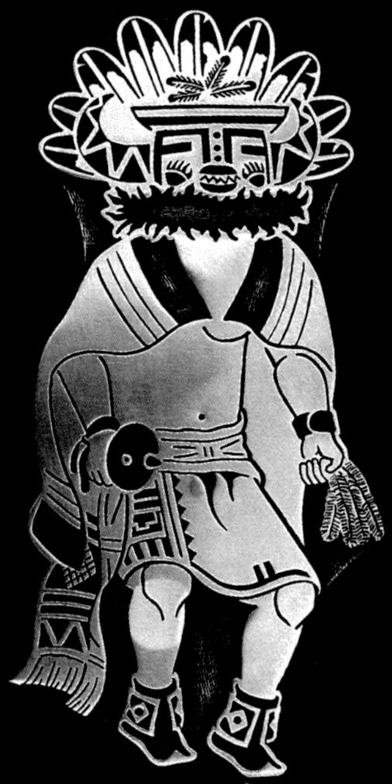

Hototo

22. Hototo is an important War Kachina on Third Mesa. On Second Mesa, he is considered a Bear Kachina when decorated with bear tracks on his cheeks. On First Mesa, he is a Wildcat Kachina if he wears a wildcat skin neck ruff. Hototo orders the people to gather wood for the kiva fire.

Pachavu Ceremony

Occurring only in certain years, with at least four years in between each performance, the Pachavu Ceremony is an historical dramatization added on to the end of the regular Powamu Ceremony. It is performed only if young men are initiated into their various clans at the Wuwuchim, or tribal initiation, held in November.

During the Pachavu, villagers cannot appear outside of their houses during certain ceremonies. All the doors and windows of the pueblo are latched tightly to prevent unauthorized viewing of the sacred rites.

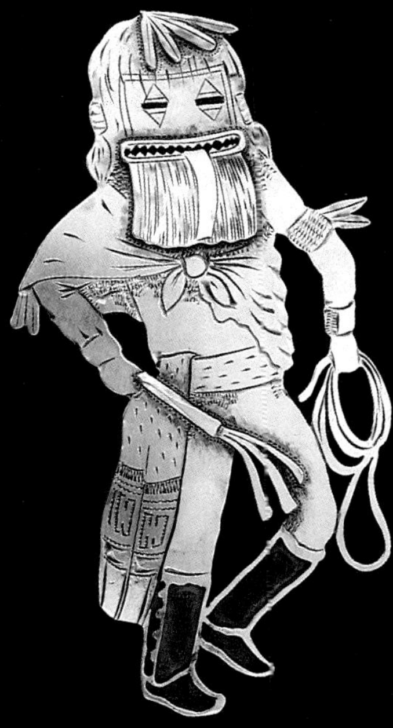

Motsin

23. Motsin is the Disheveled Kachina whose headdress features an unruly wig of sheep's wool. This kachina forces the people to attend community work parties by using his rope to lead lazy offenders to their appointed tasks.

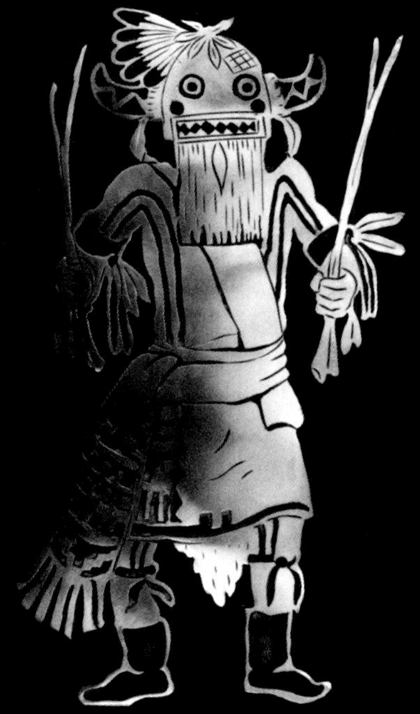

Pachavu Hú

26. Four of the Pachavu Hú together inspect the kivas' bean plants at the end of the Powamu Ceremony during initiation years. If any of the plants in a kiva have been damaged, they punish all members of the kiva with whips.

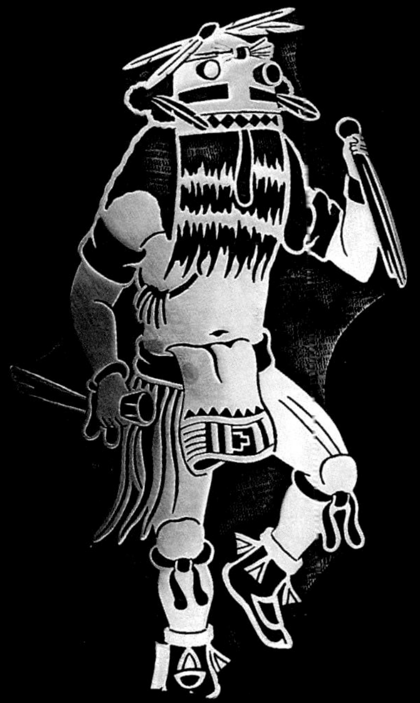

Sakwa Hu

24. Sakwa Hu is often portrayed by a young boy. Called the Blue Whipper Kachina, he serves as a guard during the Powamu on Third Mesa, joining in the procession of the Chief Kachinas through the village.

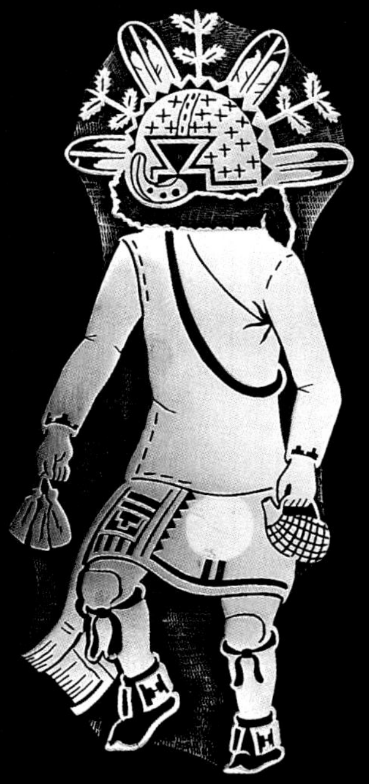

Wuwuyomo

25. The Wuwuyomo, called Mong or Chief Kachinas on Third Mesa, are ancient kachinas who appear in groups of four with the Pachavu Manas. They sing songs important for successful crops.

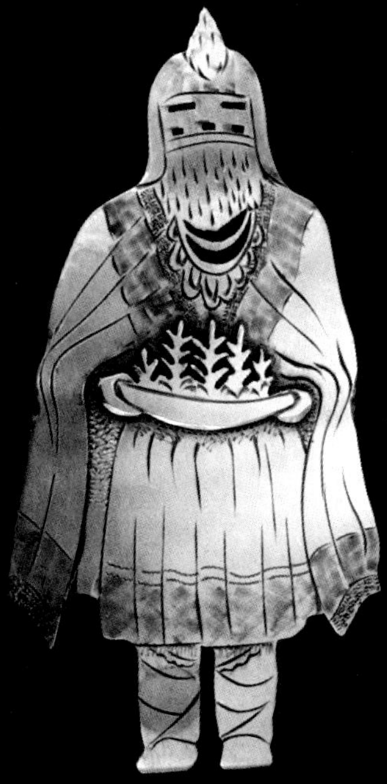

Pachavuin Mana

28. Pachavuin Mana is the only kachina spirit that is impersonated by a Hopi woman. She brings a huge load of bean sprouts into the village during the Pachavu.

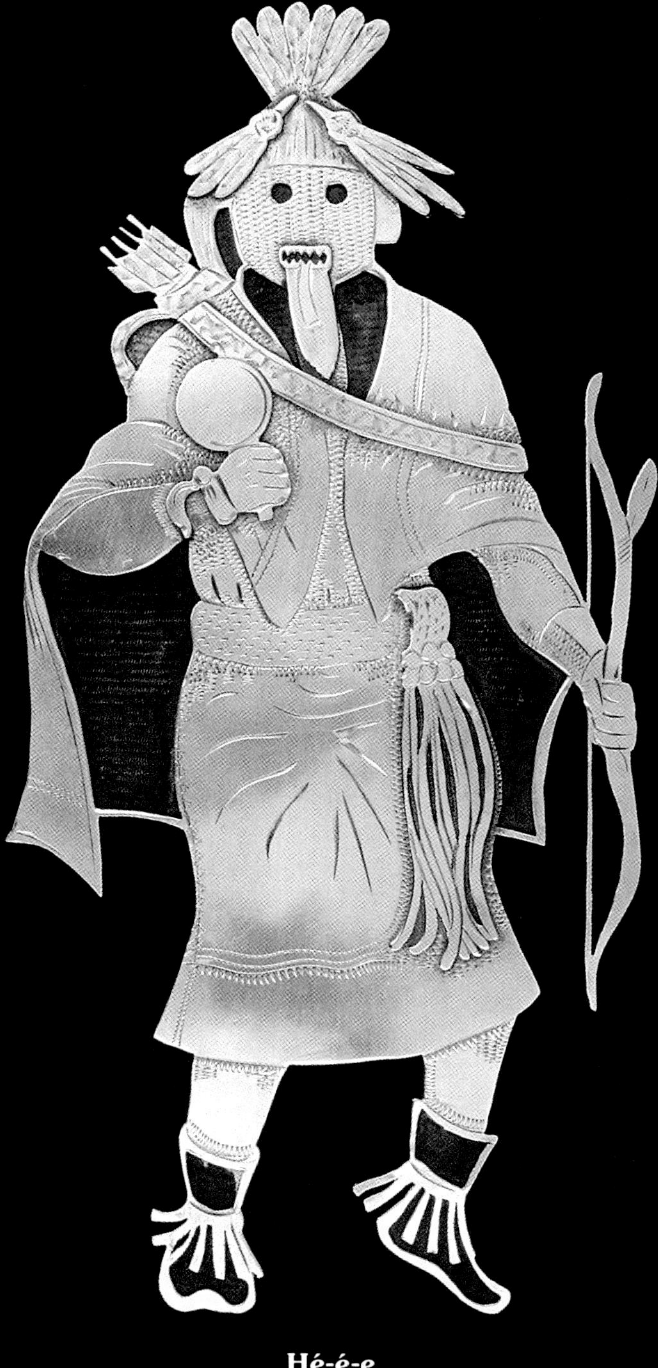

Hé-é-e

27. Hé-é-e is the Warrior Maid of Hopi legend. According to an Oraibi folktale, Hé-é-e's hair was being combed into whorls when she saw enemies of the village sneaking by. She warned her people, then led the defense of her village until the men in the fields could return to fight.

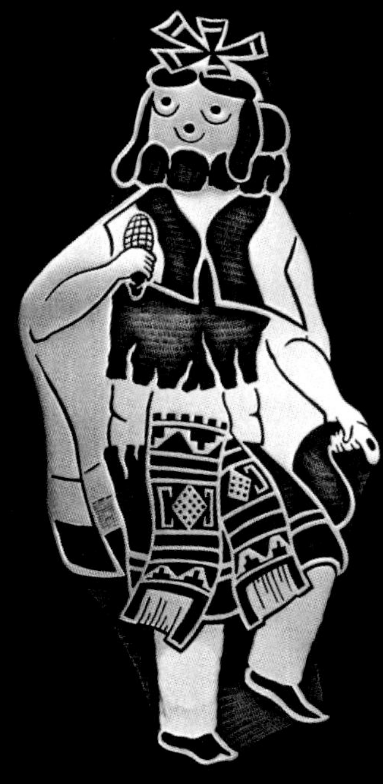

Hahai-i Wuhti

29. Hahai-i Wuhti is one of the more vocal kachinas. The mother of monsters, dogs, and kachinas, her shrill voice can be heard in many ceremonies. This kachina's tihu, or doll, is given to Hopi infants and to captive eagles.

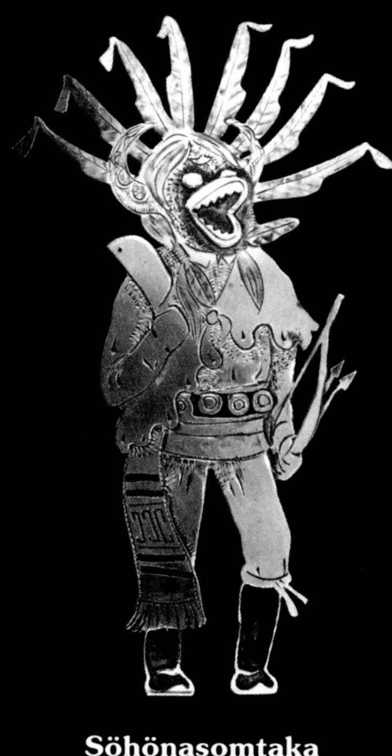

Söhönasomtaka

30. Söhönasomtaka is a warrior woman, one of the Angry Kachinas, who appears only at Oraibi. An ancient and powerful kachina, she is depicted with tufts of reeds in place of ears and a quiver filled with bow and arrows strapped to her back.

Kachina Cult Initiation

At February's Powamu Ceremony, young Hopi children are initiated into the Kachina Cult. The Crow Mother and her two sons are the essential kachinas for this rite, although other Powamu Kachinas take part in the ceremony. At this time, the kachina dancers reveal themselves to the children as men from their village, rather than true spirits.

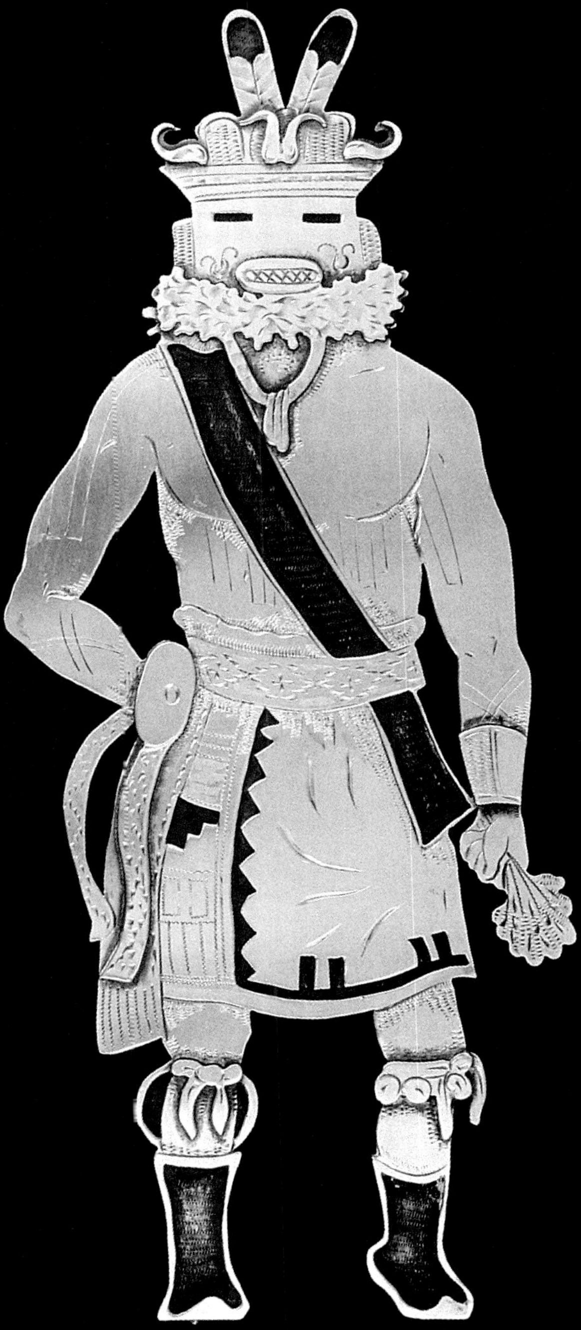

Tumoala

31. The Devil's Claw Kachina, Tumoala, is named after a plant that grows on the Hopi Reservation. Hopis believe the plant is able to hold the clouds with its hooked seed pods.

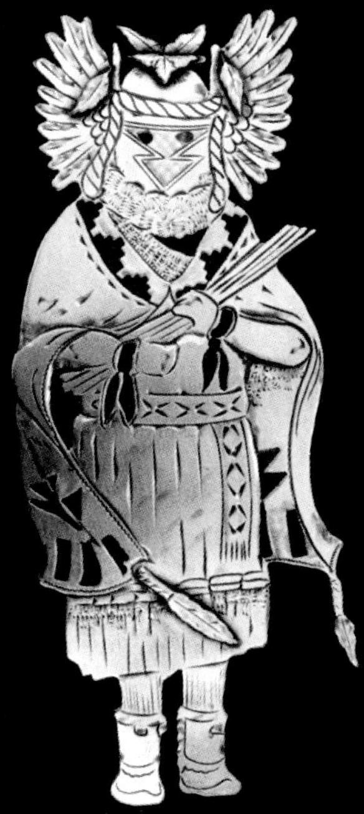

Angwusnasomtaka

32. Angwusnasomtaka, the Crow Mother, stands in dignity before a large sand painting on the floor of the kiva during the initiation rites. She holds a bundle of yucca leaf blades which are used to ceremonially whip each child, then lifts her skirts to be whipped herself.

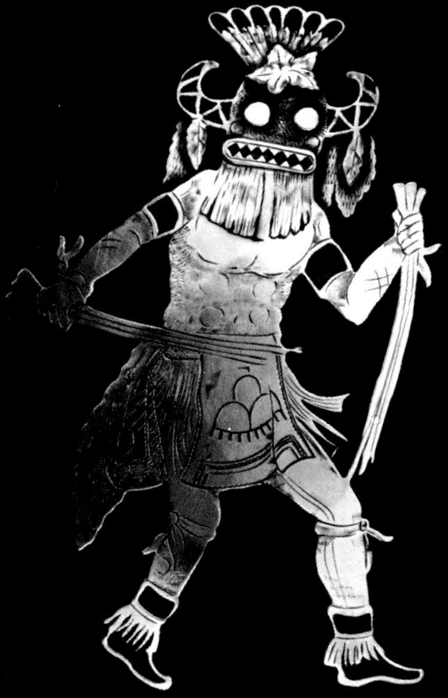

Hú Kachinas

33. The two Hú Kachinas are sons of Crow Mother who whip the young initiates four strokes each with yucca whips. This whipping is an act of purification for the Hopis.

Soyoko Ceremony

During Powamu, the Bean Dance time, very young children are visited by a terrifying ogre or Monster Woman. She threatens them into working hard at grinding corn (girls) or catching mice (boys), because four days later she will appear again and demand food. Invariably, the proffered food is rejected, the ogre demands to have the youngster instead, and a family member must defend the child, saying he or she has learned proper behavior and deserves to be spared.

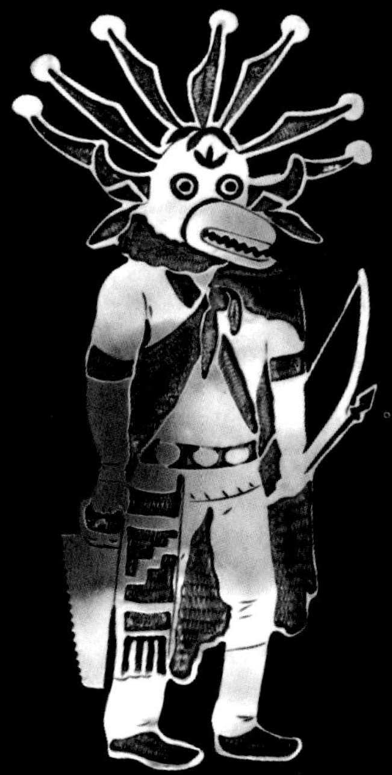

Nataska

35. The Nataska serve the same function as Monster Man. They make horrible noises by dragging saws along the ground or against the sides of houses. From infancy, Hopi children hear warnings about the terrible things the Nataska will do to them if they misbehave.

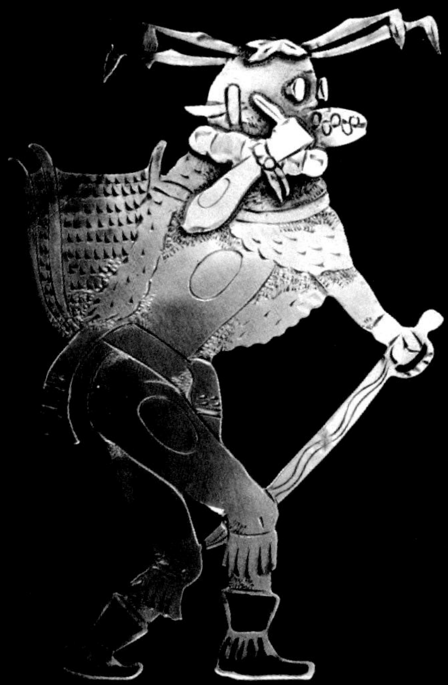

Awatovi Soyok Taka

34. The Awatovi Soyok Taka, or Monster Man, accompanies Monster Woman on her rounds to collect food from the little children. He carries a large basket, ready to stuff a child into it, and is supposed to be able to eat children whole.

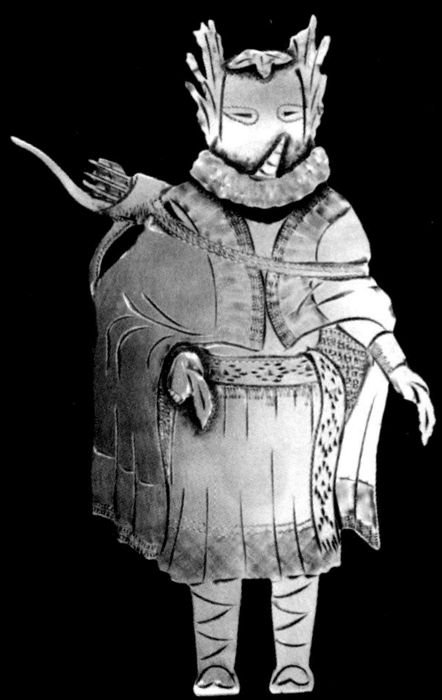

Tahaum Soyoko

36. Tahaum Soyoko is the Uncle of the Nataska. He constantly stomps his feet and shakes his weapons in a frightening barrage of sound.

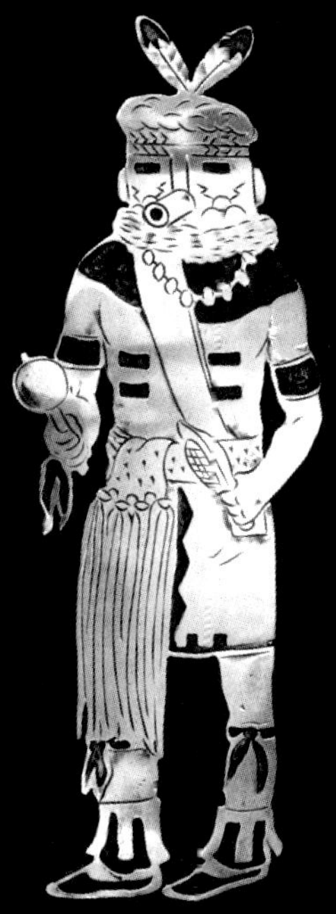

Heheya Aumutaka

37. Heheya Aumutaka once accompanied the frightening Soyoko kachinas during the Powamu Ceremony, helping them to threaten children. He now more often serves a general purpose as just one of many Powamu kachinas.

Night Dances

Between the winter solstice Soyal Ceremony and February's Powamu, dances held inside the kivas are known as Pamuya or January Dances. After the Powamu, they become Ankwati or Anktioni, Repeat Dances. All fall under the general category of Night or Kiva Dances.

Great variation between the mesas is evident in these ceremonies, and some dances are specific to only one village. The Night Dances employ a tremendous number of kachinas, many of which appear as personified animals or insects.

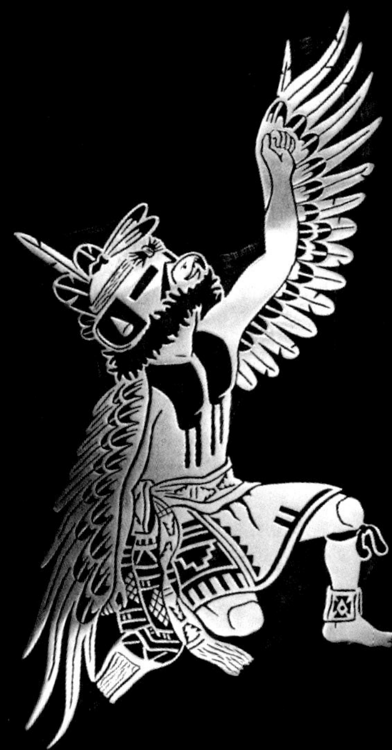

Kwahu

39. The beautiful Eagle Kachina is known as Kwahu. He imitates the movements and cries of this predator bird with startling accuracy. Eagles are thought of as honored guests and given presents.

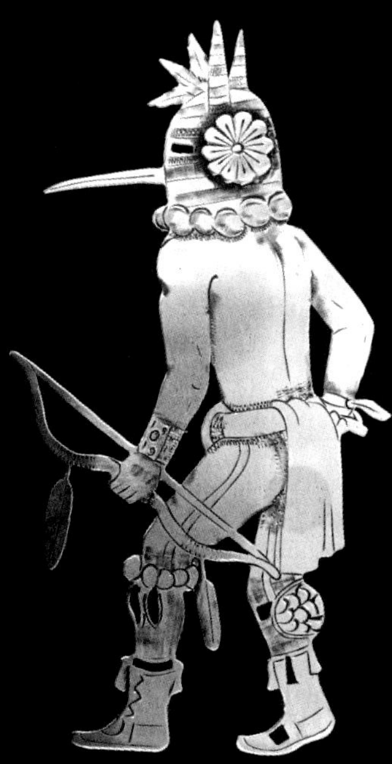

Tatangaya

38. Tatangaya, with his brightly-colored, striped headdress and long, piercing snout, is the Hornet or Wasp Kachina. He is seen either in groups or dancing alone during the Pamuya Dances in January.

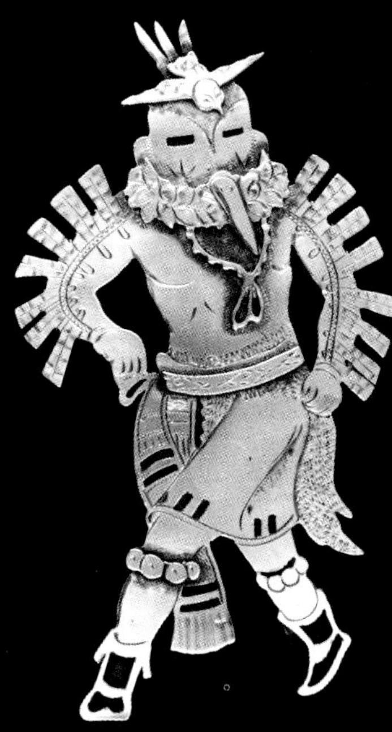

Turposkwa

40. Turposkwa is the Canyon Wren Kachina, one of many bird kachinas who participate in Night Dances. A bird is attached to the crown of his head, he wears plumage along his arms, and bird tracks are painted on his cheeks.

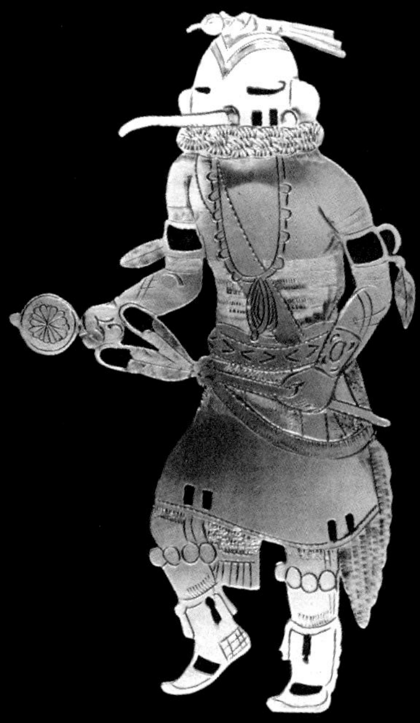

Tocha

41. The Hummingbird Kachina, Tocha, is brilliantly-colored and dances very rapidly to simulate the high-speed flapping of this tiny bird's wings. Tocha is a favorite at the Night Dances.

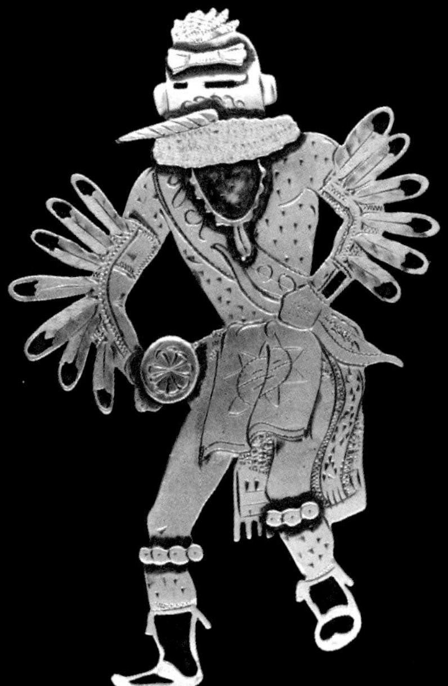

Yapa

42. The Mockingbird, Yapa, is the kachina who taught women to speak. The inverted V design over his beak is made of corn husks and seashells.

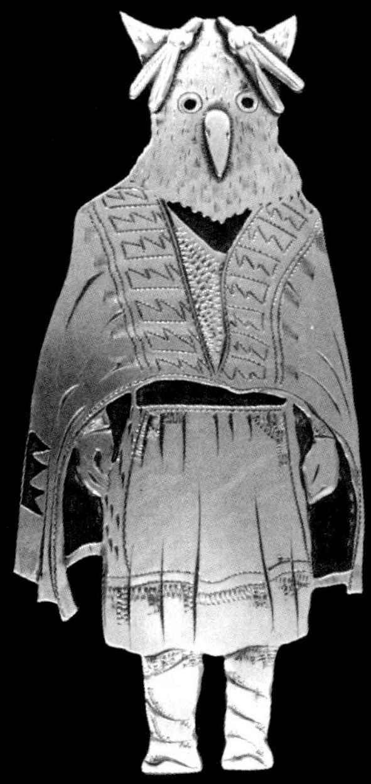

Mongwa Wuhti

43. Mongwa Wuhti is the Great Horned Owl Woman. She is not a common kachina, but when she appears, she is said to be accompanied by little owls.

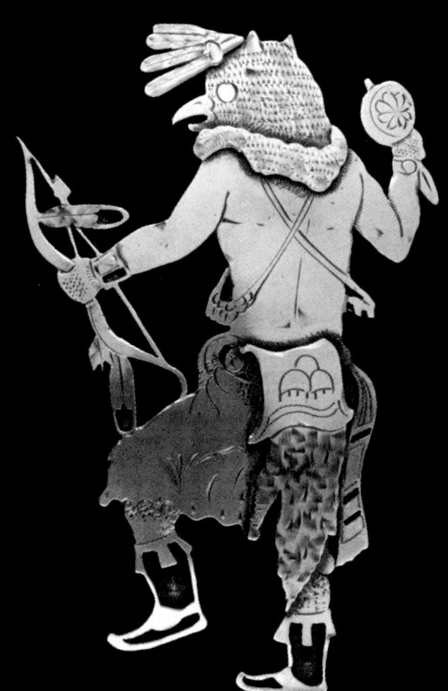

Salap Mongwa

44. Salap Mongwa serves a function similar to Mongwa, who watches over and disapproves of the clowns' antics. He is the Spruce Owl Kachina decorated with a downy head of rabbit fur and a fox skin hanging from his belt.

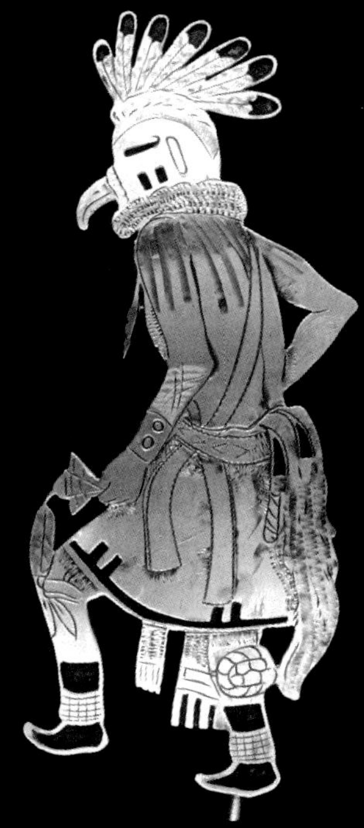

Kowako

45. Kowako, the Chicken Kachina, is a relatively recent impersonation. Generally a comic figure, Hopi legend recounts how the chicken lost his girlfriend to the Mockingbird Kachina.

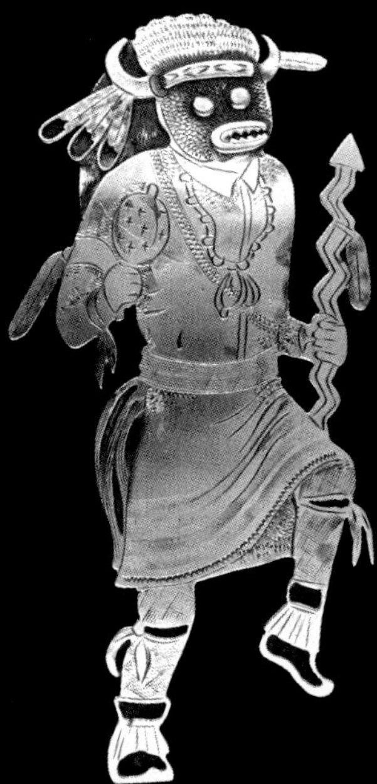

Buffalo Kachina

46. The Buffalo Kachina is the same as a Buffalo Dancer except that he wears a mask. He dances with a lightning stick and rattle in his hands, praying for an abundance of buffalo for the Hopis to hunt.

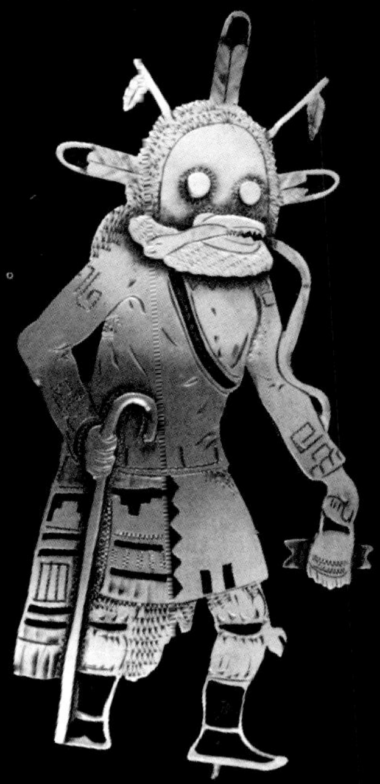

Saviki

47. Saviki carries a bullsnake in his mouth. He is considered a guardian kachina, one of the Bow Clan ancestors on Third Mesa and an ancestor from the Reed Clan on First Mesa.

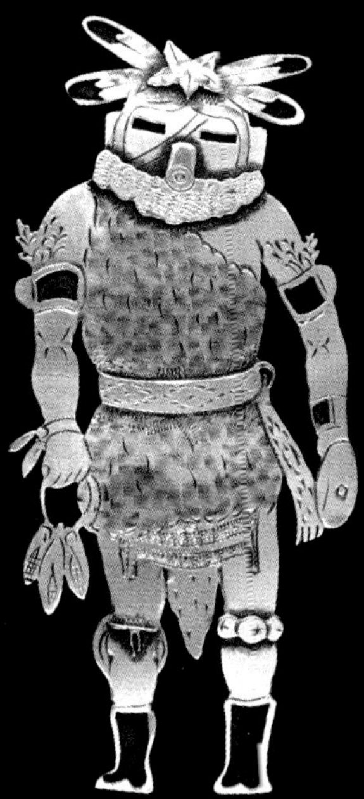

Kana-a Kachina

48. According to legend, Kana-a danced at one of the ancient villages that had turned wicked, and destroyed it with a fire cloud from Sunset Crater, which his name refers to. He only appears at Night Dances or on special occasions.

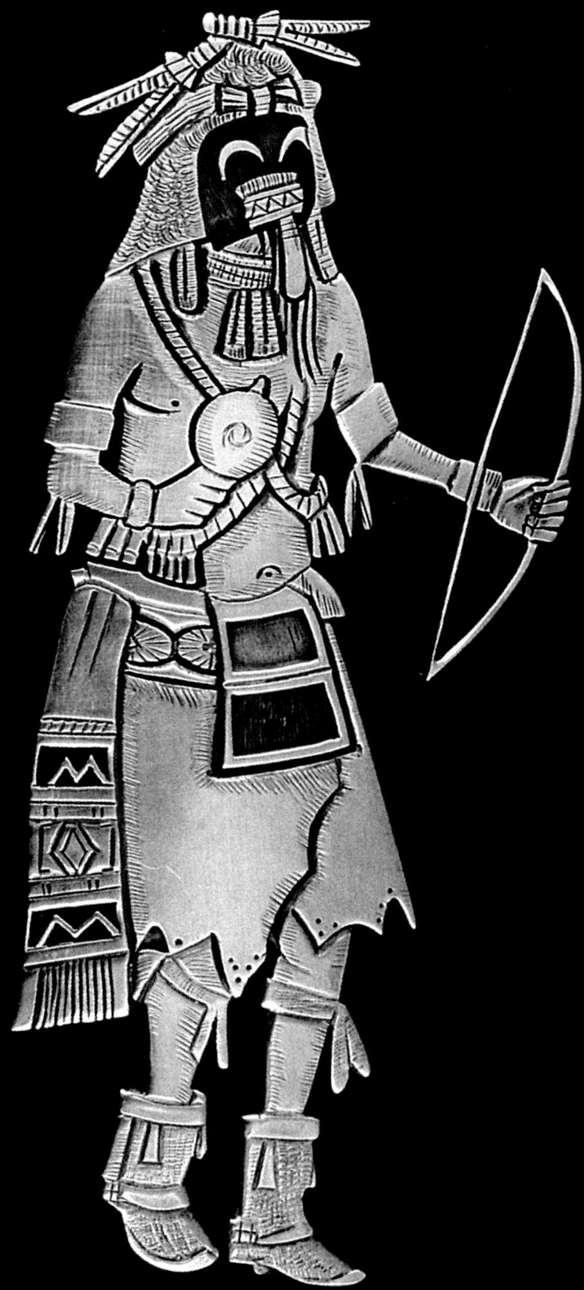

Chakwaina

49. Chakwaina is a kachina originally imported from the Rio Grande area. He is a warrior kachina with a star on one cheek and a moon on the other.

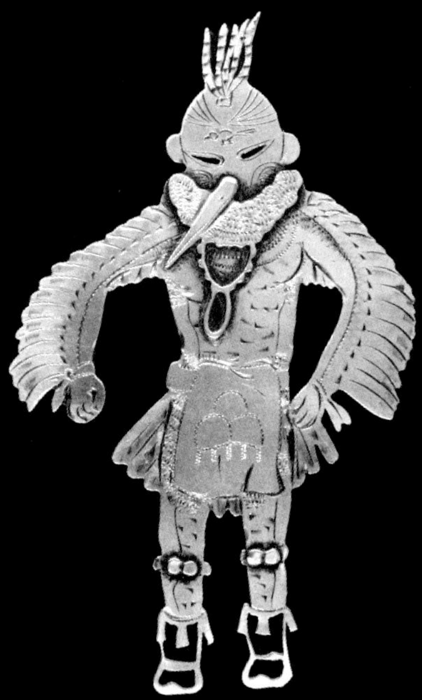

Patszro Kachina

50. Patszro Kachina represents the Snipe, a long-billed marsh bird. His cheeks are painted rainbows, and his body is dotted with small feathers stuck on with gum.

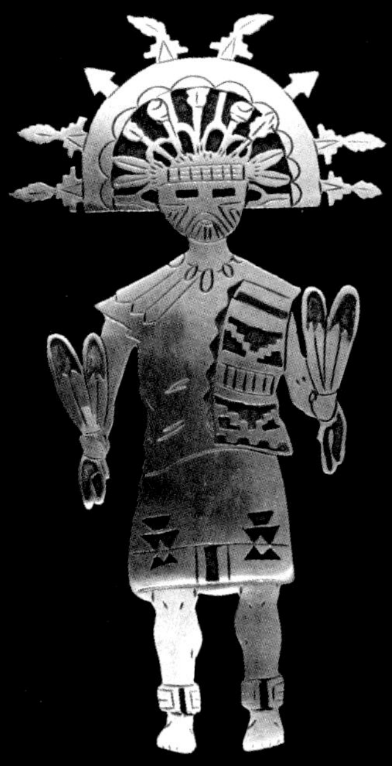

Palhik Mana

52. Palhik Mana represents the Corn Grinding Girl Kachina. She wears an elaborate tableta headdress and grinds varicolored kernels of corn.

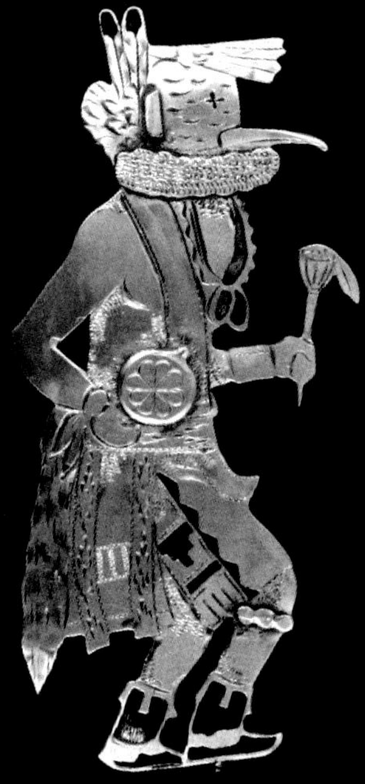

Hospoa

51. Hospoa is the Roadrunner Kachina. In Hopi ceremonies, he always wears a flat painted tablet on his back which is believed to entice the rain. Roadrunner feathers are used for certain types of prayer plumes.

Plaza Dances

With warmer weather, the Kachina Dances move from the kivas outdoors to the village plaza. Mixed Kachina Dances, or Soyohim, feature many different kachinas, while the kachinas in a Line Dance are all the same.

Plaza Dances are as entertaining as they are ceremonial; they resemble a festival complete with feasts, visits from house to house, and clown acts. The primary purpose of the kachinas is always to bring rain and fertility to the Hopis, but kachinas in the Plaza Dances usually have additional, highly-specific roles.

Mixed Dancers:

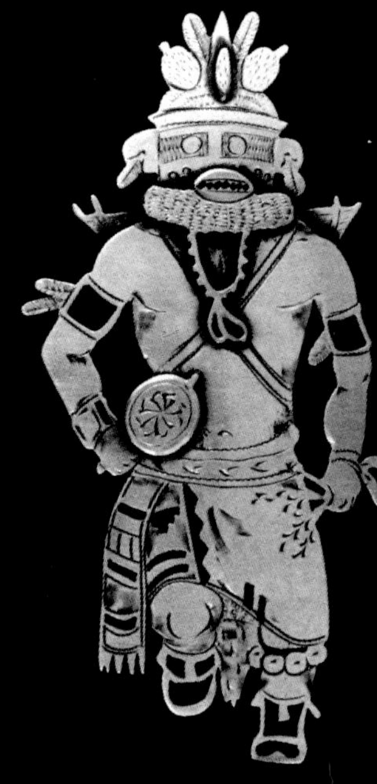

Ösök'china

53. Ösök'china forces lazy people to work. As the Cholla Cactus Kachina, he wears cactus plants on the crown of his head and his cheeks are painted with cactus designs.

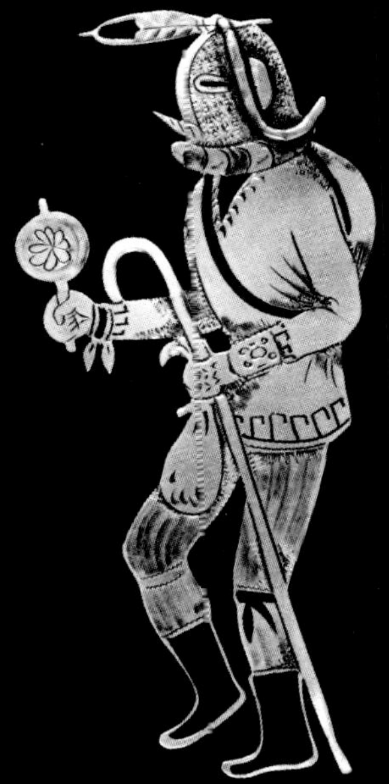

Kokopelli

54. Kokopelli, the Hump-backed Flute Player, is one of the best known kachinas. His image may be found all over the southwest on ancient pottery and petroglyphs. For the Hopis, he is the one who seduces girls, brings babies, and helps to guard the hunt.

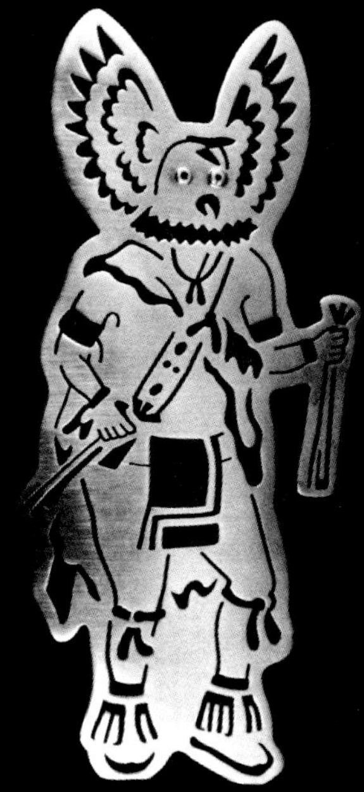

Mongwa

56. Mongwa is the Great Horned Owl who increasingly disapproves of the clowns. When the clowns' antics become intolerable, he and the other warrior kachinas finally pour water over them, beat them with willow or yucca switches, and leave them howling in the plaza.

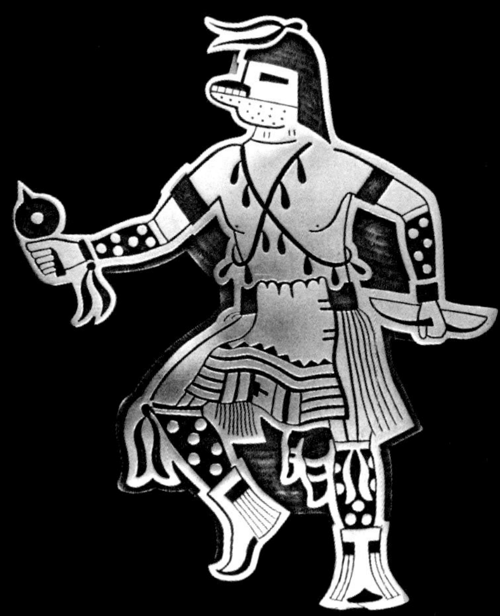

Toho

58. Toho, the Mountain Lion Kachina, appears in the lead before Deer or Antelope Kachinas because, as a predator, he is never overtaken. He serves as a side dancer for the other, grazing animals who dance in the center of the plaza.

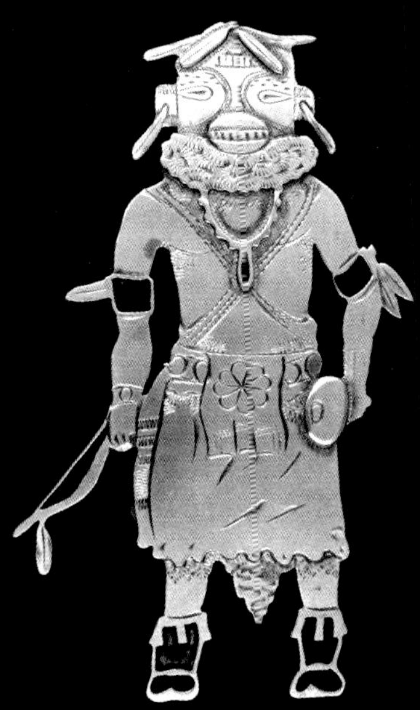

Monongya

55. The Lizard Kachina, Monongya, is one of the Fighting Kachinas who punish clowns for un-Hopi-like behavior. He represents a specific lizard of brilliant turquoise color, the Crotophytus.

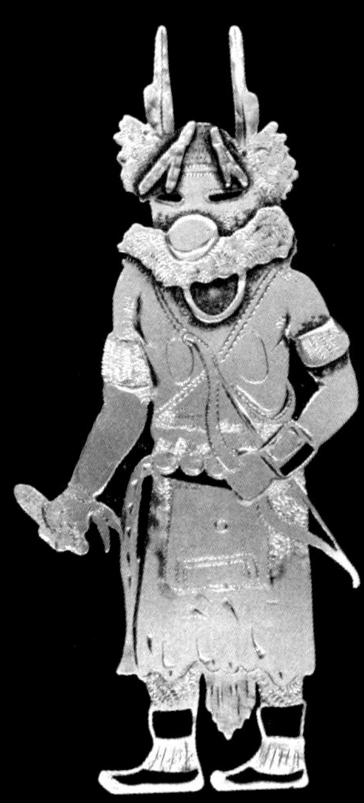

Laqan

57. Laqan is the Squirrel Kachina. He also appears during the winter Kiva Dances, where he challenges any woman to take anything from him that she covets.

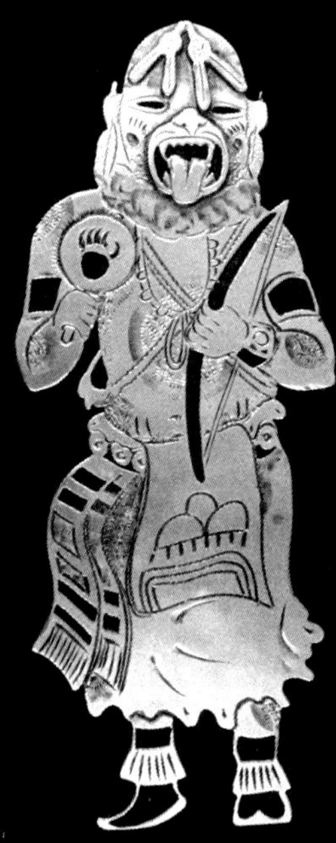

Hon Kachina

59. Besides being a great warrior, the Bear Kachina is so strong he can cure disease, according to Hopi belief. This kachina, called Hon, is distinguished by the bear track painted on either cheek.

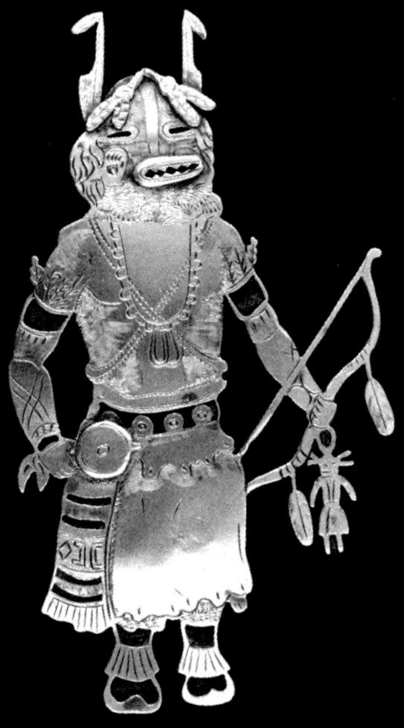

Honan Kachina

60. The Honan Kachina, or Badger Kachina, is a curing kachina. Since the badger lives underground, he receives Hopi prayers for the growth of medicinal herbs, roots, and plants.

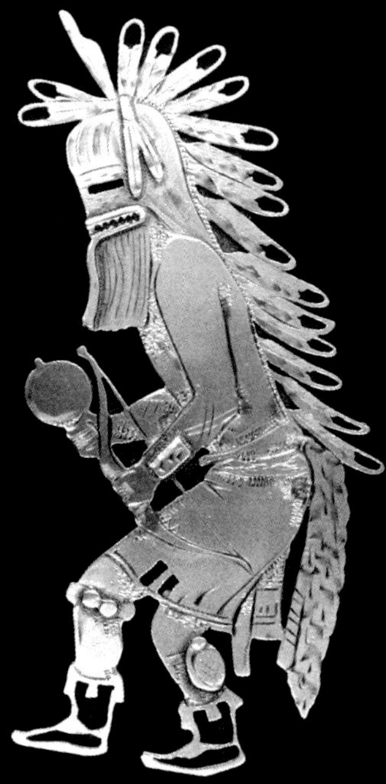

Tutumsi

62. Tutumsi is known as the Comanche Kachina. He is seldom seen in Hopi ceremonies. On occasions when he does appear, he participates in Mixed Dances.

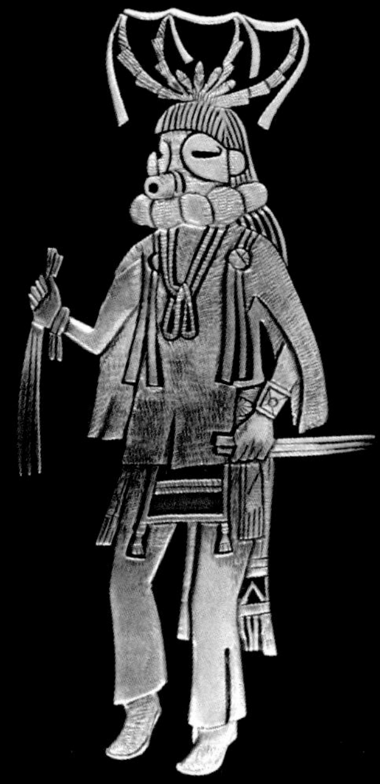

Chospos-yaka-hentaka

64. Another interpretation of Chospos-yaka-hentaka, this image is depicted wearing the traditional Hopi embroidered belt and a double-strand turquoise necklace. Both versions carry yucca whips.

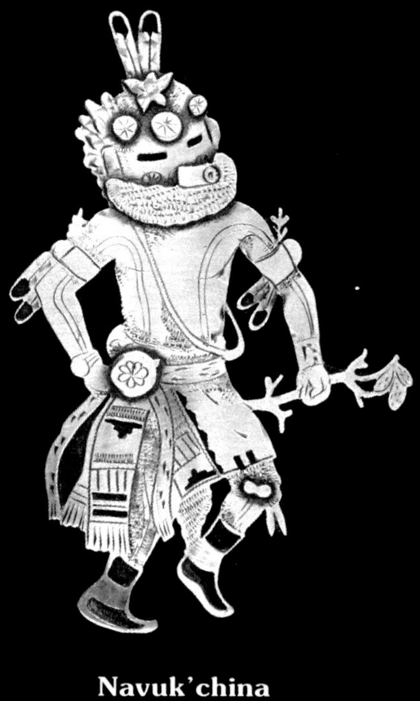

Navuk'china

61. Navuk'china is the Prickly Pear Leaf Kachina, another enforcer kachina like Ösök'china, already described. A thorny cactus pad is attached as a weapon to the end of his staff.

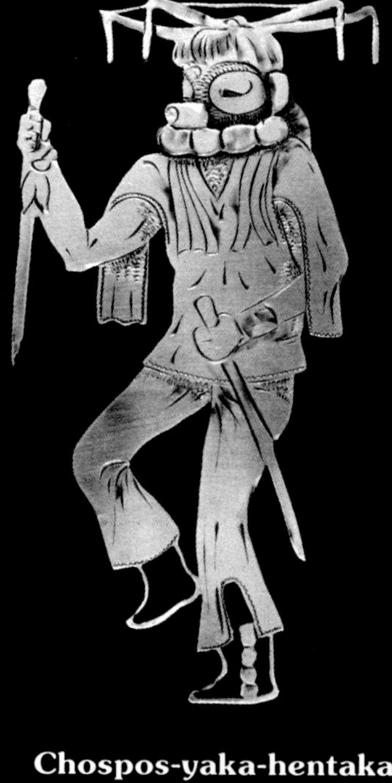

Chospos-yaka-hentaka

63. Chospos-yaka-hentaka is translated as the Turquoise Nose Plug Man. He probably originated with one of the Yuman tribes, whose members commonly wore nose ornaments made of turquoise.

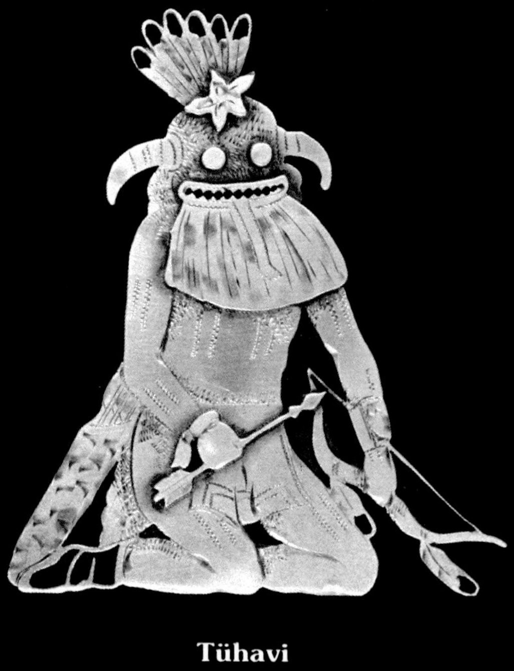

Tühavi

65. Tühavi is known as the Paralyzed Kachina. In Hopi legend, he was carried by a blind friend. Tühavi directed his friend where to walk and where to aim his arrows whenever they needed food.

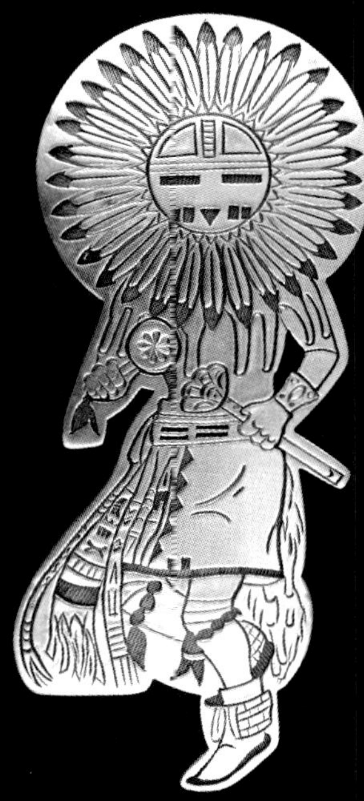

Tawa Kachina

66. Tawa is the Sun or Sun Shield Kachina, identified by a large and very beautiful feathered sunburst countenance. He is rarely portrayed in kachina dances.

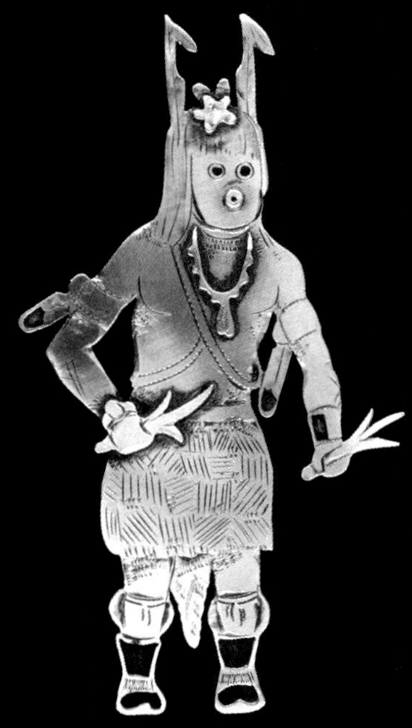

Chiwap

68. Chiwap is the Coarse Blowing Sand Kachina, more often simply called the Sand Kachina. He is a spirit not often personified in Hopi ceremonies, a teller of stories and one who criticizes at the Plaza Dances.

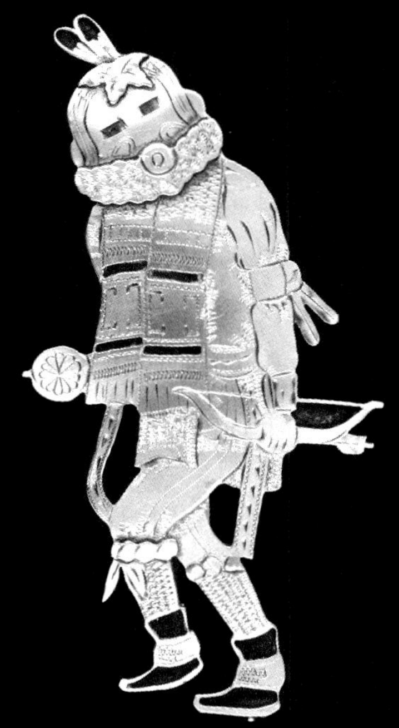

Piokak Kachina

70. The Piokak Kachina may be seen on all three mesas during the Night Dances of March. He takes his name from the sound of clapping or foot slapping.

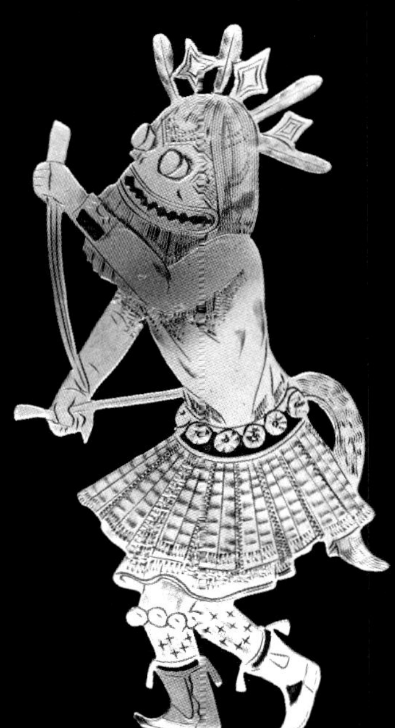

Sohu Kachina

67. The Sohu Kachina is the Star Kachina, although he wears a hunting shirt and a kilt made of turkey feathers. This kachina performs in groups during Mixed Kachina Dances.

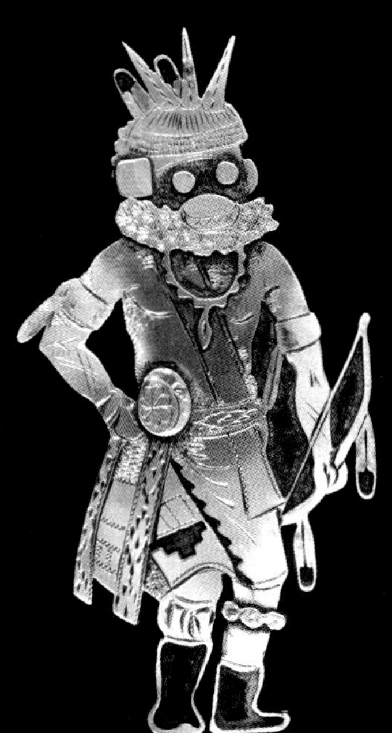

Payik'ala

69. The Three-horned Kachina is Payik'ala, identified by the three brightly-colored horns projecting upwards from the crown of his head. Payik'ala may have been adopted from a Zuni kachina early in the century.

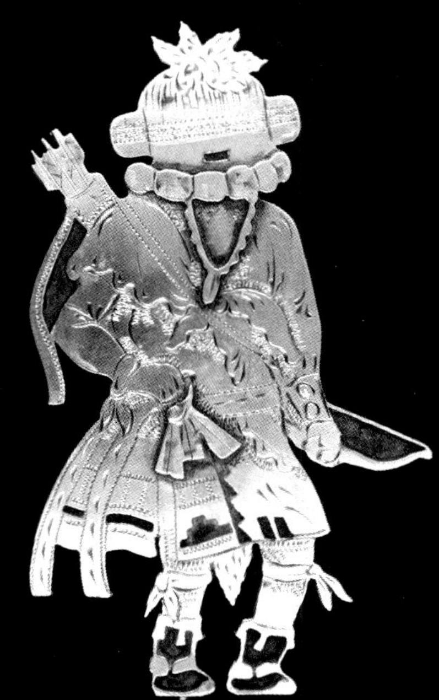

Hututu

71. Hututu is another sound-named kachina, from the cry he makes. He is one of many Zuni kachinas which the Hopis have adopted without trying to make them more traditionally Hopi-like.

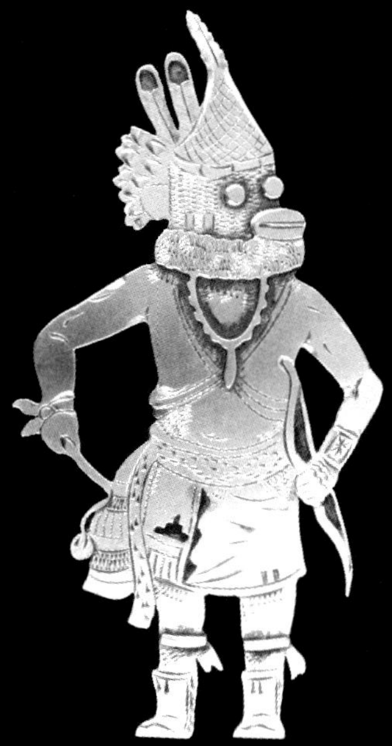

Pöökang Kwivi Kachina

72. The Pöööokang Kwivi Kachina is the Proud War God Kachina in his finest dress. He wears warrior tracks—double lines—painted on his chest and arms.

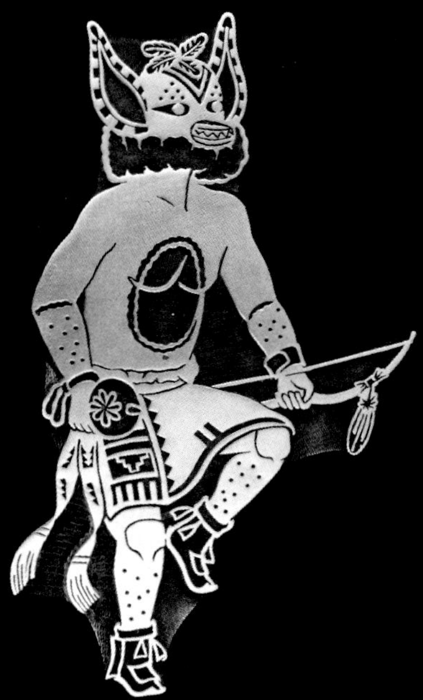

Fox Kachina

74. The Fox Kachina is usually personated as a runner, which dictates how elaborately he is costumed. He has large pointed ears lined in black with white spots, and spots painted on his forearms and calves.

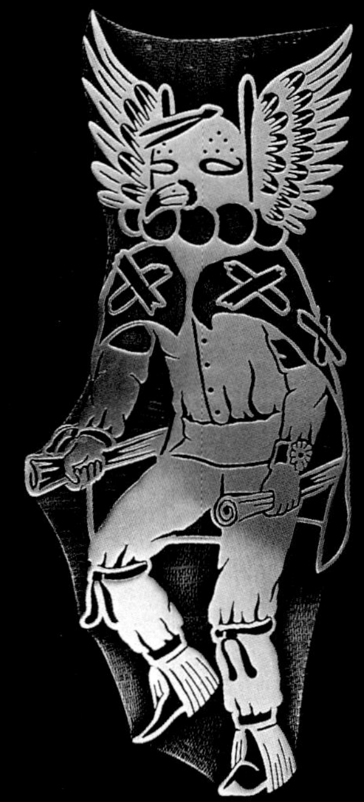

Angwusi

76. The Crow Kachina, Angwusi, helps to police the clowns during Plaza Dances. First threatening them, he finally joins the other warrior kachinas in soundly punishing the clowns for their outrageous behavior.

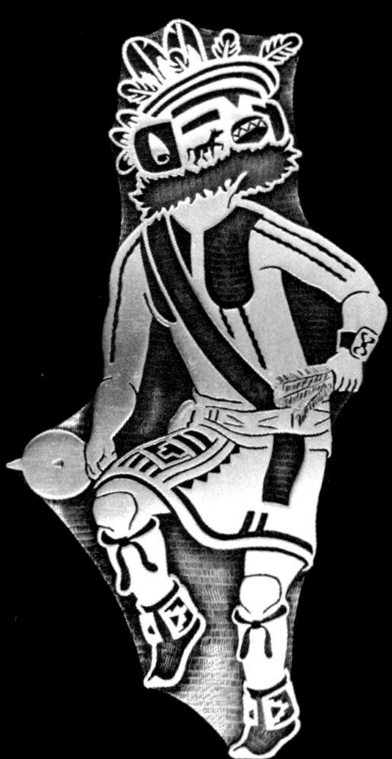

Kawai-i Kachina

73. The name of the Horse Kachina, Kawai-i, is an adaptation of the Spanish word for horse, caballo. He is a relatively new kachina, probably introduced late in the last century.

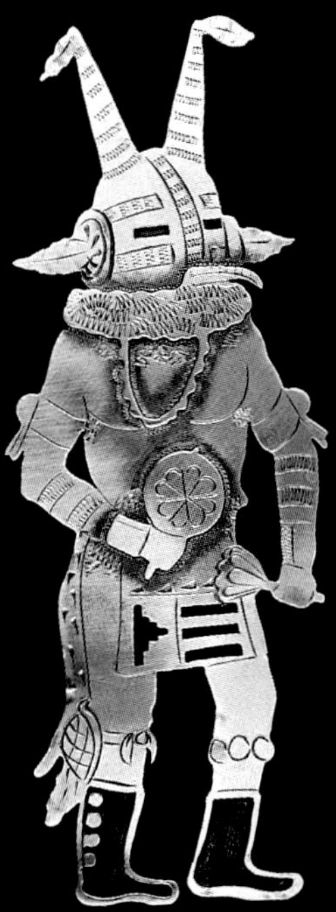

Mahu

75. Mahu is known as the Cicada Kachina. His presence serves as a prayer for the coming of summer, when these insects thrive and proliferate.

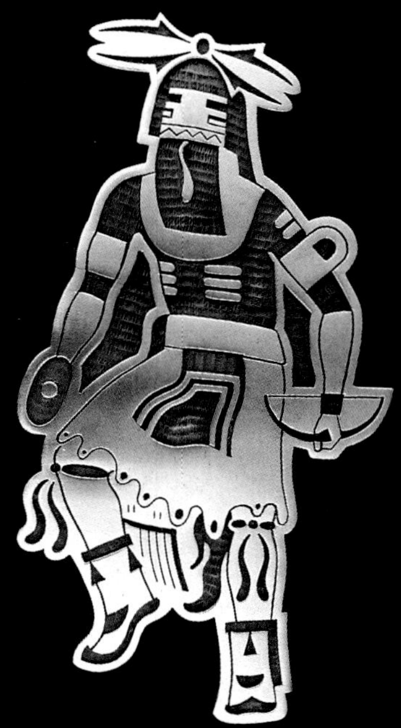

Heoto

77. Heoto can function as a guard, is one of the Warrior Kachinas, and is related to Chakwaina, previously described. Both he and Chakwaina wear deerhide kilts.

Line Dancers:

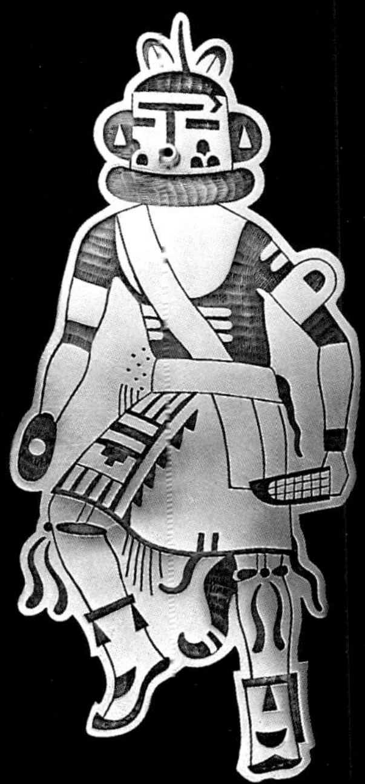

Kuwan Heheya

78. The Kuwan Heheya, or Colorful Heheya, dance in ceremonies to bring rain to growing crops. These kachinas are usually accompanied by Heheya's Uncle and the Heheya Youth, who are side dancers.

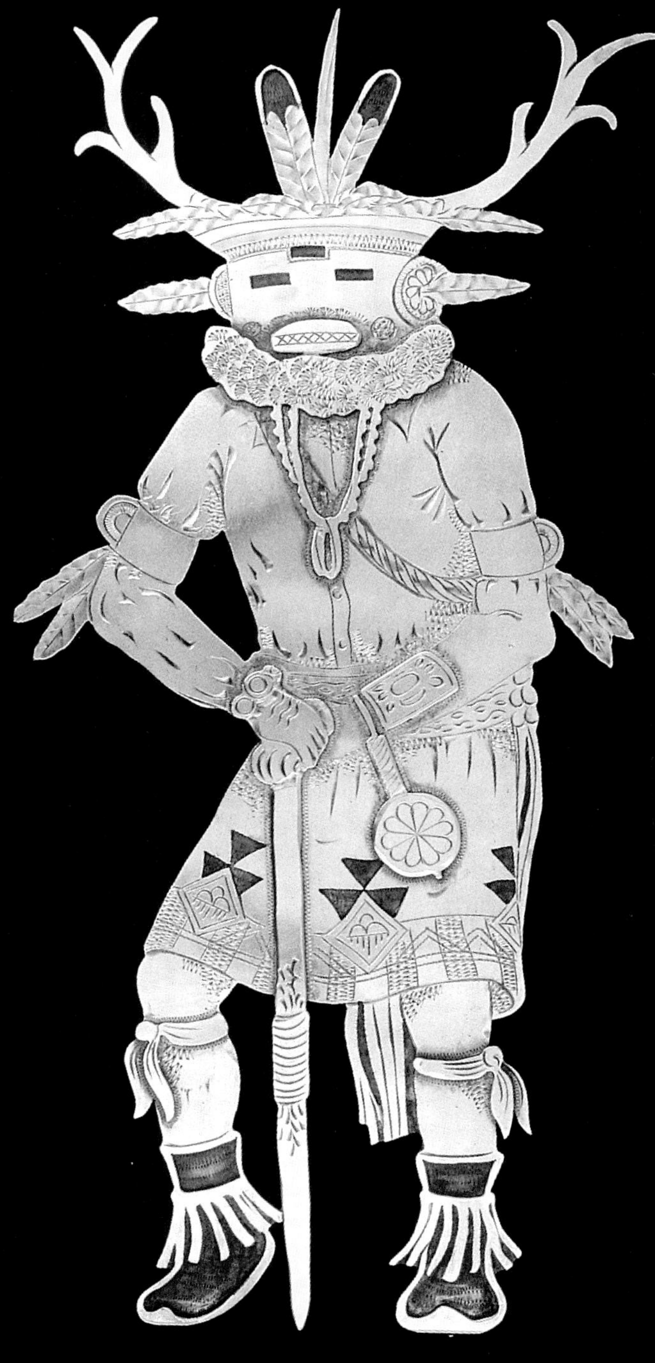

Deer Kachina

82. The Deer Kachina has power over the rain; his dancing is also a prayer that the deer population multiply for the Hopis. The Deer, like the Antelope, bends forward when he dances to lean on a short stick used to represent his front legs.

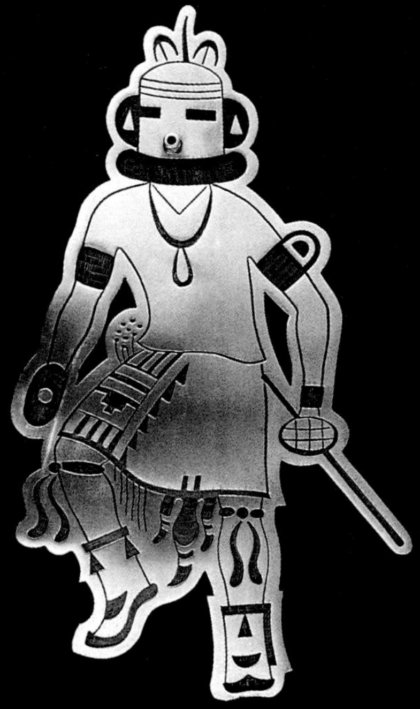

Turtle Kachina

79. The Turtle dance was supposedly transported from Acoma as a line dance before this century. Although he is not spectacular in appearance, the Turtle Kachina is enjoyed for his pleasant songs.

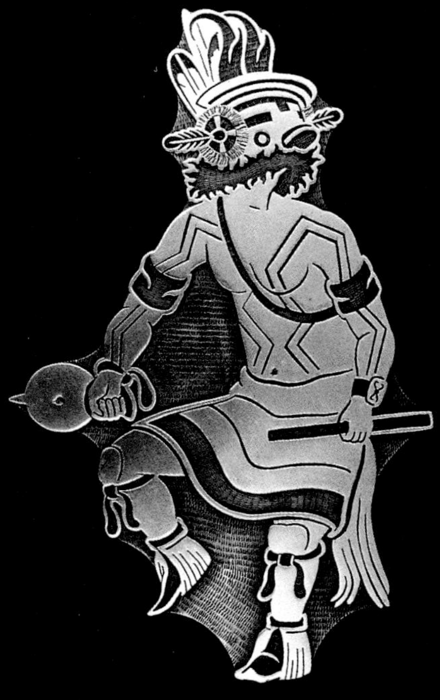

Antelope Kachina

81. The Antelope Kachina dances as a prayer for the increase of his own kind (all the game animal kachinas pray in similar fashion). He also brings rain to help the grass grow, a task all the grass- and shrub-eating animal kachinas share.

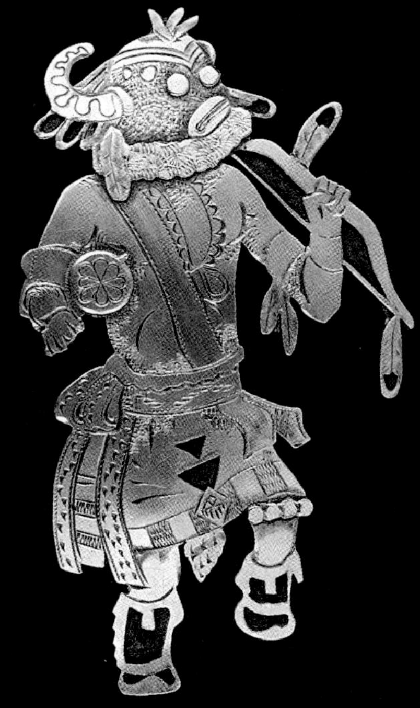

Ho'óte

84. The dance of Ho'óte foreshadows the arrival of spring's flowers. He is a popular kachina because his songs are so well-loved by the Hopis.

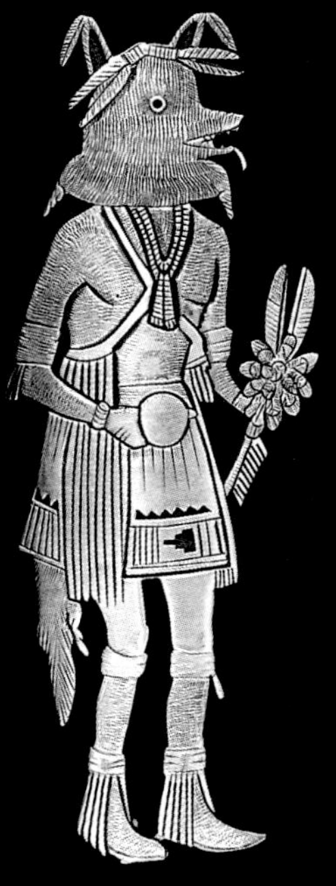

Kweo Kachina

80. Kweo, the Wolf Kachina, almost always dances when the Deer or Antelope Kachinas perform. A side dancer, his stick represents the bushes that he hides behind.

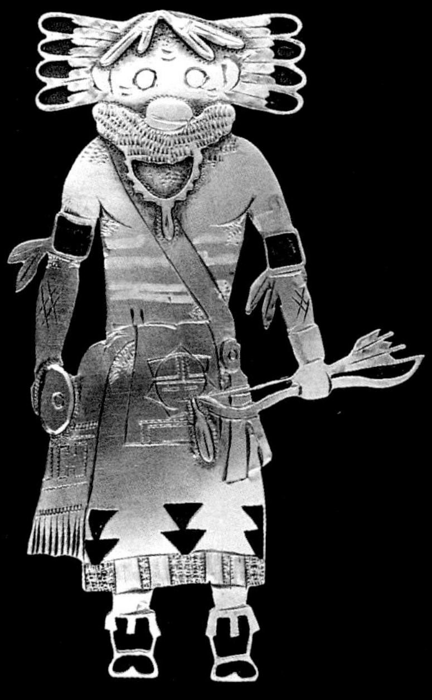

Hólolo

83. Hólolo is named for the song that he sings, and he is thought to speed the birth of children. He is often referred to as the Moon Kachina for the painted crescents under his eyes, or the Big Ears Kachina for his large ears.

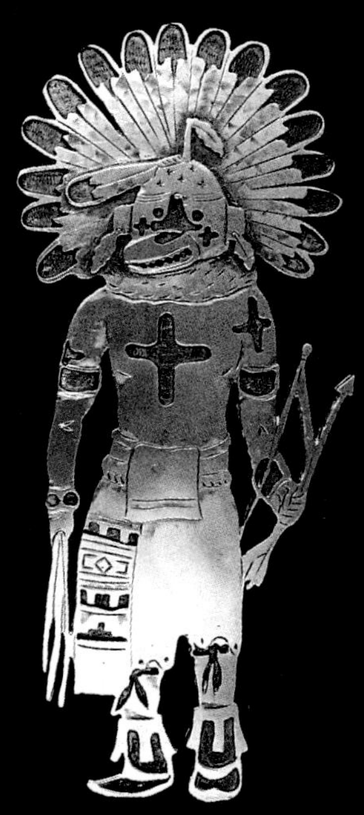

A'hote

85. A'hote represents different compass directions, depending on the color of his costume. The two most common are yellow (north), called Sikyahote, and blue (west), called Sakwahote.

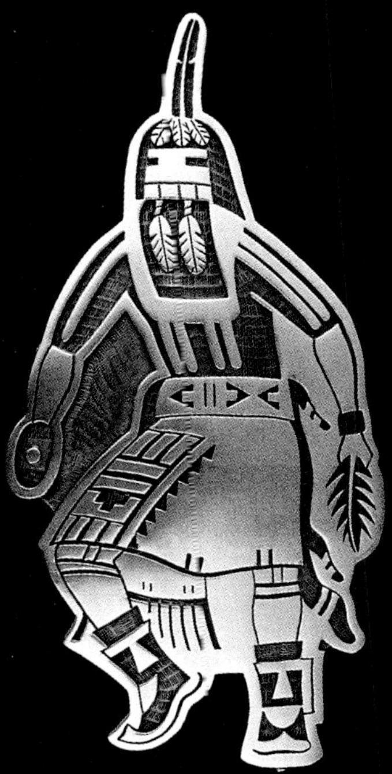

Angak'china

86. The Long-haired Kachina, whose hair corresponds to the falling rain, is called Angak'china. His purpose is to bring rain for the flowers and crops. Appearing in groups, the Long-haired Kachinas are popular because of their melodic song and beautiful dance.

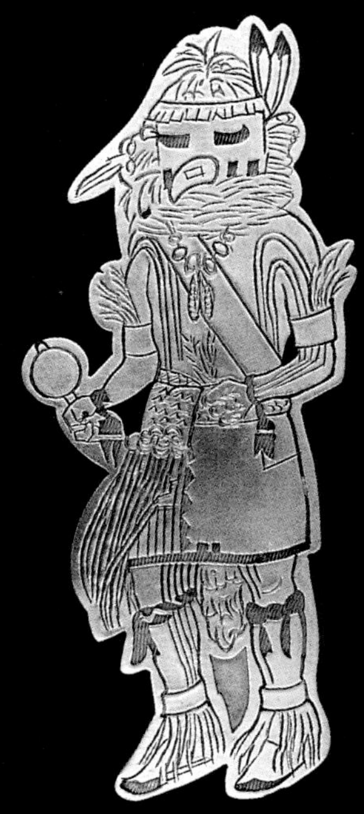

Tasap Kachina

88. The popular Tasap Kachina is a Hopi interpretation of the neighboring Navajo people. Although his dance is somewhat monotonous, it is enlivened by an occasional intricate turn.

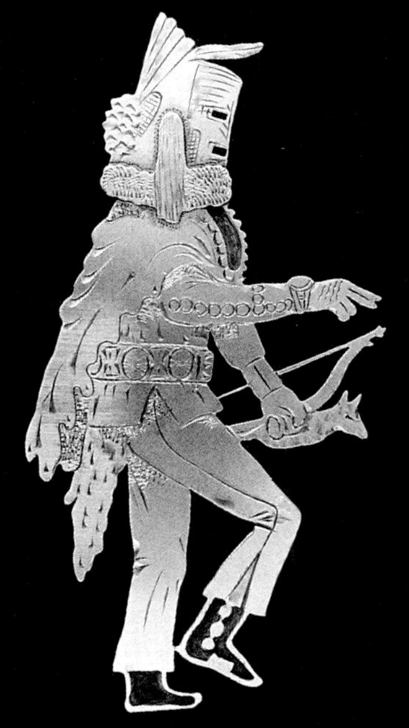

Tasap Yeibichai

90. Another Navajo-inspired kachina, Tasap Yeibichai represents the Navajo Grandfather. This kachina comically pantomimes for whatever he wants and he dances with exaggerated steps.

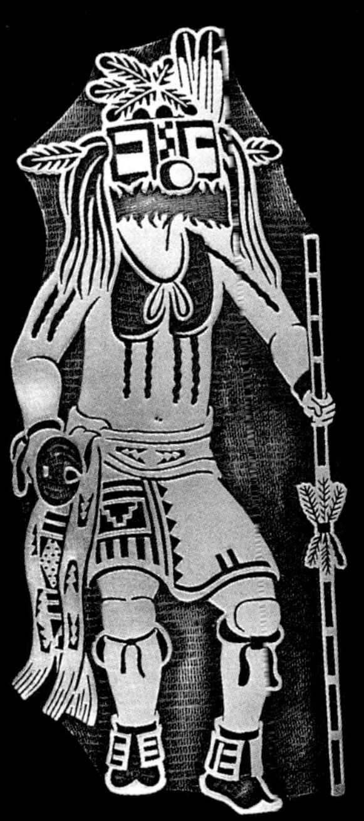

Ma'alo Kachina

87. The Ma'alo Kachina is sometimes called the Stick Kachina because he carries a straight stick in his left hand. His head is asymmetrically decorated with two feathers on the left side.

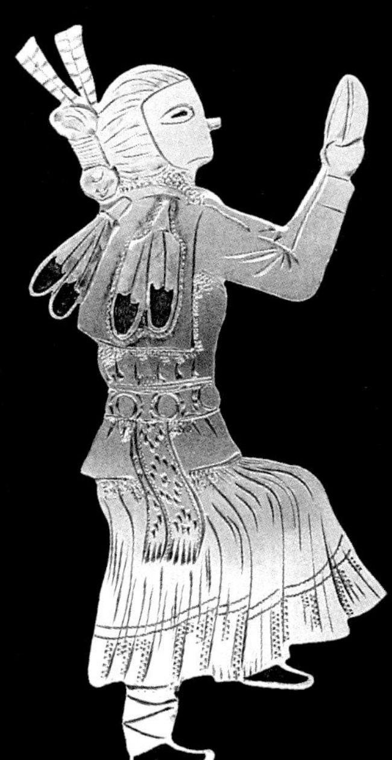

Tasap Kachin Mana

89. Tasap Kachin Mana, the Navajo Maiden, accompanies Tasap Kachina. Everything she wears—skirt, blouse, belt, moccasins—is typical of a Navajo woman's costume.

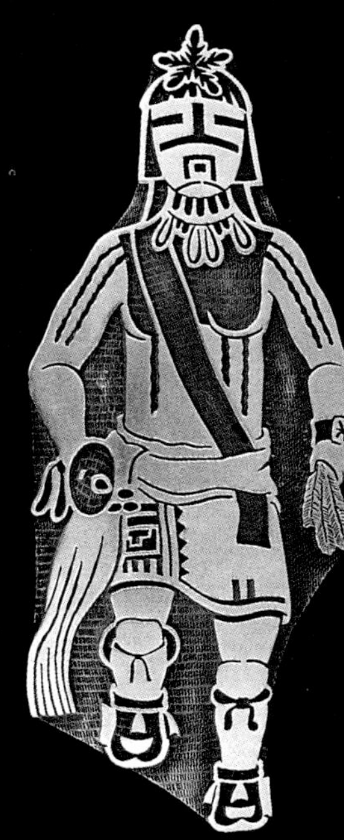

Tuma-uyi

91. Tuma-uyi is the White Chin Kachina, referring to the white clay on his chin, the same clay used to cover kachina dolls prior to painting. He is a very old kachina not seen in recent years.

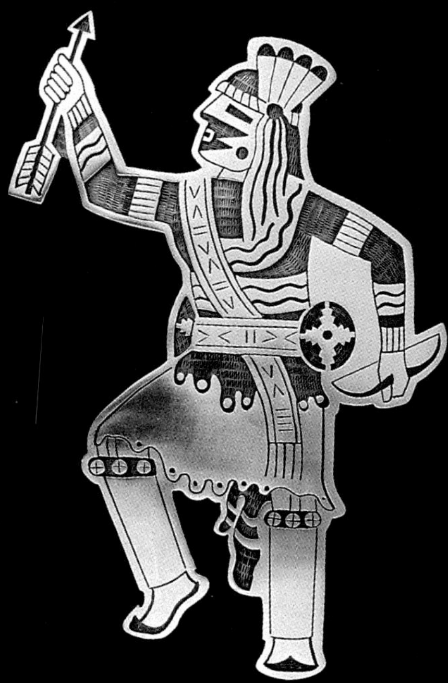

Konin Kachina

92. The Konin, or Supai Kachina, represents the Havasupai Indians living west of Hopiland. He wears small coiled basketry plaques for ears and a kilt made of fox skins.

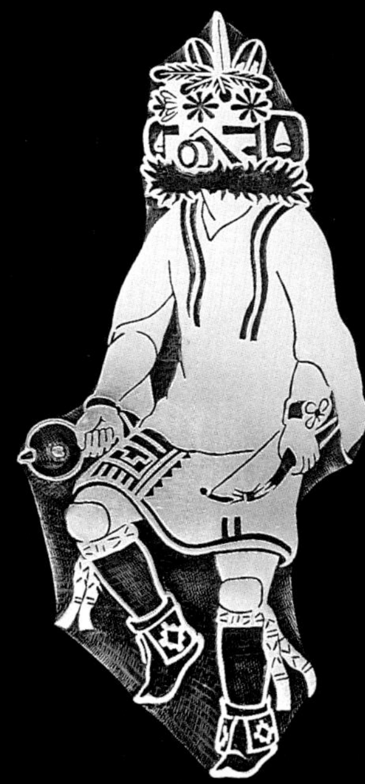

Navan Kachina

94. The Navan, or Velvet Shirt Kachina, is a fairly recent personation originating in Moenkopi. He is decorated in bright ribbons and flower designs.

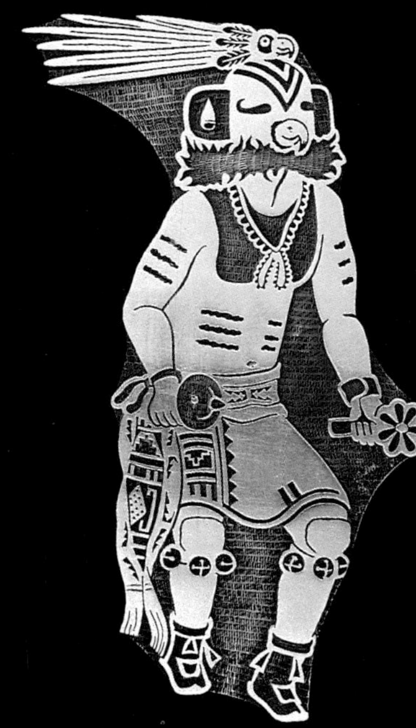

Kyash Kachina

96. The Parrot, or Kyash, Kachina was not personated for several generations until he appeared again in 1965 on Second Mesa. He brings full growth of plants in the summer as well as an increase in parrots.

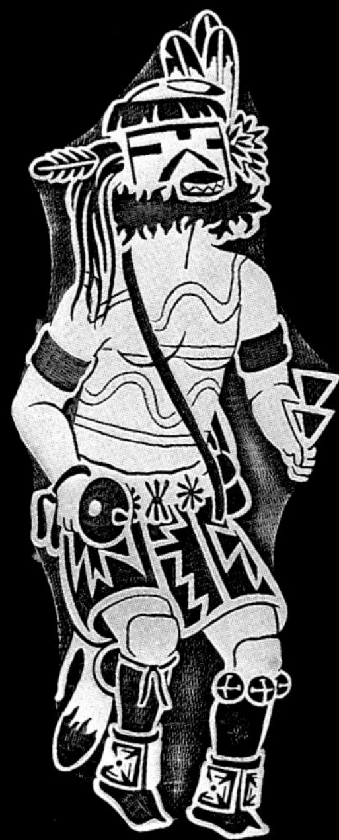

Kwivi Kachina

93. The name of a Kwivi Kachina literally refers to a "proud" or "sporty" person. The term is applied to any kachina elaborately bedecked in silver and fancy dress. Here, it refers to a type of Navajo Kachina.

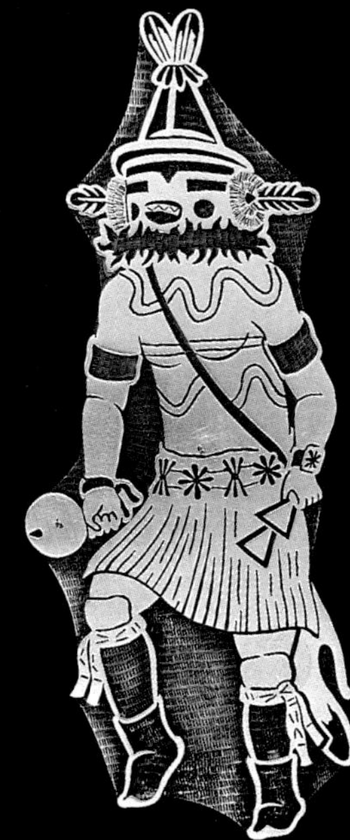

Movitkuntaka

95. Movitkuntaka is the aptly named Yucca Skirt Kachina. He is no longer seen because unseasonably cold, crop-damaging weather always followed his performance in the past.

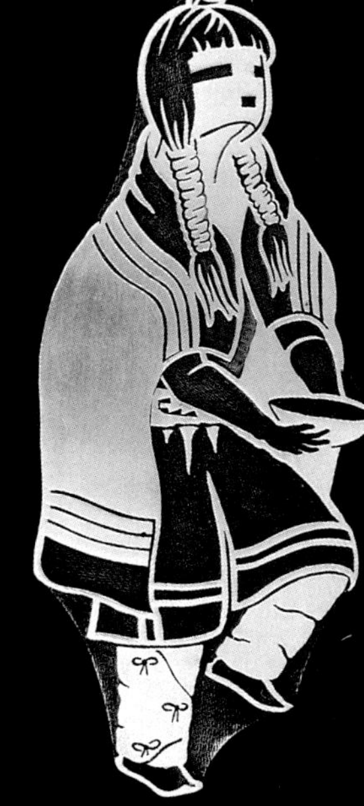

Hano Mana

97. Hano Mana may be considered one of the Long-haired Kachinas. She can be seen in regular kachina dances as a rasper, and when she dances her hand movements help illustrate the songs.

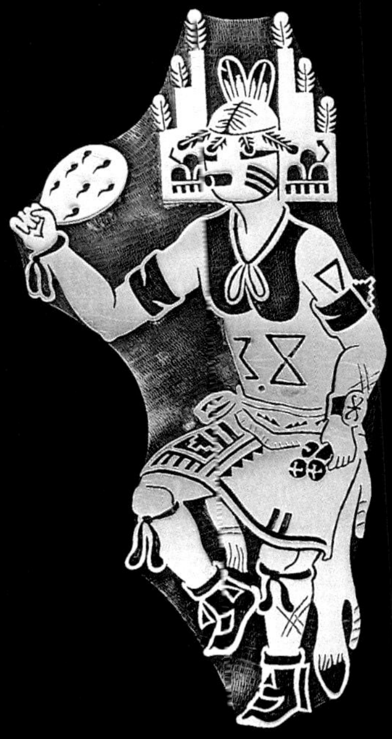

Kawaika'a Kachina

98. The Kawaika'a Kachina originated in Laguna, was borrowed by the Zunis, then taken home to Hopi by a First Mesa man who liked the dance. The kachina's name refers to Laguna.

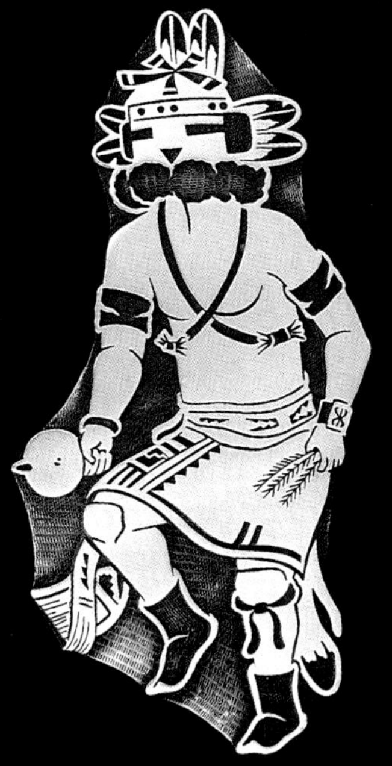

Möna Kachina

100. Möna Kachina is the River or Thunder Kachina, and he influences the flow of water. This kachina appears almost exclusively on Third Mesa, where he simulates thunder with his bull-roarer.

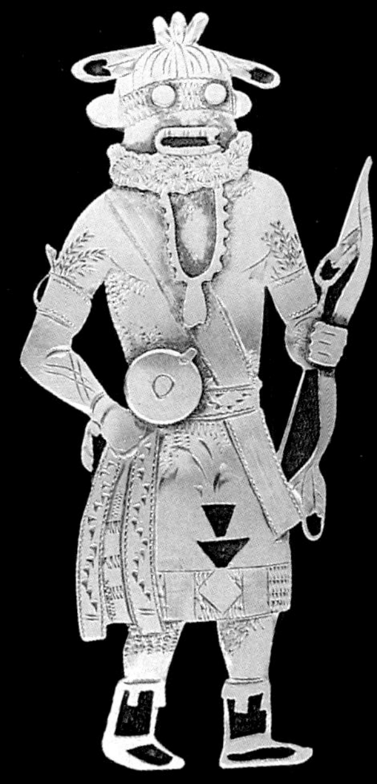

Sikyachantaka

103. Sikyachantaka is one of the ancient Hopi kachinas. His name literally means "holding entrails in the mouth." This is a reference to a time when the Hopis faced famine and a village man killed his cow to feed its entrails to the kachinas.

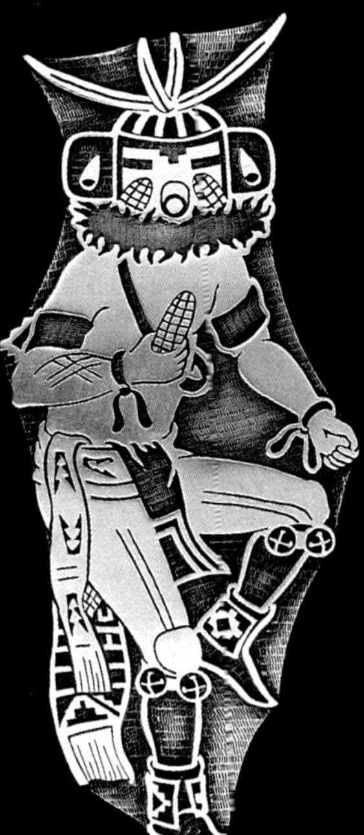

Ka'e

99. Ka'e is one of many Corn Dancers, a type of kachina that appears in many dances. Corn Dancers can usually be identified by the horizontally crossed feathers on their heads, as seen here with Ka'e.

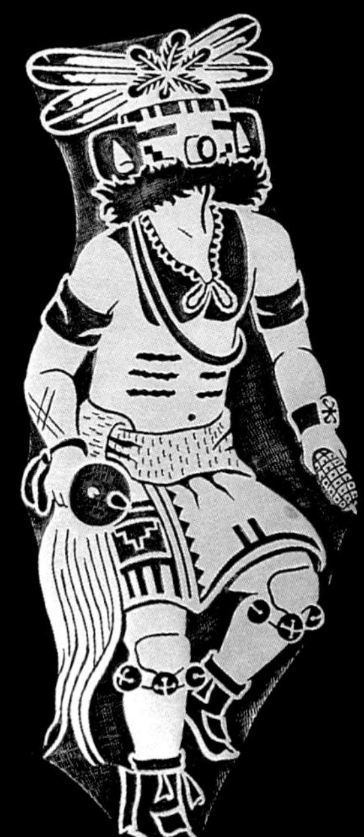

Corn Dancer

101. This Corn Dancer is one of the Rugan "Rasping" Kachinas. The Rugans are accompanied by Mana, or impersonated female kachinas, who make rhythmic rasping music with gourds, sheep scapulae, and notched sticks.

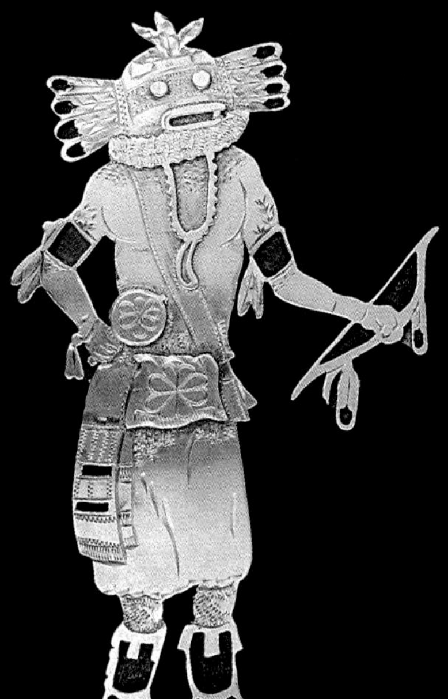

Holi Kachina

104. Holi Kachina is named for the word he constantly sings or shouts. His mask has a wide black line painted across the face over the eyes which is said to represent lightning.

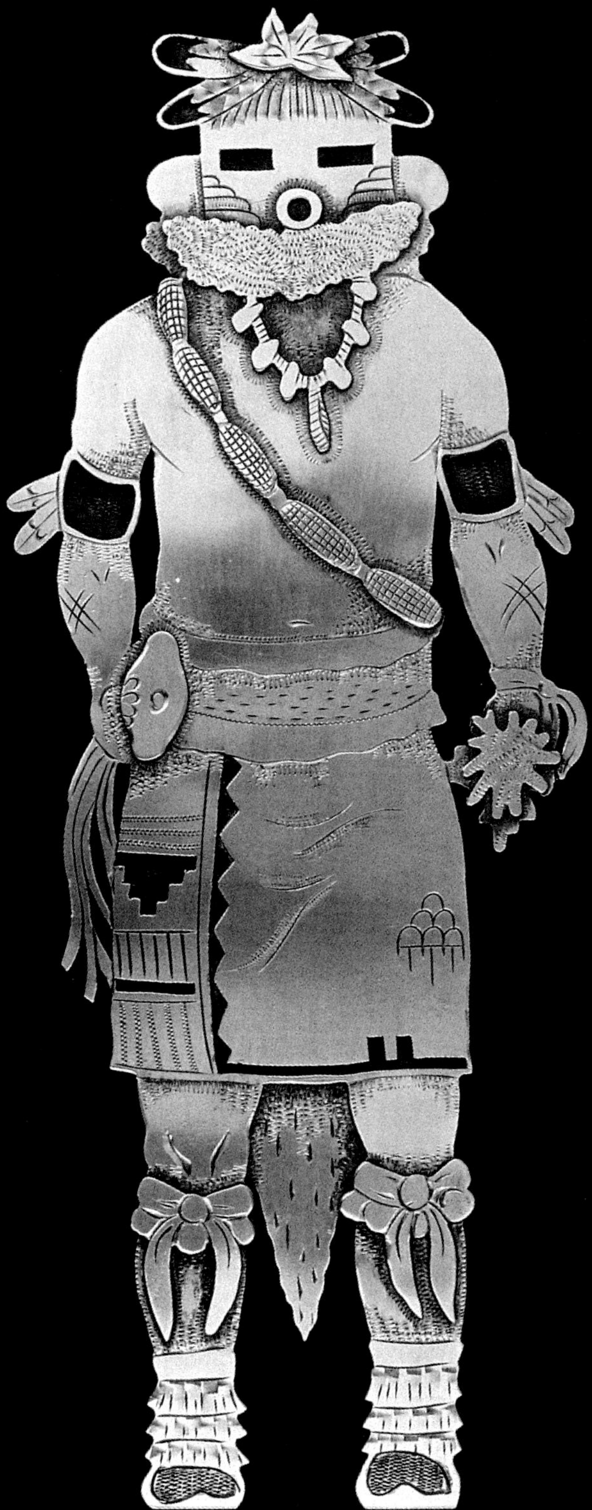

Harvester Kachina

102. The Harvester Kachina is another type of Corn Dancer distinguished by the multicolored string or belt of corn worn over his shoulder. An associated Mana who makes rasping music as described earlier also accompanies this kachina.

Niman Ceremony

The Niman is the Home Dance Ceremony to close the Kachina Season. It begins four days after the sun attains its northernmost zenith in summer, encompassing a two-week period filled with ritual activity. At the end, the kachinas are formally requested to tell their relatives to immediately send rain for the crops. They are then sent home to the San Francisco peaks in the southwest near Flagstaff, Arizona.

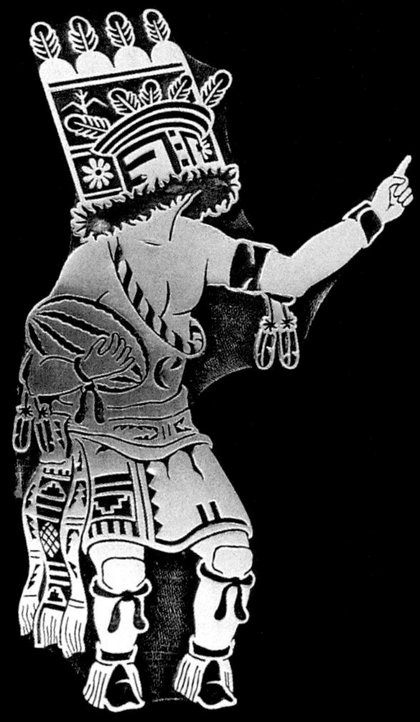

Sio Hemis Kachina

106. The Sio Hemis Kachina was introduced from Zuni before 1900. He differs little from the Hopi version except for his tableta, which depicts stylized dragonflies, sunflowers, and smaller clouds. Here he carries a watermelon.

Associated Kachinas

The Plaza Dances of late spring feature many kachinas who may not be dancers. Among them are the Wawarus Kachinas, or runners. These kachinas challenge the men and boys of the village to race. Although they exact an unpleasant punishment to the losers, they are expected to atone for plying their whips by sending rain to the germinating crops. Because they must run, the Wawarus Kachinas wear little clothing, and the eyes and mouths of their masks are usually somewhat enlarged.

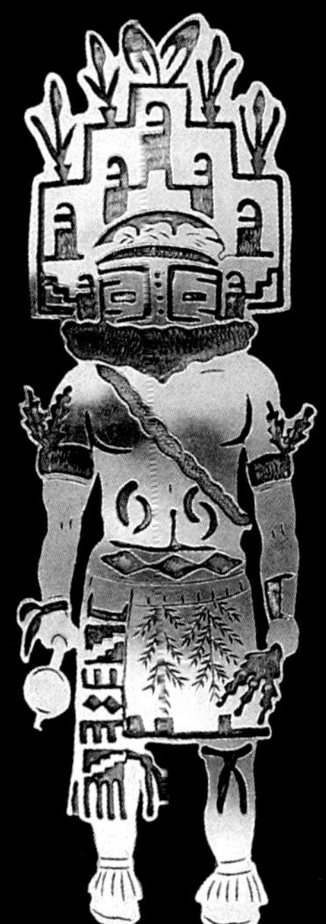

Hemis Kachina

105. The Hemis Kachina is the best known of the Hopi Kachinas. Stately and resplendent, his tableta depicts towering clouds and rain. In the company of their Manas, they bring entire corn plants to the Niman Ceremony to distribute as the first corn harvest of the year.

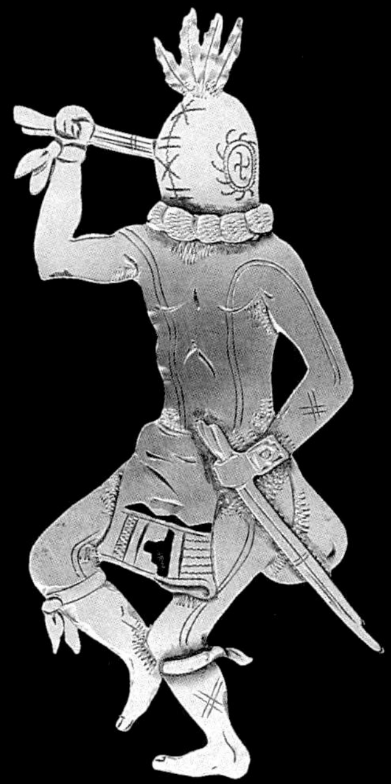

Aya Kachina

107. Aya Kachina receives his name from the shape of a child's rattle, which his helmet resembles. This kachina punishes losing racers with a stinging swat of yucca leaves, but rewards the winners with piki bread.

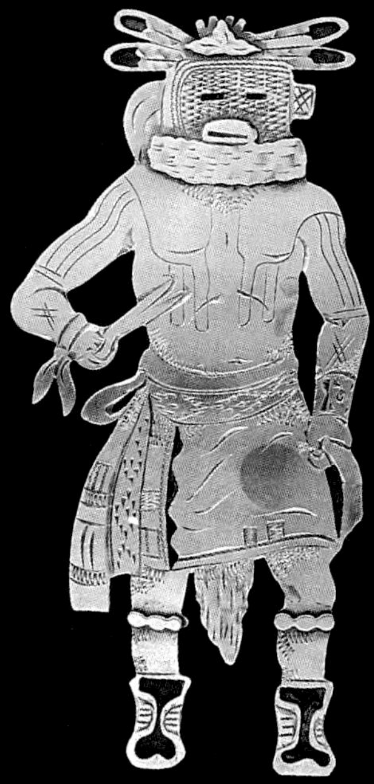

Hemsona

108. Hemsona, the "hair hungry" kachina, races with scissors or knife in hand, ready to cut the hair off of any racer he overtakes. Hemsona is the most elaborately dressed of the racing kachinas.

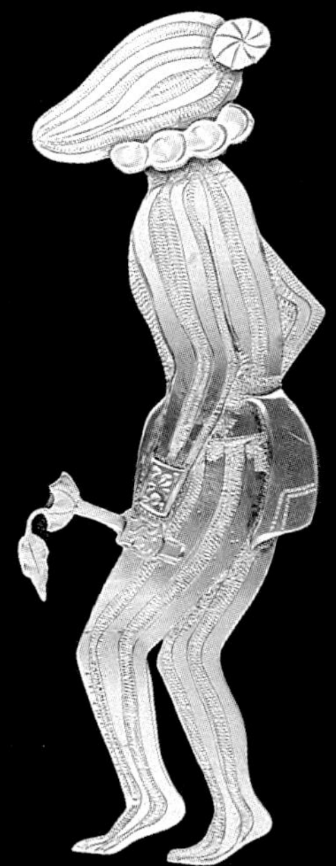

Patung

110. Patung, meaning squash, is a distinctive green and black striped kachina with a squash-shaped head. He appears primarily on First Mesa.

Clowns

Clowns are important to the Hopi Kachina Cult as comic relief and examples of misconduct, but they also may cure disease or serve as priests. They are favorites of Hopi audiences, who derive great pleasure from the humor they offer, whether it be crude or cultured.

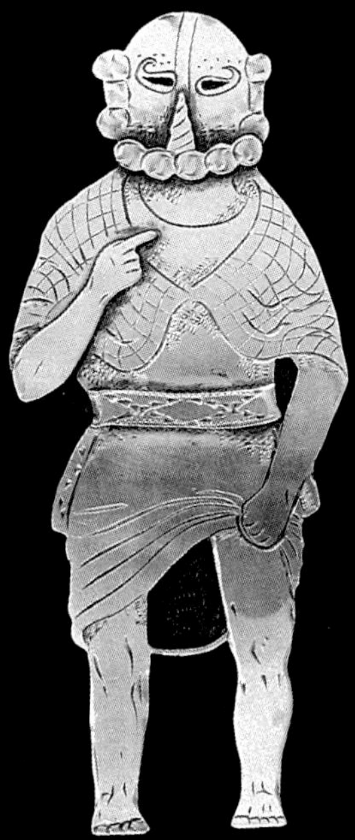

Kokopell Mana

109. Kokopell Mana is one of few "female" racers, although she is personified by a man. She first tempts someone to race, then lifts her skirts to overtake him. As punishment, she throws the runner to the ground and humiliates him by mimicking copulation.

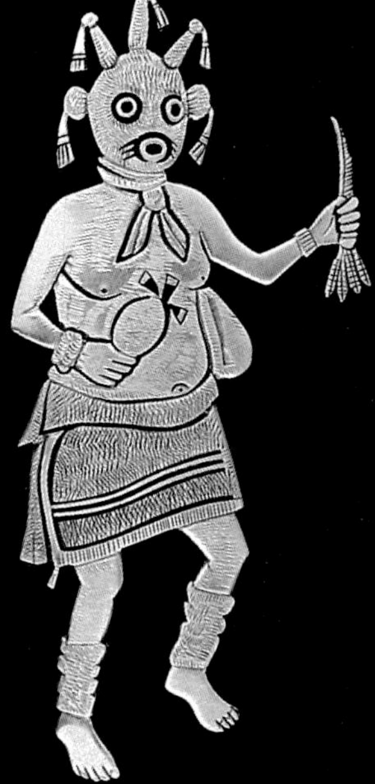

Koyemsi

111. The best-known Hopi Kachinas are the Koyemsi or Mud-heads. They appear in almost every ceremony, playing guessing games with the audience or performing simple tricks.

Hopi Salako Ceremony

The least known of the Hopi ceremonies, the Salako or Shalako, is rarely performed. Its general purpose is to bring the cloud spirits to the Hopi mesas. When performed, it occurs during the Niman activities.

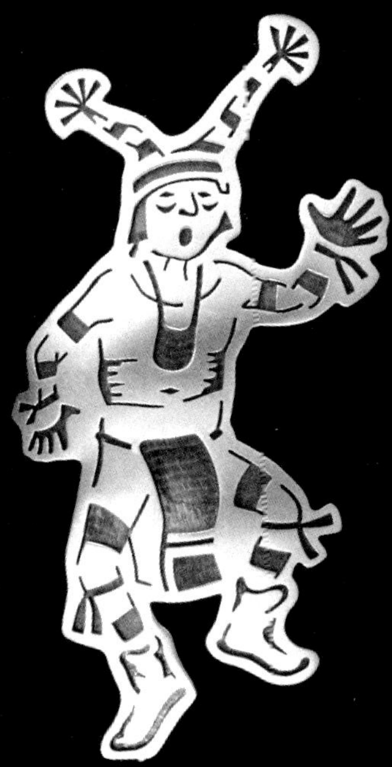

Koyala or Koshari

112. Koyala or Koshari is a Rio Grande clown as frequently called the Hano or Tewa clown. These clowns are the noisy, unrestrained fathers of the kachinas, often serving as drummers for other dances.

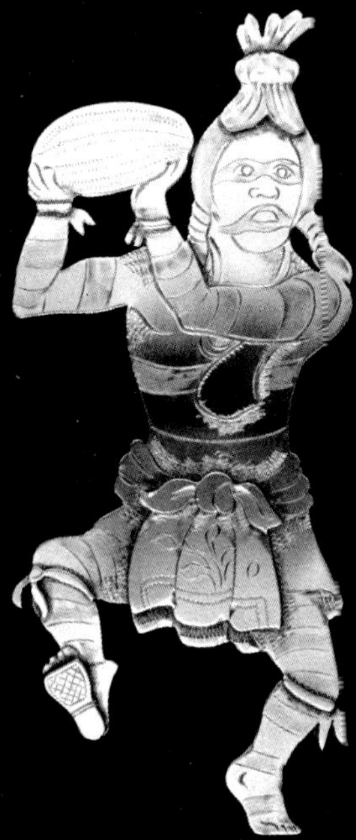

Kaisale

113. Kaisale is striped head to foot in many colors. He is a true Hopi clown, quick to improvise any act that will amuse his audience.

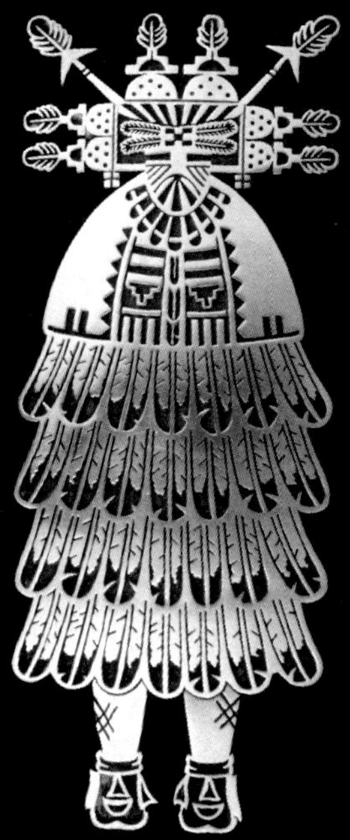

Salako Taka

114. Salako Taka stands eight feet tall, a dignified, graceful Hopi kachina. He is always accompanied by his sister, who is almost identical to him. Salako Taka and Salako Mana now appear only rarely.

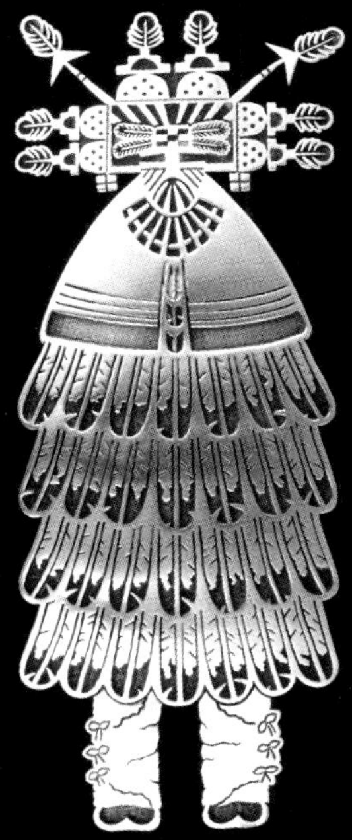

Salako Mana

115. Salako Mana is the sister of Salako Taka, identified only by her square turquoise earrings and high, white women's boots. She, like he, has a thin, sloping shape and stands very tall, although she is somewhat shorter than her brother.

Nevenwehe Ceremony

When beans are planted in May, the Nevenwehe is the final ceremony of the initiation year rituals. At its close, village youth go to "pick spinach," a ceremonial rite where boys give flowers to girls and receive packets of food in return.

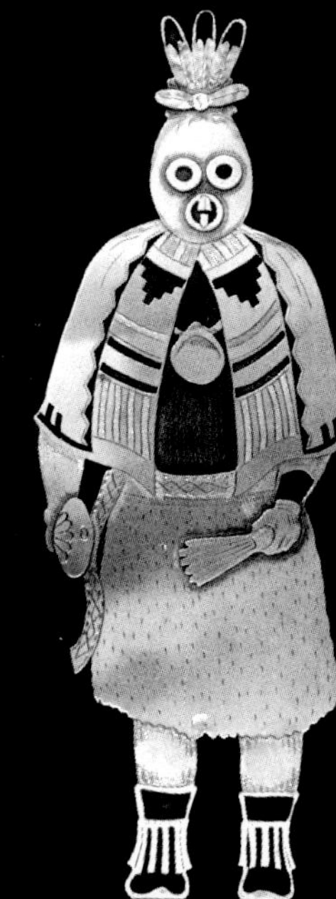

Masau'u

117. The Skeleton Kachina, Masau'u, is the only kachina who stays at Hopi after the Niman Home Dance Ceremony. As such, he may dance at any time of the year. A Death Kachina, he does many things in reverse, such as walking backward, since the world of the dead is the opposite of this world.

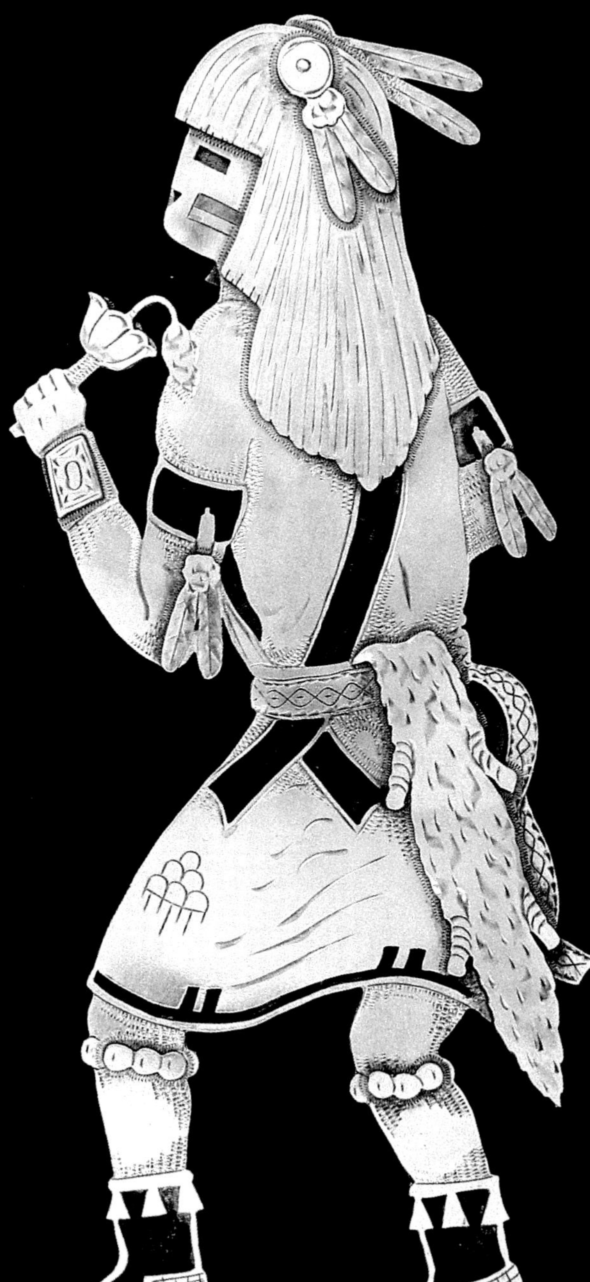

Maswik Kachina

116. The Maswik Kachina is known as the Skeleton Fetching Kachina who announces the arrival of Masau'u. His body is colored with dried blood.

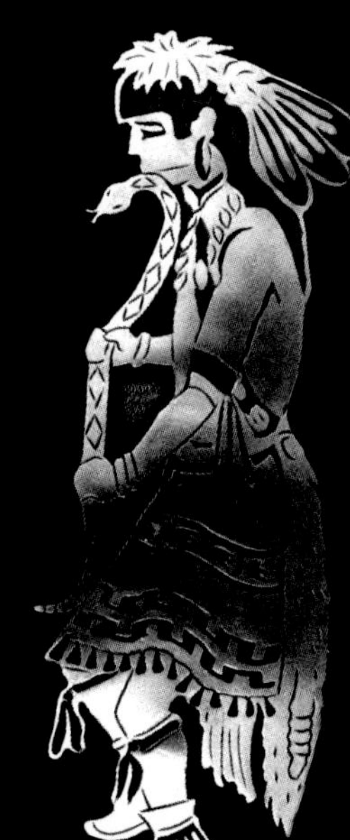

Chusona

118. Chusona, the Snake Dancer, is not a true kachina since he wears no mask. He is a very popular society personage who is as captivating to non-Hopi observers as he is to the Hopis.

HARMSEN COLLECTION: HOPI SILVER OVERLAY KACHINAS

No.	Ceremony	Kachina
	Solstice	
1		Soyal
	Soyal	
2		Ahöla
3		Ahöl Mana
4		Kaletaka
5		Ahülani
6		Sakwap Mana
7		Kachin Mana
	Powamu	
8		Eototo
9		Aholi
10		A-ha Kachin Mana
11		Angwushahai-i
12		Tungwup Ta-amu
13		Wuyak-kuita
14		Chaveyo
15		Wupamo
16		Tokoch Kachina
17		Nuvak'china
18		Talavai
19		Choshuhuwa
20		Na-ngasohu Kachina
21		Hilili
22		Hototo
23		Motsin
	Pachavu	
24		Sakwa Hu
25		Wuwuyomo
26		Pachavu Hú
27		Hé-é-e
28		Pachavuin Mana
29		Hahai-i Wuhti
30		Söhönasomtaka
	Kachina Cult Initiation	
31		Tumoala
32		Angwusnasomtaka
33		Hú
	Soyoko	
34		Awatovi Soyok Taka
35		Nataska
36		Tahaum Soyoko
37		Heheya Aumutaka
	Night Dances	
38		Tatangaya
39		Kwahu
40		Turposkwa
41		Tocha
42		Yapa
43		Mongwa Wuhti
44		Salap Mongwa
45		Kowako
46		Buffalo Kachina
47		Saviki
48		Kana-a Kachina
49		Chakwaina
50		Patszro
51		Hospoa
52		Palhik Mana
	Plaza Dances Mixed Dancers	
53		Ösök'china
54		Kokopelli
55		Monongya
56		Mongwa
57		Laqan
58		Toho
59		Hon Kachina
60		Honan Kachina
61		Navuk'china
62		Tutumsi
63		Chospos-yaka-hentaka
64		Chospos-yaka-hentaka
65		Tühavi
66		Tawa Kachina
67		Sohu Kachina
68		Chiwap
69		Payik'ala
70		Piokak
71		Hututu
72		Pöökang Kwivi Kachina
73		Kawai-i Kachina
74		Fox Kachina
75		Mahu
76		Angwusi
77		Heoto
	Line Dancers	
78		Kuwan Heheya
79		Turtle Kachina
80		Kweo Kachina
81		Antelope Kachina
82		Deer Kachina
83		Hólolo
84		Ho'óte
85		A'hote
86		Angak'china
87		Ma'alo Kachina
88		Tasap Kachina
89		Tasap Kachin Mana
90		Tasap Yeibichai
91		Tuma-uyi
92		Konin Kachina
93		Kwivi Kachina
94		Navan Kachina
95		Movitkuntaka
96		Kyash Kachina
97		Hano Mana
98		Kawaika'a Kachina
99		Ka'e
100		Möna Kachina
101		Corn Dancer
102		Harvester Kachina
103		Sikyachantaka
104		Holi Kachina
	Niman	
105		Hemis Kachina
106		Sio Hemis Kachina
	Associated Kachinas	
107		Aya Kachina
108		Hemsona
109		Kokopell Mana
110		Patung
	Clowns	
111		Koyemsi
112		Koyala or Koshari
113		Kaisale
	Hopi Salako	
114		Salako Taka
115		Salako Mana
	Nevenwehe	
116		Maswik Kachina
117		Masau'u
	Snake Dance	
118		Chusona

Index to Silver Kachinas

Recommended Reading

Books by Clara Lee Tanner

Southwest Indian Craft Arts

Indian Baskets of the Southwest

Arizona Highways Indian Arts and Crafts

Ray Manley's Indian Lands

Ray Manley's Portraits and Turquoise

Books by Barton Wright

Kachinas: A Hopi Artist's Documentary

Kachinas: The Barry Goldwater Collection at the Heard Museum

Hopi Kachinas: The Complete Guide to Collecting Kachina Dolls

The Hopi Photographs of Kate Cory, 1905-1912

Harold S. Colton

Hopi Kachina Dolls with a Key to Their Identification

Frederick J. Dockstader

The Kachina and The White Man: The Influences of White Culture on the Hopi Kachina Cult

Jesse Walter Fewkes

Hopi Katcinas

Robert C. Bishop

American Folk Sculpture

Oscar T. Branson

Indian Jewelry Making, Vol. I & II

Harmsen Collection

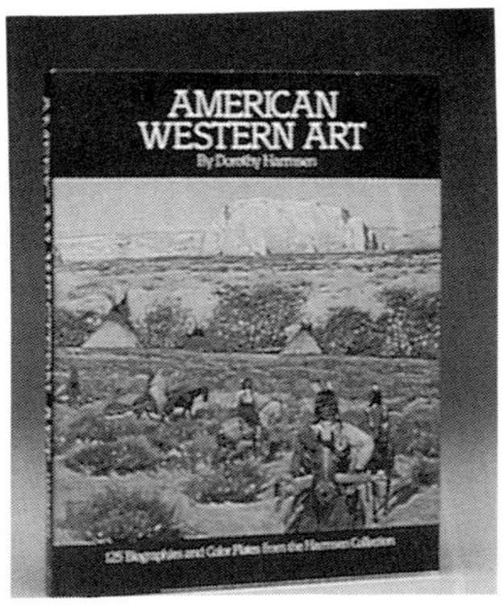

A sophisticated update of 19th and 20th century art and artists, showcasing the paintings, sculpture, and biographical profiles of 125 Western artists.
By Dorothy Harmsen

ISBN# 0-9601322-1-X
$45.00

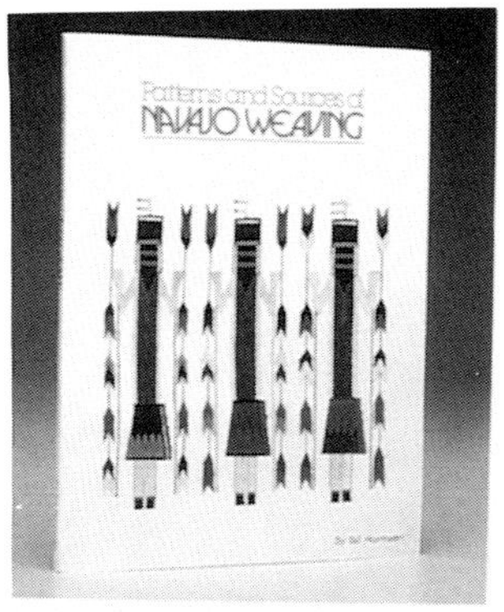

An intricate, color book of Navajo weavings and blanket patterns. Written by America's prominent authorities on Navajo history and weaving.
By Bill Harmsen

ISBN# 0-9601322-2-8
$14.95

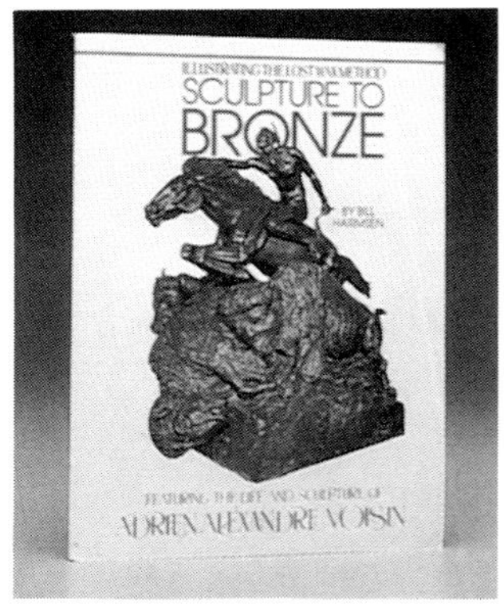

A fascinating story of the Lost Wax process, featuring the life and sculpture of Adrien Alexandre Voisin.
By Bill Harmsen

ISBN# 0-9601322-3-6
$14.95

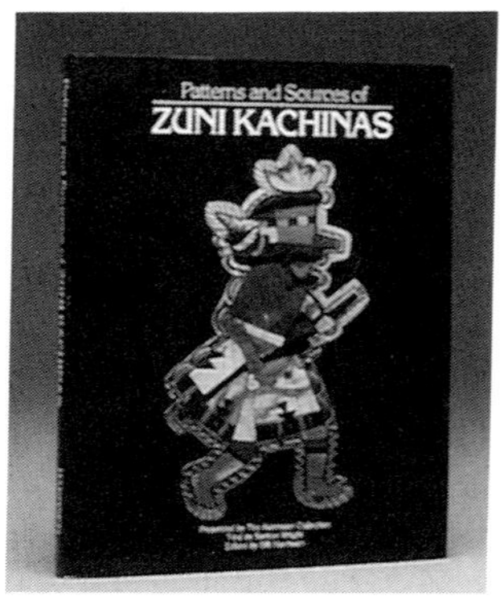

This beautiful book takes a comprehensive look at the history and traditions of the Zuni culture. These one-of-a-kind pieces are from the Harmsen collection in Tucson, Arizona.
By Bill Harmsen

ISBN# 0-9601322-4-4
$49.95

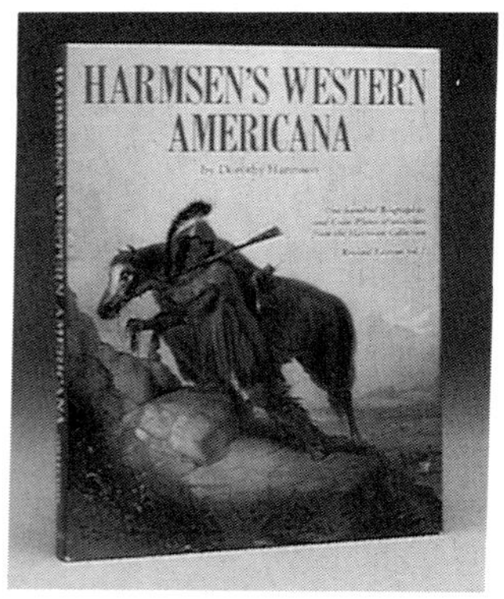

A comprehensive book on over 100 Western artists, their biographies, and full work spanning the years from 1796 to 1971.
By Dorothy Harmsen

ISBN# 0-87358-061-3
$45.00

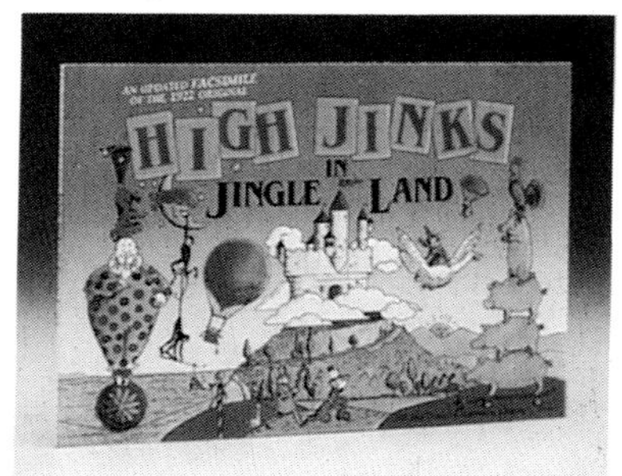

An updated version of the 1922 original, packed full of charming and clever jingles for all ages to enjoy.
By Bill and Dorothy Harmsen

ISBN# 0-9601322-7-9
$12.95

HARMSEN PUBLISHING COMPANY

3131 E. Alameda Avenue
Denver CO 80209
303/777-4030

6530 St. Andrew's Drive
Tucson AZ 85718
602/299-5502